D0340503

The Moon

The Moon

A Biography

David Whitehouse

HEADLINE

MAY   2002

523.3
WHI

Copyright © 2001 David Whitehouse

The right of David Whitehouse to be identified as the Author of
the Work has been asserted by him in accordance with the
Copyright, Designs and Patents Act 1988.

First Published in 2001
by HEADLINE BOOK PUBLISHING

10 9 8 7 6 5 4 3 2 1

All rights reserved. No part of this publication may be
reproduced, stored in a retrieval system, or transmitted
in any form or by any means without the prior written
permission of the publisher, nor be otherwise circulated
in any form of binding or cover other than that in which
it is published and without a similar condition being
imposed on the subsequent purchaser.

Every effort has been made to trace and contact the
copyright holders of all materials in this book. The author
and publisher will be glad to rectify any omissions at the
earliest opportunity.

British Library Cataloguing in Publication Data

Whitehouse, David
   The Moon : a biography
   1.Astronomy, Ancient
   2.Moon - Exploration
   3.Moon - In art
   4.Moon - Folklore
   I.Title
   523.3

ISBN 0 7472 7228 X

Typeset by
Letterpart Limited, Reigate, Surrey

Printed and bound in Great Britain by
Clays Ltd, St Ives plc

HEADLINE BOOK PUBLISHING
A division of Hodder Headline
338 Euston Road
LONDON NW1 3BH

www.headline.co.uk
www.hodderheadline.com

To my wife Jill and my children Christopher, Lucy and Emily. We are the moons that circle one another, never turning our backs.

Contents

Acknowledgements

I recall looking at the moon when I was a schoolboy, peering through a small telescope from the back garden of my home in Birmingham, England. The telescope was a small one with a tiny tripod. I was lying belly-down on the sweet-smelling grass with my eye to the eyepiece which was almost at ground level. It was July 1969, just a few days before the Apollo 11 mission, the first to attempt a landing on the moon. I remember thinking that soon the first footprints would change the moon forever. Love to my parents Derek and Ann for encouraging me and to my brothers Robert and Derick and my sister Alayne for tolerating me.

A few years later I was a junior member of the Birmingham Astronomical Society, saving my pocket money for the bus fare into town to attend their lectures. The society had a 12-inch reflection telescope about 45 minute's walk from my home and soon every Saturday night was spent there with a few like-minded friends. Well, almost like-minded. They wanted to observe so-called variable stars, stars whose light output changes. I wanted to observe the moon. Even though the telescope was just a few miles from the centre of Britain's second city, it had a remarkably good view of the sky and the wonders it showed me I have never forgotten. Whenever I am underneath the stars I am once more that dreamy little boy full of wonderment. I hope I always will be. Thank you Birmingham Astronomical Society.

For a while my life as a professional astronomer led me away from the moon, partly into the study of variable stars! But I still recall that during all-night observing sessions with the giant Jodrell Bank radio telescope near Manchester, I would sneak away across the fields for a few moments with a pair of binoculars to look at the moon. I couldn't abandon it completely.

You can know all the facts about the moon, all its measurements, the chemical composition of its rocks and the ages of its surface features, but if you just know the facts you will never know the real moon. Be it a warm full moon on a summer evening, a thin crescent in a wintry sky or the strange phases after midnight, the moon is beyond facts and figures, forever beyond the reach of science.

Many people have helped me write this book, some without knowing they did! I thank them all. Discovering them was one of the joys of this enterprise: astronauts, historians, archaeologists, astronomers, space scientists, geologists, curators, publishers, journalists, film-makers and much more, even a Druid priestess. Thanks to: Buzz Aldrin, Judy Alton, Irene Antonenko, Alex Barnett, Gordon Batho, Peter Beaumont, Kelly Beatty, Alexei Berezhnoi, Paul Blasé, David Blewett, Nic Booth, Eithne ni Bhraonain, James Burke, Bonnie Buratti, Ben Bussey, Martin Byrne, Al Cameron, Robin Canup, Alan Chapman, John Connolly, Bonnie Cooper, Gloria Correra, David Darling, Keay Davidson, Audouin Dollfus, Matt Dowd, Charlie Duke, Mike Duke, Joan and David Dunham, Sarah Dunkin, Storm Dunlop, George Eogan, Ian Franchi, Everett Gibson, Owen Gingerich, Tamara Green, David Harland, Paul Hess, Lon Hood, Sandra Jeffers, Amir Khan, Larry Klaes, Hal Levison, Lisa Lynne, Mark Maimone, Jean-Luc Margot, Jonathan McDowell, John and Jayne McNish, Jay Melosh, Charles Meyer Jnr, Scott Montgomery, Sir Patrick Moore, John North, Stu Nozette, Wubbo Ockels, Gregory Ojakangas, Carol Oliver, Emma Restall Orr, Louise Page-Bailey, Richard Pailthorpe, Mark Parmentier, Matt Pritchard, Michael and Barbara Rappenglueck, Jeffrey Robinson, Mark Rosiek, Clive Ruggles, Olaf Schmidt, Khalid Shaukat, the late Alan Shepard, Peter Shelus, John Shervais, Thomas Stair, Phil Stooke, Larisa Starukhina, John Sved, Janet Thorn, Chris van den Berg, Mark Wade, Marita Waehlisch, Lionel Wilson, Shijie Zhong.

I thank my agent Lavinia Trevor for her belief in this book and her expert handling of all its aspects; Kelly Davis for her editing and her many wise comments and Doug Young, Ian Marshall and Juliana Lessa at Headline. I must also thank two journalists who changed my life and taught me so much about writing and journalism, Bob Eggington and Tim Radford. Thanks, too, to Mike Smartt, the editor of the best news website in the universe.

Without the support of my wife Jill and my children Christopher, Lucy and Emily this book would not have been written. It is one of the greatest joys of my life that they share my fascination with the night sky and the moon that inhabits it. I hope that, in a way, I have given it to them.

David Whitehouse
Hampshire, England
April 2001

CHAPTER ONE

The Moonwatchers of Lascaux

A full moon rose into a cloudless Dordogne sky that September evening. Twenty thousand years ago this place was a small temperate oasis on the southern edge of the great Würm glacier. The ice age that had gripped Europe would continue to hold it for many thousands of years yet. Ancient man made his home here and left behind something extraordinary. As we sped along deserted country lanes, through darkening forests of oak and chestnut, the moon peered over the limestone cliffs that seem to be everywhere littered with evidence of the Cro-Magnon. Soon, across the valley, we saw what we were headed for. 'There,' said my guide pointing at it, 'there is the Hill of Lascaux.'

The moon still played between the trees as we made our way to the entrance of the cave. As I descended the steps I noticed the sudden drop in temperature, as if signifying the portal to another world, another time. Above ground it was a warm, balmy autumnal night, considerably more pleasant than the damp and misty England I had left earlier that day. It took a few moments for my eyes to become adapted to the cave's half-light. I had heard about this place of course and seen the pictures of it but as I entered the 'Hall of the Bulls' I knew instantly that nothing could have prepared me for its powerful, overwhelming beauty. Outlined in black and coloured with vivid brown, ochre and rusty-red, bulls and antelope were stampeding across the walls. They seemed to be converging on some significant point in the cave with their movement captured so well that I would not have been surprised to see them move. The prehistoric cave paintings of Lascaux are surely one of the greatest artistic achievements of my species.

I was here with Dr Michael Rappenglueck of Munich University, a man who has studied these caves, and many others, and has begun to uncover some of their mysteries.

Above the shoulder of one magnificent bull there was a collection of small dots. Their familiar shape meant that Dr Rappenglueck did not have to convince me that they were the Pleiades (or the 'Seven Sisters'). To me it is staggering that the constellation of Taurus the Bull is so ancient that it stretches back over 15,000 years to the time these caves were painted. These people looked up at the same stars that we see today and bequeathed us a bull with a tiny cluster of stars on its shoulder. I will never look at Taurus the same way again. But there was more.

To one side of the main chamber was the so-called 'Shaft of the Dead Man'. If you look at it in the right way you can see the three bright stars that are known today as the 'Summer Triangle'. This is by far the world's oldest star map but not a star map as we know it. Some stars are there but this prehistoric cosmos was also full of animals and spirit-guides.

The moon was here as well.

Back to the main chamber and down slightly to the entrance of a spectacular passageway adorned with bulls and horses and strange symbols. 'Look here,' said Dr Rappenglueck pointing up at the ceiling.

Beneath a horse so lifelike that you just know these people loved their animals, I could see a row of dots, some of them forming a loop. This is believed to show the moon going through its monthly cycle. It is the oldest lunar calendar yet discovered. I pointed to the loop looking puzzled. 'Perhaps a representation of the brightness of the full moon,' he speculated.

Another group of dots may also be connected with the moon. 'It shows half of the moon's monthly cycle,' Dr Rappenglueck said. 'At the new moon, when it vanishes from the sky, they have painted an empty square, perhaps symbolically representing the absent moon.'

'Did you know,' said my guide glancing around, 'in many ancient cultures such as Assyria's, a bull represents the moon god? I suspect the antlers of these bulls may be also symbolically representing the moon, as they did ten thousand years later in ancient Egypt.'

We left the cave with a sense of loss. You felt you wanted to get to know these people. That they would be waiting at the entrance uttering strange words with their flat stone lamps that burned animal fat just extinguished, their hands still covered in ochre and black pigment. I almost felt that the answers to my questions would be just a few steps away and that the outside world had changed. But the moon was a little higher as we made our way back through the still and silent trees. I felt that in a way I had become one of them, one of the moonwatchers of Lascaux.

The moon has accompanied us since the dawn of time. Every creature that has ever lived has done so under the moon. It was here long before we arrived and, who knows, may be here long after we have gone. It has been the Earth's faithful companion since the chaotic birth of the sun and its planets and there are some who believe that, without it, the Earth would not be the bountiful world it is. On its ancient surface is a record of the solar system's life, a chronicle long since obliterated from the face of the Earth. It is a history we have learned to read.

Throughout the ages it has been praised and feared but never underestimated, except perhaps today. There was something hidden, almost sinister, about its changing phases and its relation-ship with water and fertility. Its influence was beneficial yet unsettling, an unseen power that was darker and more mysterious than the unsubtle sun. Its life in night-time skies meant that it was not just an observer of human affairs but a participant in them as well as an accomplice to the strange forces of the night. 'What is there in thee moon that thou shouldst move my heart so potently,' wrote Keats. 'This is the light of the mind, cold and planetary,' added Sylvia Plath.

It has had many names. In Mesopotamia it was Sin or Ishtar; in Egypt, Hawthor; for the Greeks the triple deity Artemis, Selene and Hecate; to the Romans it was Diana; to the Chinese Kwan-Yin; to the Hindus it was Shiva, unstable and as mysterious as madness; and to the Alaskan Inuit it was Igaluk, the supreme being of the universe. She has been a mirror to the world, a stopping-place for the souls of the dead, the ruler of the tides and the temptress of time.

Her changing phases marked out time although they were not in concert with the seasons, as is her way. All ancient calendars were lunar calendars. The practice of starting a month by the first sighting of a crescent was observed by the Babylonians and the Hebrews as well as the Germans and the Celts.

Her influence is pervasive and unappreciated. So many of our words and customs stem from the moon. Sabah is an early word for the moon and Sabattu was the full-moon day from which we get the word Sabbath. There are some linguists who believe the origin of the word 'men' comes from an earlier word for moon. The familiar nursery rhyme of Jack and Jill going up the hill to fetch a pail of water is a modification of a far more ancient Norse tale of Hjuki and Bil who represent the waxing and waning of the moon. So many legends say that without the moon man would be nothing. Neither would woman. The sometimes dim-red light of the eclipse was when the goddess Ishtar menstruated, said to be the time of the blood of the great mother's wisdom. Fertility is the moon's gift.

In France some women who wish to become pregnant gather at a certain prehistoric stone and lift their skirts to the moon; in South America mothers take their children out under the moon and give thanks. Even today many people believe that the full moon has an effect on us. Had there been a full moon on that fateful night the lookouts on the *Titanic* might have seen the iceberg. The moon in the water is a favourite Zen metaphor for human life. What we experience depends upon reality as well as our senses; and it is our senses that mediate between the internal and the external world, like ripples in the reflection of the moon. In China, during the Han dynasty, the emperor Wu Ti (140–87 BC) had a terrace built overlooking a royal park. It was called *fou-yue-t'ai*, which means 'for viewing the moon from below'. To do this he added a lake. There is something stirring about drawing down the moon in water.

It is not far away. For some ancient Greeks it was just beyond a spear's reach or the wings of Icarus. It is really only 400,000 km or three days away by spaceship. How many have had the breathtaking experience of looking at it through a telescope, let alone taken the time to understand its rhythms? Despite the adventure of going there, modern man has lost touch with the moon.

Far from the Dordogne, the full moon also rises over the African savannah as it has done since before man counted time. In the fading light, it sees the creatures of the day seek their shelters and those of the night begin to stir. Here, on the game-rich savannahs of sub-equatorial Africa, is another of the places where it all began, where the first steps on our journey to the moon were paced out.

We are high on the escarpment that is the Lebombo Mountains in northern KwaZulu, Natal, which means 'Place of Heaven'. Above the green cane fields and their irrigation systems, there is a placed called Border Cave. It is difficult to reach and was until recently the playground of baboons, but now its only inhabitants are a huge rock python and archaeologists. 'Place of Heaven' seems apt. It has magnificent views of the surrounding country-side and watching the moon rise up from the horizon is breath-taking.

Excavations of the sandy floor of this giant, volcanic cave have uncovered the remains of what may be the oldest known evidence of anatomically modern man. *Homo sapiens sapiens* lived here 150,000 years ago and probably earlier than that. The layers of dust on the floor, which archaeologists sift and call 'horizons', are pages from the very first chapter of the book of modern human-ity. The upper horizons tell of Iron Age inhabitants, probably ancestral Swazis, that lived here a few centuries ago. There is evidence of Stone Age occupation, five adults and a four- to six-month-old child in a shallow grave. Few places on Earth have been lived in for longer than Border Cave.

They were hunter-gatherers scratching out a living on the vast plains, stalking game and anything else they could keep up with. In the cave are the remains of at least forty-three mammal species, including leopard and elephant, and several species that are now extinct. Perforated seashells, possibly used for ornamen-tation, have also been found. It was from caves such as this that our distant ancestors began to migrate north towards Europe and Asia 100,000 years ago, displacing the more archaic Neanderthal man who already lived there. Over many generations, they moved into Europe, through Asia, on to Australasia and across the land-bridge that still existed between Asia and the Americas. Over tens of thousands of years they migrated down the spine of North and South America. Some branched eastwards and settled in a place that tens of thousands of years later would be called Florida. From there, some of their offspring would depart for the moon.

In the 1970s a small piece of the fibula of a baboon was found here. As the dirt was rubbed from it, twenty-nine clearly defined notches were seen. It was soon suggested that it had something to do with the moon. The changing phases of the moon recur every twenty-nine days.

At 37,000 years old, this carved bone ranks with the oldest mathematical objects known. It resembles the calendar sticks used by Bushmen clans in Namibia. Tens of thousands of years later, on the other edge of this continent, Euclid's *Elements* were published in Alexandria and heralded as the greatest mathematical achievement of mankind. But, for me, the tiny bone unearthed in Border Cave eclipses it. Mathematics was born in Africa and its midwife was the moon.

Another incised bone, called the Ishango bone, now to be found in the Institute for Natural Science in Brussels, was discovered in the 1960s on the shore of a lake in north-eastern Zaire. It was originally thought to be a record of prime numbers and doubling, perhaps a forerunner of the ancient Egyptian system of multiplication by doubling. But others think it is a six-month lunar calendar recording the phases of the moon. It is thought to have been carved about 20,000 BC or earlier. Similar calendar bones have been found in Europe.

On the island of Gotland, in the middle of the Baltic Sea, strange grooves have been cut into the bedrock and into large stones, over 3,600 of them. They are up to a metre long and up to 10 cm deep. It is thought that they were cut by some form of pendulum. They were a mystery until it was realized that they were not random in their direction. They were directed at the most northerly and southerly points on the horizon of moonrise and moonset. This is not a straightforward thing to do as the moon has a cycle of almost nineteen years during which its rising and setting points migrate along the horizon.

Some grooves were clearly in groups and that enabled the date they were cut to be estimated as March 3152 BC. This is about the time that Stonehenge was built and that has some definite lunar alignments as well. It seems that understanding and marking the motion of the moon was important to our ancestors. But our ties with the moon go back even further, as we shall see.

Neil Armstrong, the first man on the moon, has said: 'There are secrets on the moon, there are things to see beyond belief.' So come and read its story. For a while, think of the moon and pay no worship to the garish sun.

CHAPTER TWO

Landscape of the Past

A slender crescent hanging in the evening sky, a sickle moon, is always a mesmerizing sight; Shakespeare called it a 'silver bow, new-bent in heaven', for Shelley it was something 'from the great morning of the world when first God dawned in chaos'. Sometimes there is the faint hint of the ashen glow of earthlight, caused by sunlight reflecting from the Earth's oceans onto the night side of the moon. When I see it, I think of Leonardo da Vinci who explained it. At this time, the moon has a haunting beauty unmatched at any other phase of its cycle or indeed by any other object in the sky. There is something ageless about the crescent moon with its renewed promise of a new month to come. Long ago the first humans looked up at it with recognition and wonderment. We still do so today.

They are all waiting in the dark. The astronomers we shall meet have been gathered from the scattered centuries and placed on its face. One by one, over the next fourteen days, as the earthward side of the moon is unveiled, the sun will reach them. Its light will reach craters, plains, valleys, mountains and many strange formations. It will come up over broken space probes and six times it will rise over human footprints.

Once each month in its orbit around the Earth, the moon disappears and becomes what is called 'new' when it lies between the Earth and the sun. For ancient peoples this was a time when the great unseen power of the moon made itself felt and when the cycle of heaven was renewed. The moon disappeared from the sky but was brought back to life after three days, a powerful image. Sometimes when the precise alignment is satisfied, the moon actually passes across the face of the sun and a solar eclipse takes place. This occurs because by some coincidence the sun, being 400 times larger than the moon, is also 400 times further away, so that the disc of the moon fits over the disc of the sun, allowing the queen of the night an attempt to extend her dominion to the daytime sky. Most months, however, the moon passes a little above or below the sun so no eclipse takes place and the moon's cycle begins anew with a thin crescent. For some it is important to catch the crescent moon as early as they can.

As time passes from the instant of the new moon, the angular separation between the sun and the moon increases. Each day it moves 13 degrees further from the sun. If the moon were a smooth sphere we would be able to see it as a very tiny sliver of light but in practice we do not see a crescent until it is about 7 degrees from the sun. The earliest a crescent moon has been seen with the unaided eye is 15 hours and 30 minutes, with binoculars 13 hours and 32 minutes, and with a telescope 12 hours and 7 minutes. In 1966 a camera on a missile launched from the White Sands Missile Range in New Mexico snapped the moon when it was just 2 degrees from the sun and just a few hours old.

For centuries men have scanned the horizon in the region of the setting sun for the first sighting of the moon's thin crescent. Excavations have uncovered Babylonian clay tablets that record narrow crescent moons as long ago as 750 BC but we know that the Sumerians were searching for the crescent at least a thousand years earlier.

These days there are computer programs that predict when and where the crescent can first be seen. But for me, the computer-generated maps of the Earth's surface that show the regions from where the moon's crescent will first be glimpsed, are dull and sterile. I prefer to imagine an Islamic holy man squinting and straining his eyes against the evening glare to see a tiny arc of light. If he sees it, and even today a computer prediction must be followed by an actual sighting, he can officially sanction the start of a new month. By the first crescent sighting Muslims align the beginning and the end of the months in their lunar calendar. For them the moon symbolizes the power of God: 'Allah offered it to Man to help him measure time.' The Fast of Ramadan occurs during the ninth month of the Islamic calendar. It begins with the first sighting of the crescent and ends the next time it is seen in the evening sky. The Muslims are the guardians of the crescent moon.

Viewing the moon so close to the sun represents a great challenge and a risk. Being close to the sun, it is a slender crescent against a bright background, close to the horizon and seen through a considerable thickness of atmosphere that can distort and obscure. The most favourable times are in the spring in the northern hemisphere and the autumn in the southern hemisphere, when the moon is at its greatest angle to the horizon. Never sweep for it with binoculars or a telescope when the sun is in the sky – that way can lead to blindness. But when you do find it, slender and newborn, you can begin to follow it through its lunation, just like the moonwatchers of Lascaux did 15,000 years ago.

When the moon is a day-old crescent, craters appear as dark elongated streaks and the border between day and night, called the terminator, is delicately ragged. Appearances can, however, be deceptive. Despite what you will see on the moon, the craters are not really the deep, steep-sided holes they appear to be. Because they are features on a vast scale, they look more dramatic from afar than they do from the surface of the moon itself. Even the most spectacular ones rarely have slopes that exceed 40 degrees and most of them are shallower. If you stood inside one of the great walled plains you would have no impression of being in such a place because its ramparts would be far over the horizon. The moon is a smaller globe than the Earth and its horizon curves away more sharply, leaving the observer with the impression that they are standing on a flattish plain.

On the first day of the 29-day cycle of the moon, or the lunation, the sun unites centuries of lunar study by rising over astronomers from the early as well as the modern phase of lunar observation. It greets the 68 km crater Plutarch, named after the first-century writer who had a good idea of what the moon was like with its mountains and valleys. It also shines upon the smaller crater named after the Nobel prize-winning chemist Harold Urey who in the 1950s wrote an important book about the planets and ushered them out of the astronomical doldrums in time for the space age. However, you would be advised not to search too hard for these craters on the thin crescent, as they are difficult to see and for dedicated lunar observers only. Pass them by this time, we shall hear of them later.

The moon travels round the Earth in an almost circular orbit. In our century its greatest distance will be 406,707 km on 14 March 2002 and the shortest will be 356,509 km on 14 November 2016. It would be more accurate to say that the Earth and the moon orbit their common centre of gravity called the barycentre. This point is located some 4,800 km from the Earth's centre, that is, about 1,500 km beneath your feet. The actual location of the barycentre changes constantly during the moon's orbit.

The moon spins on its axis in the same time it takes to orbit the Earth, 29.5 days (called a lunation or a synodic month). But if the moon's orbit is measured against the stars then it takes only 27 days and 7 hours to complete one revolution. This is the sidereal month and the difference between the two – two days a month – is about how long each full moon will lag behind the calendar. Look at it in the sky and it will take just two minutes to slide its own diameter across the sky to the west. Its rotation is tidally locked to the Earth and so it keeps the same face pointing towards us as it has probably done for billions of years. There are slight variations in the moon's rotation and orbit that cause the Man in the Moon to nod and shake his head so that over time we can see about 59 per cent of the surface even though its edges are highly foreshortened. Over the centuries astronomers have often wondered what the far side was like – and what a surprise it turned out to be.

It was in 1651 that an inspired Jesuit priest, the complicated and troubled Giovanni Riccioli, named the lunar seas. The romantic and evocative names he, and the others who followed, chose add a new dimension to the moon. On day one of the lunation, sunlight finds Mare Marginis, the Border Sea, and moves towards Mare Undarum, the Sea of Waves, and then on to Mare Spumans, the Foaming Sea. Later we will find the Lake of Dreams; the Bay of Rainbows; the Marsh of Decay; the Sea of Nectar; the Ocean of Storms; the Sea of Cold; the Marsh of Diseases; the Lake of Death. On some old maps there is near the edge, or limb, of the moon a Stagnum Glaciei or Frozen Pool, which was prophetic – given the discovery of ice near the moon's poles in 1998.

By the second day, the sun is rising over the magnificent Mare Crisium, the Sea of Crises. Few sights on the moon are as spectacular as watching the sun's rays illuminate the mountains that surround this vast oval-shaped, lava-filled basin. In many ways, its story is typical of the moon. Nearly four billion years ago, when the solar system was young and still swarming with rocky debris, something large, perhaps a few tens of kilometres in size, slammed into the moon here. The resulting explosion scooped out a depression almost 600 km across, scattered across the moon pieces of debris ranging from house-sized boulders to fine dust, and sent shock waves pulsing through the surface. Mare Crisium, about the size of Great Britain, is a relatively young feature, although it is older than the two most recently formed: Imbrium, the Sea of Rains, and Orientale, the Eastern Sea.

Once, Mare Crisium was indeed a sea but of lava not water. Between 300 and 500 million years after the Crisium impact lava seeped up through the lunar crust and filled the basin, obscuring some craters and partially drowning others. The lava erupted episodically, so we can see flows superimposed upon flows and sometimes ridges where one flow petered out on top of an older one. It is one of the small lunar 'seas', but one of the most interesting. Certainly, by grazing light (when the sun shines along the lunar surface instead of down upon it) it is one of the most beautiful. As the moon's crescent grows it is the first prominent spot to be revealed, and to disappear after full moon.

If you are lucky and catch the moon at just the right time, and there are astronomers who spend their lives watching through telescopes and waiting for the correct lighting conditions, you will see the peaks of Crisium's eastern wall greet the lunar dawn. For an hour or two, when the myriad points of light grow as sunlight races down their slopes, they appear as a strange constellation of stars. Then comes a moment, perhaps my favourite moment of the whole lunation, when the sun pokes its head above Crisium's eastern rim and stretches across the Mare itself. Sunlight pours into the dark abyss and throws the wrinkles and ridges in the Mare's surface into high relief.

From Crisium's mountainous south-east border rises a promontory, Cape Agarum. It has been reported that this cape sometimes takes on a delicate misty appearance when the moon is between two and three days old. One seasoned observer noted that the pass to the east of the cape appeared to glitter as the sunset approached. The highest peak in this region rises some 3,350 m above the Mare surface. And from Agarum a long ridge runs concentrically with the low and indefinite border of the Mare, as far as a ring, the remnant of an ancient crater that formed after the Crisium basin but before the lava flooded it. Just beyond Cape Agarum, in the mountains that surround the Mare, can be found the crater Alhazen formed by the impact of a 5–8 km object. We will hear more about Alhazen.

You need a high-powered telescope to perform the journey around Mare Crisium, but even if you look through a small telescope or a pair of binoculars the view is enthralling as it dominates the moon's shimmering crescent low down about the horizon. You can never look very long at these features on the moon. When illuminated like this they stay for an hour or so and soon follow the setting sun.

Moving north along Crisium's eastern shore, you pass several high peaks and mountains. There is a long, narrow valley-like depression, the Mare Anguis, or the Serpent Sea, and beyond, the shoreline consists of a broad, gently sloping plateau with wide passes that reach up into the mountains. These eastern lands are riven with narrow cutting valleys. Some of the mountain massifs protrude into the Mare and disappear beneath the lava like the foothills of nunataks beneath Antarctic ice. The northern border of Mare Crisium is a fascinating coastline and when the air is still, when, as astronomers say, the 'seeing' is good, you can discern triangular mountains separated by narrow winding valleys penetrating many kilometres into the highlands. When will explorers venture across this region I wonder?

The surface of Mare Crisium, a solidified mass of lava floes several kilometres thick, is by no means smooth. Under a low light numerous wrinkles or ridges, at most only a few hundred metres in height, can be seen. They are termed Dorsa and they cast long shadows. Follow one of them, the Dorsa Harker, south and it will lead you to the site of Luna 24, the last moon lander and the third in the Soviet Union's automated sample return missions. Not far away lies the damaged Luna 23 craft, designed to carry out the same task but crippled during a very rough landing two years previously. Its sample return canister may still be attached forlornly to the main body of the craft, or sunlight may come across it piece by piece scattered over the lunar plain.

Under a higher sun there appear many minute bright spots and delicate white lines on the Mare, deposits laid down billions of years ago by distant impacts and local volcanoes. These, together with the wonderful fan-like rays emanating from the magnificent crater Proclus that lies just beyond the borders of Mare Crisium, make the south-west portion appreciably lighter than the rest of the surface. As you will see later, you can read much of the moon's history in the layers of material on its surface.

Follow another wrinkle, the Dorsum Termier, south and it will bring you to the wreckage of the mysterious Luna 15. The Luna 15 landing was one of the strangest in the history of lunar exploration. While Apollo 11 was en route for the first manned lunar landing, an unmanned Soviet craft was already in lunar orbit – attempting to steal its thunder. Just a few hours after Neil Armstrong and Buzz Aldrin touched down on the Sea of Tranquillity Luna 15 was coming in to land on the Sea of Crises.

There are craters on Mare Crisium itself, though nowhere near as many as can be found on the surrounding highlands. From their numbers astronomers can deduce the age of the surface – the older a surface is, the more craters it is presumed to have. The largest crater on the Mare is Picard – some 23 km across. It has bright walls that rise 1,500 metres above its floor. East of Picard is a sinuous ridge. Variable in altitude and running alongside the border of the Mare, it curves east, ending in a large, partly buried crater-ring. This is indeed a landscape of the past.

Mare Crisium is one of several regions of slightly stronger than average gravity that can deflect orbiting spacecraft. These mass concentrations, or 'mascons', were discovered in the 1960s when spacecraft began orbiting and surveying the moon. The mascon presumably consists of buried fragments of the asteroid whose impact created the basin. The gravity anomaly makes the already complex task of computing the orbits of lunar space probes all the more difficult. It also causes satellites orbiting at low altitudes either to impact the moon or to be flung out into interplanetary space after a few years.

Some astronomers still speak of the vast natural bridge they have seen in a corner of Crisium, between the Promonitorium Lavinium and Olivium. Some claim that there is a huge arch 30 km long and 2 km wide that straddles two mountain ranges. One veteran observer said: 'It looks artificial. It's almost incredible that such a thing could have been formed in the first instance, or if it was formed, could have lasted during the ages in which the moon has been in existence.' Another astronomer claimed in the 1950s that it was not natural and in fact made of iron! But close-up images of the region taken by Lunar Orbiter spacecraft that surveyed the moon prior to the manned landings show no bridge there. It is an illusion caused by the eye straining to see fine detail at the limits of perception. The bridge on the moon has gone the same way as the Canals of Mars.

The brightest crater in the vicinity is Proclus, the second brightest object on the moon. It was formed only about 50 million years ago when an asteroid, approaching at a shallow angle from the south-west, slammed into the moon, and scooped up bright highlands material, scattering it across the surface in a series of brilliant rays. From orbit, Mare Crisium and Proclus are even more spectacular than through a telescope. Only a few people have seen them 'up close and personal'; one of them was Apollo 15 command module pilot Alfred Worden who said: 'It is almost like flying above a haze layer and looking down through the haze at the surface. Ejecta from that crater [Proclus] does not look like it is resting on top of Crisium. It looks like it is suspended over it.'

Go south now and look at the sun rising over the magnificent ramparts of a 136 km crater on the eastern shore of Mare Fecunditatis, the Sea of Fertility. This crater is called Langrenus, after a Dutch mapmaker, Michael van Langren, who drew the first map of the moon in 1645. In 1992 the veteran lunar observer Audouin Dollfus of the Observatoire de Paris was observing Langrenus, using the 1 m Meudon reflecting telescope, when he noticed a series of glows in the crater. Each time he returned to the telescope he noticed that the shape of the glows had changed. He believes they were due to escaping gas that lifted the dust above the surface into the sunlight – perhaps the gas vented from the extensive series of fractures that can be seen on the floor of Langrenus. The moon, it seemed, was not such a dead world as had been supposed.

By day three of the lunation Mare Crisium is visible in all its glory and ghost craters show up in pale outline on its floor. By now its southern neighbour, the Sea of Fertility, is emerging from the lunar night, larger than Crisium but without its well-defined borders. Towards the south it peters out into the highlands near the crater Petavus. To the north a small patch of highland provides the border with Mare Tranquilitatis, the Sea of Tranquillity. From Langrenus you can take your telescope into the southern uplands. Here the terminator is constantly changing as it moves across uncountable craters. Beyond Petavus lies Funerius and the spectacular Rheita Valley which always looks different as the sun never catches it the same way twice.

Some in the ancient world looked up at the moon and believed it to be a mirror that reflected an image of the Earth's lands and seas. Later Leonardo da Vinci (he has an inconspicuous crater with a disintegrated wall not far from Crisium) argued against the idea but it crops up many times over the years. If the spots on the moon, the dark maria, were really a reflection of the Earth, did they correspond with actual lands? Perhaps, with some imagination admittedly, the eastern maria (Crisium, Fecunditatis and Nectaris) could be seen as reflections of Africa, and the western maria (Imbrium, Nubium and Oceanus Procellarum) could be Asia. Did any of the ancients who believed this look at the moon's image reflected in a mirror in the hope of seeing the Earth's unknown lands? Perhaps they did.

In the Bodleian Library in Oxford is an unusual Arabic map of the world as it was known in 1570, a few decades before the telescope showed the moon to be a place with features like the Earth. A comparison of it with the moon shows Africa as a great double peninsula, quite unlike the true shape of Africa but more similar in appearance to Maria Fecunditatis and Nectaris. There is even a large island in the South Atlantic that might be Mare Crisium. Curiously, another island on the extreme west edge of the Bodleian map is described as the place where the souls of the dead reside, another long-held belief about the moon. Some other Arab maps of the period also show southern Africa as a pair of peninsulas. I wonder if the Mountains of the Moon, the name given to the sources of the Nile on maps of Africa drawn two thousand years ago, was given because it was thought that they could be seen reflected in the moon?

Galileo said of the moon at this time: 'On the fourth or fifth day after conjunction, when the moon displays herself to us with brilliant horns, the boundary dividing the light from the dark does not form a uniformly oval line, but is marked by an uneven, rough, and very sinuous line. For several, as it were, bright excrescences extend beyond the border between light and darkness into the dark part, and on the other hand little dark spots enter into the light.' He knew exactly what he was seeing. 'And just as the shadows of the earthly valleys are diminished as the sun climbs higher, so those lunar spots lose their darkness as the luminous part grows.'

★ ★ ★

By day four Mare Crisium is now fully visible. Proclus is very prominent, the Sea of Fertility is now visible, and the sun is just beginning to rise over the Sea of Tranquillity, the site of the first manned landing. Many space probes litter this place. It was one of the favourite regions for Soviet spacecraft because of limitations in their ability to manoeuvre when in lunar orbit. Luna 16 landed here in 1970 and became the first spacecraft to automatically return a rock sample. Later Luna 20 returned a sample from the highland between Crisium and Fecunditatis.

The first of the human footprints to see the sun's rays during the lunation were the last ones to be placed on the lunar surface. Apollo 17 touched down in the valley of Taurus-Littrow on the south-east edge of Serenitatis in December 1972. It is one of the darkest regions of the moon, and many of the small craters the astronauts visited in the valley had been made as a result of the formation of the distant crater Tycho over a hundred million years ago. Under a high magnification you can sometimes see a bright landslide that the astronauts visited.

Look for the sharply defined crater Taruntius on the highland between Serenity and Tranquillity. As Armstrong and Aldrin began their descent to the lunar surface for the first lunar landing in July 1969 they looked down on this region and searched for familiar landmarks to guide them across the south-eastern shores of Tranquillity until they landed near the lunar equator. A part of this region of the moon was recreated on Earth. As astronauts were being trained for landing on the moon, the United States Army took a high-resolution map of a small section of Tranquillity, the area beneath Apollo 11's flight path, and recreated the crater field in the Arizona desert by means of a series of explosions. Then the astronauts were flown over it in a light aircraft. The crater field is still there.

The moon was about four days old when, in 1178, a

Canterbury monk called Gervase and five other monks saw something unusual. There was a bright young moon, and he says its horns were tilted towards the east as is usual for that phase. Suddenly, the upper horn split in two.

Gervase wrote:

> This year, on the evening of 18 June, when the moon, a slim crescent, first became visible, a marvellous phenomenon was seen by several men who were watching it. Suddenly the upper horn of the crescent was split in two. From the midpoint of the division a flaming torch sprang up, spewing out over a considerable distance fire, hot coals and sparks. The body of the moon which was below writhed like a wounded snake. This happened a dozen times or more, and when the moon returned to normal, the whole crescent took on a blackish appearance.

Some believe that what Gervase had seen was something large striking the moon. It is estimated that craters big enough to be seen from Earth are formed at a rate of about one every ten thousand years. During the time they operated, until 1977, seismometers left on the moon by the Apollo manned landings detected about a thousand moonquakes a year. A small fraction of them were the result of impacts by meteoroids, but these impacts were much smaller than the one that June evening so long ago.

Just around the north-east limb of the moon is the crater Bruno, thought to be the youngest crater on the moon. Bruno has a very sharp rim, giving it a new, fresh look. It also has an extensive ray system formed by material scattered in all directions during its formation, and it has the longest rays for its size of any crater on the moon. The longer a crater has existed, the more that subsequent impacts cover or destroy its rays. The continuous assault of micrometeoroids and the solar wind also eats away slowly at the surface, softening contours and obliterating details. With such an extensive and sharp ray system, Bruno must be young indeed.

As well as seismometers the Apollo crews left another instrument at each site, a retro-reflector, whose highly polished, closely aligned mirrors allowed Earth-based lasers to determine very precisely the Earth–moon distance. They're sensitive enough to measure any wobble remaining from the postulated impact. As a result, we know that the moon is still shuddering from the slam of the object that struck it 800 years ago.

It is an interesting story, but not entirely clear-cut. Recent analysis suggests that the moon would have only been just over a day after new and difficult to see on that June night. Also an impact that caused Bruno crater would have showered the earth with ten million tonnes of material, perhaps a trillion meteors in all. The moon's 'wobble' may also be due to internal motions. But the question remains, what did Gervase and his fellow monks see?

By day five, the magnificent crater Theophilus can be seen where Mare Nectaris meets Mare Tranquilitatis. Theophilus is one of the moon's finest craters with a grand central peak complex. Nearby are the equally magnificent Cyrillus and the dramatic Atlai Scarp, formed at the same time as the impact that gouged out the Nectaris basin. Only a few miles east of Theophilus can be found the medium-sized crater of Mädler, named after the German astronomer Johann Mädler who, with his colleague Wilhelm Beer, used a relatively small telescope to produce an excellent map and in 1838 one of the finest books ever written about the moon, *Der Mond*.

By now the broad crescent of the moon is visible during the afternoon and for most of the evening. It will transit, or pass across the meridian, around sunset, so the best time to observe is during the first hours of darkness. The whole of the Sea of Tranquillity and almost all of the Mare Serenitatis, which joins it to the north, are now visible. On the north-western edge of

Serenitatis, the eastern end of the 5,200 m Caucasus mountains are revealed. Travel north and you will reach the mighty crater Aristotle, named after the Greek philosopher who believed the moon to be a perfect, unblemished body. The smooth area immediately north of here is the eastern end of the Sea of Cold (or Mare Frigoris), a long, narrow plain that will take some six nights to emerge from the lunar night.

There is in Serenitatis a tiny crater called Linne, named after the Swedish botanist Karl von Linne. It is small but it is in a sparse part of the Mare so it is easy to see. This seemingly undistinguished feature has probably caused more controversy than any other crater in the history of lunar science (or, as it is sometimes called, selenography).

It is only about 3 km across and 500 m deep but on lunar maps prior to the mid-eighteenth century it appears as a very deep crater. On 16 October 1866 the German observer Julius Schmidt raised the alarm: Linne had changed from a crater to a white spot. It caused a sensation. Suddenly it seemed that the image of the moon as an unchanging world could be wrong, and over the next few years hundreds of telescopes were turned towards this unassuming crater. We shall tell Linne's story later.

The shapes of craters on the moon change with increasing size. The larger the object that strikes the moon, the larger and more complicated will be the crater. Those with diameters of less than 10–15 km have simple shapes. They are like a bowl, about a fifth or sixth as deep as they are wide, and have rims elevated above the surrounding terrain. In the diameter range 20–30 km they have flat floors, and around 40 km in size we begin to see central peaks and terraced walls. The central peaks are important because they consist of rocks that come from 10–20 km below the surface and as such they tell us what the crust is made of. Above about 250 km in size the central peaks become more complex and sometimes form a mountain ring structure. These craters are on the way to becoming basins, the largest and most fundamental structural features on the moon. Above about 330 km in size there are no central peaks. The largest structures on the moon are the multi-ring basins which are over 1,000 km across.

In the south-west of Tranquillity lies the most famous of the many human artefacts left on the moon: the base section of the Apollo 11 landing module, Eagle, from which Neil Armstrong made the 'small step' in 1969. Nearby are three small craters, now called Armstrong, Aldrin and Collins after the crew. Normally lunar features are named posthumously but these are the only nearside features that break that convention. Only 40 km to the north lies the Surveyor 5 craft, a soft lander. Turn north-east, travel a further 60 km and you will reach the place where Ranger 8 struck the moon and formed a small crater as it was vaporized.

The sun now rises on Apollo 16, the only manned landing in the highlands and away from the maria. It is the most difficult of the six landing sites to locate through a telescope. You have to crater-hop westward from Theophilus to identify the spot but when you do you can actually see the splash pattern of South Ray crater. The astronauts tramped over this region and the material they brought back was found to be only two million years old.

The moon is approaching its first quarter, when half the Earth-facing disc is illuminated. This is the most popular time to observe it, as the craters along the terminator are thrown into sharp relief. It will rise around midday and set around midnight and is bright enough to be conspicuous in daylight. Newly revealed tonight is the Mare Vaporum, the Sea of Vapours, roughly the same size as the Mare Crisium but less well defined. It is bounded to the north-east by the Haemus Mountains which form the southern border of Mare Serenitatis. To the north-west are the spectacular Apennine Mountains, a treat to come. Adjoining the Sea of Vapours to the south-west is Sinus Medii (or the Central Bay), the nominal centre point of the lunar disc from which latitude and longitude are measured. Two United States Surveyor craft, numbers 4 and 6, lie within a few km of each other in Sinus Medii. Contact with Surveyor 4 was lost but it may have landed safely. Surveyor 6 was successful and came to rest near a small ridge. You could walk from one to the other in less than an hour.

Between Tranquillity and Vaporum is the Ariadaeus Rille, a magnificent feature, especially when shadows dance along its straight, almost 300 km length. It is up to 5 km wide and some day perhaps visitors will make a magnificent journey along it in a surface rover.

To the south-south-east of Sinus Medii by roughly its diameter is the giant crater Albategnius. An ancient formation, its walls are interrupted by many more recent craters. This may be the most prominent crater on Galileo's first drawing of the moon in 1609. We suspect it was but cannot be certain because Galileo's drawing, while impressive, was not that accurate. In 1962, it was the target of the first experiment to project a laser beam onto the lunar surface. As is usual for such old, rounded features, its current sharp relief will appear to diminish considerably as the full moon approaches and the shadows disappear.

To the west of Sinus Medii is a wrecked crater with a disintegrated wall some 34 km across, named after another lunar mapper, Johann Schröter. In 1822 Franz von Paula Gruithuisen, a German health official (who invented a device for crushing gall stones!) and moon observer, saw what he thought was an entire city inside Schröter. In twenty-five thick logbooks he wrote that he could see what he called a fortified structure with regular walls. Here was proof that the Selenites, as he called them, were defending themselves against something:

In all probability we have before us a city with underground vaults where the Selenites are forced to live to protect them from the intense heat of the day and the cold of the night . . . two straight dykes must have been constructed to block the cold passing wind that rages through the south-western mountains . . . there is a well sheltered park where the Selenites can catch their breath from time to time . . . you can make out a star-shaped configuration . . . it might be a kind of temple, dedicated to the stargazers . . . don't forget that on the moon the stars can be seen during the daytime.

Gruithuisen's city is just a ruined mountain and a wrecked crater but it is fascinating to focus on it and imagine what he thought as he stared down upon it. Unfortunately there are many who, even today, cling to the belief that they have found artificial structures on the moon and that space agencies have been engaged in a big cover-up. There are many websites that show unconvincing, fuzzy, overblown images which are claimed to be structures or monoliths. They are all nonsense, all unconvincing, all wishful thinking. I would like to find an alien artefact on the moon, placed there because it would survive unmolested by weather for far longer than it would on the Earth, only to be reached if we attained spaceflight. There is no evidence that we have seen one, but then again we have explored so little of the moon.

Now comes the hour that everyone who knows the moon even a little has been waiting for. The eastern end of the enormous and majestic Mare Imbrium, the Sea of Rains, is glimpsed for the first time. So vast is this Sea that it will take a further three nights to emerge from the darkness. Someday explorers will visit the grave of Luna 2 that lies hereabouts. It was the first man-made object to touch the moon over forty years ago. But, despite Soviet propaganda at the time, there will be no scattered field of Soviet metal pennants. The impact would have been so great that there is probably only a small crater there. Any metal in the vicinity would have been vaporized.

Here lives the magnificent crater Aristullus and north-north-west of it can be seen Piton, an isolated mountain inside Imbrium that is an eerie sight when the sun catches its summit. Very few such features exist on the moon – most lunar mountains belong to ranges such as the mighty Alps that guard the northern edge of Imbrium. Cutting through the Alps can be seen the sharp gash of the Alpine Valley that stretches north-east across the uplands to Mare Frigoris, the Sea of Cold. With a powerful telescope, a narrow river-like rille may be seen winding along its floor. At the moment the huge oval plain that is dark-floored Plato lights up the terminator, along with another mountain, Pico. Here is also Mont Blanc which can look so dramatic nestled close to the main wall of the Alps north of the crater Cassini. It is 3,600 m high but, being 30 km across, the average slope is only 15 degrees, so walking up it would require little effort in one-sixth of Earth's gravity. The view from the summit must be magnificent, as you would be able to see more than 100 km in all directions. Look north and you would see a great parting in the mountain front, the start of the Alpine Valley.

Apollo 15's remains lie not far from here in the most dramatic of manned landing sites. The region is best seen a day or two after first quarter. Hadley Rille, a winding gash across the surface, probably a collapsed tube that once held lava, lies in shadow for a while after local sunrise. Look at a photograph of the lunar surface, or with a strained eye at the eyepiece, and if you are lucky you will see the elbow where astronauts David Scott and Jim Irwin looked into the chasm. Johann Mädler's colleague, Wilhelm Beer, has his crater hereabouts. It is 250 km from the base of the Apennines. It is circular with a sharp rim, only 10 km across, one of the simple craters I mentioned; perhaps a bit paltry considering his contribution to lunar science, but not as paltry as some.

I guess it's no surprise that I often daydream about visiting the lunar surface: walking along in one-sixth gravity across that pristine, elemental landscape, aware of my breathing behind my faceplate and the internal reflections of my visor. What would it be like to stand on top of Mons La Hire before local sunrise? Picture yourself on a sunlit lunar hill, surrounded by the black lunar night, when on the eastern horizon you see a dazzling bright point of light. The limb of the sun is just peeping over the horizon. Looking downwards, you see the sunlight race over the sun-facing slope and over you.

Now the moon is gibbous, that phase between quarter and full. It's visible throughout the afternoon and evening, and bright enough to be conspicuous in daylight. It is now that the moon's finest mountain range, the Apennines, is revealed in its true glory. The westward march of the terminator has revealed half of Mare Imbrium as a smooth semi-circle. On the northern shore of Imbrium lies the distinctive dark circle of Plato. Archimedes, not far away, echoes the larger and darker Plato, said to be one of the centres of mysterious obscuration effects such as strange mists.

North, across the long horizontal ribbon that is Mare Frigoris, resides the not-so-large but still interesting crater Anaxagoras. It is just one degree outside the moon's equivalent of the Arctic circle. Because of the tilt of the moon's orbit the sun can vary in altitude by about 12 degrees, meaning that the seasons are slight on the moon. The maximum altitude of the sun, as seen from Anaxagoras, is about 25 degrees. This, combined with the crater's considerable depth, means that the sun will never clear its southern rim sufficiently to illuminate its whole floor, and it may, like many other polar craters, contain a pool of permanent, freezing darkness. The Lunar Prospector probe obtained evidence of large quantities of ice near the poles. If humankind ever build a base on the moon, and I expect we will, it will probably be within walking distance of these ice fields.

At the centre of the disc you will now see a chain of three imposing craters: Ptolemaeus, Alphonsus and Arzachel. Now watch the sunrise over Ptolemaeus. When sunlight strikes its floor at a grazing angle (shining along rather than down) you can see an amazing variety of features, depressions, hills, tiny craters. Alphonsus is named after the thirteenth-century Spanish king Alfonso the Wise, who once said: 'Had I been present at the creation, I would have given some useful hints for the better ordering of the universe.' In 1965 the probe Ranger 9 transmitted a series of spectacular images of Alphonsus before impacting north-east of its centre. In 1956 an American astronomer thought he saw what looked like a cloud hanging over its central peak. Two years later Russian astronomer Nikolai Kozyrev saw a cloud with a reddish glow while watching the same area from the Kharkov Observatory in the Crimea. Evidence of weak volcanic activity, perhaps.

Kozyrev was arrested by Stalin's police in 1936 during a purge of 'dangerous' intellectuals. His wife, along with the wives of other astronomers, was also imprisoned. He was sentenced to two years in a labour camp but soon the sentence was altered – to death. He was saved because there was no firing squad at his prison. Fortunately his second appeal was successful and he was sentenced to ten years in prison. He died in 1983 and has a crater, on the moon's far side, named after him.

Although Imbrium is glorious do not ignore the other end of the moon for it has wonders of its own. Set into the southern edge of the Mare Nubium is the old walled plain Pitatus, on the western edge of which is the smaller and similarly old Hesiodus. There is a breech in their shared wall which, when the morning terminator is nearby, produces the Hesiodus Sunrise Ray – a beam which briefly arcs across the floor of the crater. Adjacent to this is the smaller Hesiodus A, an example of an extremely rare double concentric crater, the result of an impact being followed by another, smaller impact on exactly the same spot. I suppose, given the number of impacts on the moon, it had to happen some-where.

Look to the south and you may see the crater Tycho. It is a

modest feature now, but in just a few nights it will become the centre of a huge ray system that will dominate the entire moon. In 1968 Surveyor 7 landed on its northern rim. By Surveyor 6 the Surveyor mission goals had been achieved (to understand the nature of the moon's surface for the manned landings), so Surveyor 7 was given to the scientists to land just where they wanted and they chose Tycho. Two diameters to the south-east of Tycho is the massive Maginus, a 185 km wide walled plain, its walls still 5 km high despite hundreds of millions of years of battering by meteorites. Look at it well for it has an impressive grandeur but by the time Tycho reaches its full glory, mighty Maginus will have become almost invisible. Apollo 17 samples of ejecta from Tycho show it to be 108 million years old.

By day nine of the moon's cycle the terminator has reached one of the moon's finest sights: the magnificent terraced crater Copernicus. Although not the largest crater (this title belongs to Bailly in the southern uplands) or the deepest (probably Newton), or the brightest (Aristarchus) or with the largest ray system (Tycho), it is undoubtedly one of the most dramatic features on the moon. In 1966 the United States Lunar Orbiter 2 was only 45 km above the moon when it looked northwards across Copernicus. The picture it took was called the 'picture of the century'; you can see the ramparts and the intervening plains and the 400 m central peak. Before it was cancelled, Apollo 20 was due to have landed on that central mountain and sampled material thrown up from inside the moon. Look on it now and wonder at what could have been.

A billion years ago or so an object several km across smashed into the moon on the southern shore of the Sea of Rains. The asteroid penetrated so deep into the moon's crust, and the explosion was so enormous that Copernicus, a crater nearly 100 km wide, was gouged out. Streams of vaporized rock flew upwards and clouds of minute glassy particles were thrown all

over the moon. Having been compacted, the lunar crust
rebounded and thrust great blocks of crust upwards to form the
central mountains that were then surrounded by vast lakes of
molten lava. The great seventeenth-century astronomer Hevelius
called this crater Mount Etna and Van Langren called it Félipe IV
of Spain and set it in King Philip's Ocean.

South of Tycho, which is becoming more prominent with each
passing hour, is the huge Clavius. Even foreshortened by its high
latitude it is a dramatic sight, and it can be clearly seen that its
floor is convex because of the moon's curvature. Across its floor a
series of diminishing craters runs in a pretty curve from the south
to the west wall. There are six in all and they make an interesting
test of a telescope's power to count how many are visible.

Day ten is the night of the young craters Copernicus and Tycho. To
the north of Copernicus the whole of Mare Imbrium is seen, a
smooth ellipse bounded by mountain ranges, the Alps, the Caucasus, the Apennines and the Carpathian Mountains. What a titanic
impact it must have been to create the Imbrium basin? On the
north-western edge of Imbrium lies the Sinus Iridium or the Bay of
Rainbows. Ringed by the Jura Mountains, this is one of the most
enchanting sights on the entire moon. Its sunrise, when the floor is
in shadow and the Jura Mountains are illuminated so they seem to
protrude into the blackness and give a 'jewelled handle effect', is
heartbreakingly beautiful. Some day, someone will be the first to
stand in this bay, on the almost black lunar surface. In the west there
will be a wavy, horizontal sunlit band of lunar mountains; in the east
the glow of the solar corona and the zodiacal light (sunlight
reflected from dust in between the planets) will herald the dawn.

The western arm of the bay is the Heraclides Promontory and
there is an intriguing drawing of this region by Jean Dominique
Cassini, Director of the Paris Observatory in the seventeenth
century, discoverer of a gap in Saturn's rings and mapper of the

moon. On one of the drawings the promontory appears as a lady's head looking out into the Mare. These so-called 'moon maidens' can be seen from time to time, though none are as enchanting as the one drawn by Cassini. The eye likes to see patterns; we are programmed from birth to see faces, in carpets and curtains and on the moon. Nearby, about 50 km to the south-west, lies the silent Lunokhod 1. In 1970 it was the first wheeled vehicle on the moon. Remotely controlled from the Earth, it roamed across 11 km and saw over 200 lunar panoramas. It survived several lunar nights.

The sun now reaches the landing site of Apollo 14 at Frau Mauro, a region of battered craters with broken rims inundated with lava. Only 150 km to the west lies Apollo 12 with Surveyor 3 right alongside. Frau Mauro is an interesting, old-looking region. Several Apollo rockets and discarded Apollo Lunar Module ascent stages were deliberately crashed here, although their impact-craters are too small to be visible from Earth.

By day eleven the gibbous moon is visible for the evening and for much of the morning, and it will transit during the few hours before midnight. By now the mighty Oceanus Procellarum is showing more of itself each night. You can also witness sunrise over Kepler which, although only 32 km wide, is a complex young crater with a marvellous ray system. North and slightly west from Kepler can be found intriguing Aristarchus. At full moon this is the brightest object on the lunar surface. Measuring 43 km wide and 3 km deep, it is also the centre of an extensive network of rilles. In 1969 the crew of Apollo 11 saw a luminous glow in this region. The largest sinuous valley on the moon is nearby. Schröter's Valley, named after the German astronomer Johann Schröter, starts about 25 km north of the crater Herodotus. It resembles a dry river bed with numerous meanders and eventually opens up to form what observers call a 'Cobra's head' which is thought to be a collapsed lava tube.

For centuries there have been reports of TLPs (Transient Lunar Phenomena), reddish or bluish glows, mists and sometimes bright flashes near certain craters and valleys. There are several explanations: weak volcanic activity, perhaps; or the escape of gases trapped beneath the moon's surface; or impact by meteors. Many lunar geologists have doubted their existence. The moon, they have argued, is a dead world. There might perhaps be a rockfall here and there, or a small impact by a meteor, but not volcanic activity.

In 1996 the Clementine lunar orbiting satellite returned over two million images and provided an unprecedented opportunity to study the question of TLPs. As Clementine photographed the moon from orbit, a team of amateur astronomers were mobilized to provide almost continuous observations of our satellite and in at least four cases Clementine images were obtained before and after reports of TLPs by ground-based observers.

One exciting case concerned an incident near the so-called Cobra Head on the Aristarchus plateau. On 23 April 1994, amateur astronomers noticed a 'possible obscuration over the region'. Clementine images taken on 3 March and again on 27 April do indeed show a change; part of the region is a slightly different colour. It is also a region where TLPs have been seen in the past. Perhaps pockets of gas seep up through the ground and, when caught by the bright rays of the lunar dawn, glow in reds and blues. Or perhaps heating effects cause sub-surface explosions. Either way, as a world, the moon is dead. But it seems that occasionally, in specific places, something does stir.

By now the crater Gassendi is almost fully illuminated. Nearby craters Grimaldi, Riccioli and Hevelius, named after early mappers of the moon, can be seen significantly positioned on the other side of the moon from Langrenus. Grimaldi, first seen last night, stands out conspicuously dark and tonight it is joined by

Riccioli just to the north-west. Here another cluster of spacecraft lies scattered across the lunar plains: Luna 9, which made the first landing on the moon and sent back the first picture from the lunar surface, as well as Luna 8 and 13. On the edge of Procellarum, not far from Luna 9, is the tiny light speck of the crater called Galileo, hardly a fitting tribute to the man who first saw the moon for what it was: a mountainous, three-dimensional world.

The southern shore of Oceanus Procellarum is one of my favourites. Here, in a wrecked, almost classical landscape, are vast ancient craters deluged by lava. Letronne is half there and half not. And the surface of the Mare ripples occasionally, outlining a crater's rim buried below the surface. Below mare Humorum is the large crater Schikard with a dark, convex floor. Its curvature is so extreme that its walls cannot be seen from its centre. Nearer the limb than Schikard is one of the weirdest objects on the moon. Until fairly recently astronomers puzzled over Wargentin, which appears as a crater filled to the brim with lava, like a plateau. The twentieth-century astronomer Harold Urey used to keep pictures of it in his study and say, 'Wargentin worries me.' But nowadays we see it as something quite simple. At some point in its history, lava welled up from inside and was contained by its even and unbroken walls. Then, just before it reached the rim, the flow stopped and the lava set. The result is a smooth, flat-topped disc, which has been nicknamed 'The Thin Cheese' due to its resemblance to a huge Camembert.

We are almost at full moon, when the shadowless moon takes on an entirely new appearance. The full moon is visible throughout the night and transits around midnight. Such a bright light in the sky, when combined with the right atmospheric conditions, can create some interesting optical effects — such as the ghostly lunar rainbow or a moonbow whose colours are less intense but no less impressive than a daytime rainbow.

When ice crystals are present in the high atmosphere a lunar halo can sometimes be seen. Because the crystals have six sides they normally refract light at an angle of 22 degrees, creating a halo around the moon of that diameter. But sometimes a halo is produced by other light refractions through the ice crystals and a halo can appear at 46 degrees. If you are ever lucky enough to see one of these look carefully at it. You will notice that its pale colours are reversed; the inner edge of the 46-degree ring is reddish and its outer edge blue, just the opposite of the 22-degree ring. With the right combination of humidity and angle sometimes a mock moon or a moondog can be seen at one of several angles to its side.

When high in the sky the moon will appear much smaller than when it is rising or setting – a phenomenon known as the moon illusion.

When viewed close to the horizon the moon appears to be strikingly larger than when it is high in the sky. In reality, there is no difference; the effect is one of perception. But why we should perceive the low-down moon as larger is a question that has puzzled scientists and philosophers for thousands of years. Ptolemy proposed the notion of 'filled space', saying that when the moon is near the horizon our brains can see it next to familiar landmarks whose size we know. Later the Arab astronomer Alhazen developed this theory. This comparison, which is not possible when the moon is high, allows our brain to judge the moon as being larger. In 1913 an Italian psychologist, Mario Ponzo, tried to explain the phenomenon using a drawing of a railroad track. Imagine a photograph of a railroad track going off into the distance and take two thin strips of paper each the same length. Place one at the foot of the photograph over the nearest rails and place the other one over rails that are some distance away. Now stand back and look at the strips of paper, the upper strip appears to be bigger because it spans a greater apparent distance between the rails and the brain compensates for this effect.

Other scientists have pointed out that airline pilots flying at very high altitudes also experience the moon illusion, so perhaps foreground objects are not the whole explanation. A more recent theory is that the brain interprets the horizon moon as being much farther away than the elevated moon because it has no clues as to its real distance. When we look at a distant person or motor car our brain automatically estimates its distance from how large humans or motor cars should be. Next to the person or car there are usually many other clues that enable an accurate perception of distance to be computed. But our brains just do not have the experience or point of reference required to estimate the distance to the moon.

The glorious moon of autumn, the harvest moon, is no ordinary full moon. Throughout the year the moon rises about 50 minutes later every night but near the autumnal equinox the night-to-night difference is only about 30 minutes, meaning that for a few nights the full moon will rise up just after sunset. For farmers racing to harvest their crops this is a natural blessing, unless you live in the southern hemisphere where the effect is reversed.

The full moon of 22 December 1999 was rather special. That full moon occurred at the time of the northern hemisphere winter solstice, when the Earth–moon system was closest to the sun, and at the time when the moon was at its closest to the Earth in its orbit. It's a line-up that happens from time to time. This full moon was about 25 per cent brighter than the average full moon. But not many were able to see such changes. I remember going out to look at it on that night, and because I had nothing to compare it with could not draw from my memory how bright it normally appeared. But something strange does happen to the moon when it is full, something that tells us about what its surface is like.

In the day before full the moon jumps in brightness by 30 per cent so that the full moon appears somewhat brighter than it would if the brightness of the moon's illuminated surface was merely spread out across its entire face. The mechanism responsible for this 'lunar opposition' effect is still a subject of debate among astronomers and recent studies have yielded contradictory results. A few years ago it was suggested that it was due to an effect called coherent backscatter which causes light to be reflected more in one direction by the lunar soil than in others. Another suggestion that has some support is that a simple lack of shadows, when the sun is overhead, makes the moon much brighter. Perhaps unsurprisingly, very recent studies suggest that both mechanisms have an influence.

Near the eastern limb, north of the Mare Crisium by about its width, is the large walled plain Gauss. With extremely favourable libration, a small crater may be glimpsed to its east at an apparent separation of just over twice its width. (Libration is the rocking of the moon that turns one side of it, then the other, towards the Earth, allowing us a better view of features near the limb.)

When the moon is tilted towards the Earth more than usual, and if you have a really good telescope, you can look beyond the dark oval that is the crater Grimaldi and towards the mysterious Cordillera Mountains that stand along the edge of the moon. Some of these peaks rise to over 6,100 m. They are part of the rugged outer ring surrounding the dramatic Mare Orientale, the Eastern Sea, a gigantic, relatively young, far-side feature whose importance is not realized from this aspect.

By day sixteen of the lunation Mare Crisium will be visible in its entirety for the last time before the terminator sweeps westwards across it. To the south, Langrenus shows in strong relief and looks very different from the way it did just a few days ago during the full moon. As Mare Crisium goes you can take a closer look at the Rheita Valley. It has a strange shape, and is thought to be a series of craters that have run together. The gibbous moon is visible during the late evening and for much of the morning, and will transit during the last hours of darkness. The Sea of Tranquillity is now half in darkness. To the north of it, the rough oval of the Sea of Serenity is still complete. At their junction, the crater Pliny stands out well against the smooth darkness and at the north-east section of Serenitatis, the larger Posidonius shows as a bright ring. To its south, the sun is setting on the last footprints to be placed on the moon. As Apollo 17 astronaut Gene Cernan raised his foot from the moon in December 1972 and started to climb the ladder to the cabin of the Lunar Module he threw down a challenge for others to place their footprints on more distant worlds. His challenge remains unanswered.

By day twenty-one, and about a third of the way down the terminator, Mare Serenitatis is lost to the darkness. The Caucasus Mountains on its north-west edge and the Apennines that border Mare Imbrium are thrown into spectacular relief by the setting sun. The moon has just passed its last quarter, rising around midnight and setting around noon, and is bright enough to be conspicuous in daylight. Mare Imbrium is next to go into shadow and the lengthening shadows make the Apennines look especially three-dimensional. Look for the last time now at Autolycus, and, to the north-east of Archimedes, Aristullus. The flooded floor of Archimedes is still almost entirely in light, but the interiors of its smaller neighbours are totally black, indicating their much greater depth. The area bounded by these three craters has been named Sinus Lunicus, to commemorate Luna 2.

The broad crescent moon of lunation day twenty-three is visible for most of the morning until the afternoon. The best time to observe it will be during the last hours of darkness. The last quarter is not nearly as often observed as the first quarter, a consequence of its unsocial hours, but it is just as rewarding. The late phases of the moon have an emotional power because they are the phases we do not normally seem. Familiar features lit by sunlight coming from the other side see strange to those who have only looked at the moon before midnight. Tonight you can see sunset approaching the Sea of Rains. Few sights on the moon compare to the mighty Mare Imbrium entering shadow.

When Galileo first looked at the moon through a telescope four centuries ago, it is probable that he saw it as it appears tonight. Certainly, this is how he drew it in three of the five illustrations in his *Sidereus Nuncius* ('The Celestial Messenger') of 1610. In his drawings you can clearly see the bright arcs of the Alps and the Apennines reaching out into the dark side from the northern and southern edges of Mare Imbrium. This is his commentary:

Let us speak first about the face of the moon that is turned toward our sight, which, for the sake of easy understanding, I divide into two parts, namely a brighter one and a darker one. The brighter part appears to surround and pervade the entire hemisphere, but the darker part, like some cloud, stains its very face and renders it spotted. Indeed the darkish and rather large spots are obvious to everyone, and every age has seen them. For this reason we shall call them the large or ancient spots, in contrast with the other spots, smaller in size and occurring with such frequency that besprinkle the entire lunar surface, but especially the brighter part. These were, in fact, observed by no one before us.

How fascinating it is to peer through a telescope with a copy of the *Sidereus Nuncius* and read these words while looking at the moon's last quarter. All astronomers and students of astronomy should read it, for its passion and sense of discovery are inspiring. But, as for no one else observing the 'other spots' on the moon before him, Galileo was wrong.

Near the terminator and about a quarter of the way north from the southern cusp is the irregular Mare Nubium, the Sea of Clouds. In its south-east region a light hairline may be seen running north-east to south-west. This is the Straight Wall (Rupes Recta), a 95 km long fault that, despite its sharp appearance, is not a precipitous cliff. In fact it is never more than a moderate slope reaching only a few hundred metres in height. It faces towards the west, and consequently is at its brightest at this time. The deep interior of Tycho now displays strong contrast but its dramatic ray system which made it the focal point of the full moon has all but disappeared. Now the huge oval of Mare Imbrium lies half in darkness. The moon is returning to a crescent again.

By day twenty-five the best time to observe the moon is during the last hours of darkness. Despite the beauty of its crescent form there is somehow a feeling of loss when you observe the moon at this time. Copernicus is absent and the focal point is the striking crater Kepler which is level with the mid-point of the terminator. Aristarchus is magnificent. To the south-west of the western end of the Jura Mountains, on the plains of Procellarum, is the site where the Soviet Luna 17 soft-landed in 1970. Its payload was Lunokhod 1, the first vehicle to travel on lunar soil. Tonight, if you could see them, its tyre tracks would be a fine chain of small shadows stretching across the wasteland. Follow them and you will eventually reach the rover, sleeping now, its only contact with its home planet the occasional laser beam that strikes the retro-reflectors on its roof before returning home after a round trip time of just three seconds.

On day twenty-six the crescent moon is easily seen during the last hours of darkness but it is fading, getting smaller, and will soon be gone. In this light, the contrast between the dark maria and the bright uplands is slight. And by day twenty-seven it will only be visible for a short while before sunrise, low in the east. Soon the moon is gone. Each month the moon disappears from the sky for three days – I wonder if the ancient biblical prophecy that the Messiah will rise again on the third day is something to do with the moon's absence and rebirth?

Galileo, Hevelius, Grimaldi, Riccioli and the other craters belonging to each of the astronomers we shall soon meet are now in darkness. But there is one crater that, being on the far side, is still in sunlight. Until 1970 this particular crater was without a name but now we call it Harriot. Remember it.

CHAPTER THREE

A Light Not Its Own

Today there is only one surviving column of the Temple of Hera on the Aegean island of Samos. Hera was the goddess of women and marriage and queen of heaven. In some accounts she was even older than Zeus himself. She was an ancient mother goddess he never quite conquered. Two and a half thousand years ago the temple was a place for her worship. She married Zeus and they honeymooned here, it is said, not far from the site of the temple. On a clear night on Samos you are reminded of her presence because when she was with child her milk spilt across the heavens to form the Milky Way. But also in the sky over the temple, sometimes brilliant, sometimes out of sight, was a goddess far older than Hera, a strange, complex and mysterious goddess.

For the Greeks the moon was a holy trinity. When growing in the sky she was Artemis, goddess of the hunter and friend to mortals. When full she was beautiful Selene, from the word *selas* meaning 'light', sister to Eos the dawn, known for her love affairs and the three daughters she had by Zeus. When waning or new she was the mysterious and brooding Hecate, which means 'influence from afar', in later years said to be the daughter of Zeus and Hera. She dwelt in the underworld but had power everywhere. The Greeks regarded her as supreme, both in heaven and hell; the owl flying through the moonlit sky was her messenger.

The first renaissance took place on the small islands of the Aegean. Samos must have been an exciting place to be in the sixth century BC. Its political system allowed those rare privileges, free speech and worship, and the introduction of the

Phoenician alphabet led to widespread literacy. It was at the geographical crossroads of Asia, Africa and Europe; it was also at an intellectual crossroads. One day, perhaps someone who stared at the many-columned temple of Hera, the finest in Greece, had the idea that the moon might not be a god.

The free thinkers of Samos started along a path that would lead them to very modern ideas about the universe. Philosophers like Democritus, who came a century or so later, believed in many worlds wandering through space – sometimes he thought they must collide – but he never thought that such an idea would apply to the birth of the moon. He did think about the moon and speculated that the dark markings on its face were mountains. He was right. His 'modern' notions of the physical world included a belief that nothing existed except atoms and the void. Naturally, he did not believe in Hera's milk; the Milky Way was made up of unresolved stars.

So many ideas, so many people asking questions. Thales of Miletus, a city in Asia not far from Samos, is said by some to have been the first person to suggest that the moon's light was reflected from the sun. Another Greek philosopher, Parmenides, was later to write of the moon that it had 'light not of its own', and was 'always gazing towards the rays of the sun'. Thales believed that water was the basic element of the universe and was aware of the moon's special relationship with water. Heraclitus says Thales predicted the solar eclipse of 585 BC and he is credited with discovering the seasons of the year and developing a 365-day calendar. There is a story that one night he fell into a well while out walking and staring up at the night sky.

The Greeks were the great geometers, able to probe the universe with simple theorems. They made observations of the sky, combined them with lines drawn in the sand, and discovered that the logic of geometry reached into the heavens. They were the first to show that man could comprehend, explain and in a way master the universe. They measured the distance to the moon using logic. On Thales' tomb was the inscription: 'Here in a narrow tomb great Thales lies; yet his renown for wisdom reached the skies.'

The great Pythagoras, he of the theory of right-angled triangles and much more, was born on Samos. It is said that when young he visited Thales and the old man created a strong impression, inspiring him to study mathematics and astronomy. He attended lectures given by Thales' pupil Anaximander who had definite views about the moon: ' . . . the moon appears now to wax and now to wane because of the stopping and opening of passages [in the sky]. The wheel of the sun is 27 times the size of [the earth, while that of] the moon is 18 times as large. The sun is the highest of all, and lowest are the wheels of the stars.' Pythagoras was unconvinced; he had his own ideas.

He travelled to southern Italy and in 518 BC founded a philosophical and religious school at Croton. Although his followers had many strange customs, at the core of their philosophy was something quite remarkable and profound. They believed that, at its deepest level, reality is mathematical. To them astronomy and music were sister sciences and there was a music of the spheres that only Pythagoras could hear. Caused by the planets moving through the cosmos, each had its own distinctive musical pitch and the moon was but a single bass tone in this celestial fugue.

The Pythagoreans called the moon the counter-Earth and believed it to be a mirror-like body. Some Pythagoreans said that the reason the moon went through its phases was because it was a spreading flame kindled until it became the full moon and thereafter slowly dying. Some said that its appearance was due to its being inhabited by animals and plants, like those on our earth, only greater and more beautiful. Some believed that the moon was the place souls passed through on the way to the paradise fields of the stars. Some Greeks located the Elysian Fields, home of the blessed dead, in the moon, and the shoes of senators were sometimes decorated with ivory crescents to show that after death they would inhabit the moon. Later Rome would teach 'the souls of the just are purified in the moon'. Whatever it was, for Pythagoras, and many others who followed him for two thousand years, the moon marked a fundamental boundary in the cosmos. All things below it were subject to change and decay, while from the moon upwards there was only eternal, unchanging perfection. Some suggested that the stained face of the moon indicated that it was inside the realm of decay but this view did not gain as much currency as the notion that the moon was perfect, despite its spots.

In about the fifth century BC the divorce took place between the calendar month and the moon, although even today we have relics of the old lunar way of marking time. For instance, the moon still governs movable feasts such as Easter, Passover, Rosh Hashanah and Hanukkah. Today the Islamic calendar is still lunar, an annual round of lunar cycles, 10–11 days short of the western solar-based one. Hence, the Islamic seasons move around the calendar every thirty-four years.

In the fifth century BC the Greek astronomer Meton discovered that the dates of the phases of the moon repeated almost exactly after a period of nineteen years. He found that in nineteen years there were about 235 lunations. This was one of the secrets of eclipse prediction but he may not have been the first to recognize this regularity. All over north-western Europe are stone circles whose alignment suggests that the nineteen-year secret of the moon was known to far more ancient people than Meton.

In 450, when Anaxogoras was asked what the purpose of life was, he answered: 'the investigation of the sun, the moon, and the heavens'. In 467 BC he observed a meteorite fall to Earth and suggested that stone-like masses originally solidified as the Earth and were then flung back into space. (Remember that description, we will hear of it again later.) But the intellectual climate started turning colder. Soon it was dangerous to believe that the moon had anything in common with the Earth and Anaxogoras' manuscript had to be distributed in secret. When it was discovered he was imprisoned and when eventually released he travelled to Ionia where he established a school. In many ways, the climate would remain inhospitable until the Renaissance arrived almost two thousand years later.

In 413 BC a lunar eclipse affected the outcome of the Battle of Syracuse. The Carthaginians and the Greeks had settled along the southern coast of Sicily and there were occasional conflicts. In the Peloponnesian War between Athens and Sparta the Athenians had a major force near Syracuse. Commander Nicias was in charge. Plutarch takes up the story in 'Nicias, the Slave of Fear'.

> . . . the Athenian soldiers heard the news that the Syracusans had just received more men and supplies from the fickle Sicilians, who now were backing Syracuse again. Nicias realised that the situation was hopeless, and he gave orders to pack up and sail back to Athens. But just as the Athenians were about to hoist anchor, there was an eclipse of the moon. Nicias called off the departure until the omens were more favourable.

It was a fatal delay for Nicias whose forces were defeated. He was captured and stoned to death in Syracuse. Depending whose side you were on, eclipses of the moon, and the sun as well, were often useful in battle. Years later the Romans used a lunar eclipse to their advantage at Pydna in 168 BC, a battle crucial to their control of Greece.

Plato was driven by the same faith that drives today's physicists who search for a fundamental theory of everything: the faith that nature is basically simple. Plato believed that the world was constructed with a geometric simplicity and elegance and he was certain that the sun, moon and planets would have a natural circular motion, since that is the simplest uniform motion that repeats itself endlessly. The 'fixed stars' moved in simple circles about the North Star, but the sun, moon and planets traced out much more complicated paths across the sky or, according to Plato, paths that only appeared to be more complicated. Their motions were reasonably well known, as they had been followed closely since early Babylonian times. Plato suggested that perhaps their complicated paths across the sky were actually combinations of simple circular motions, and he challenged his Athenian colleagues to prove it.

At Plato's academy, Eudoxus placed all the fixed stars on a huge sphere, with the Earth on a much smaller sphere fixed at the centre of all things. The huge sphere rotated about the Earth once every twenty-four hours. Eudoxus assumed the sun to be attached to another sphere, concentric with the fixed stars' sphere and also centered on the Earth. This new sphere, lying entirely inside the sphere that held the fixed stars, had to be transparent, so that the fixed stars could be seen through it. The sun sphere went around every twenty-four hours but, in addition, it rotated slowly about the two axis points where it was attached to the big sphere, and this extra rotation was also once a year. This ingenious device showed that complicated motions in the sky could be explained by combinations of simple motions, almost. Aristotle wrote a summary of the idea that included fifty-five concentric transparent spheres. He believed the crystal spheres were real, although Eudoxus may have viewed them as simply a computational device.

Aristarchus of Samos also lived in the third century BC but he believed that the Earth was one of the planets and that the stars were very far away. Others had argued that the Earth was a sphere, which was, after all, the most perfect shape. Some had even suggested that the spherical Earth moved but it was Aristarchus who attempted to shatter the crystal spheres by suggesting that the Earth went around the sun. His universe was larger than many of his contemporaries. It would be almost 2,000 years before his idea took hold. His treatise 'On the Sizes and Distances of the Sun and Moon' was a breakthrough in finding distances to objects in the universe. We recognize Aristarchus' universe: his moon received its light from the sun as it circled the Earth. According to Archimedes:

> Aristarchus of Samos produced a book consisting of some hypotheses, in which the premises lead to the result that the universe is many times greater than it is now called. He believed that the fixed stars and the sun remained unmoved, that the Earth revolves around the sun in a circumference of a circle, the sun lying in the middle of the orbit.

He was right.

To determine the sizes of the sun and moon, Aristarchus used an ingenious method. He started with the observation that the disc of the moon just covers the sun during a solar eclipse. He knew that this was not always true; sometimes the sun appeared a bit larger or smaller but that was a secondary effect to be accounted for afterwards. His second observation was that during a lunar eclipse the shadow of the Earth appears to be about twice as large as the moon at the moon's distance. Armed with these simple facts, he constructed an Eclipse Diagram which he used to show that the Earth is approximately three times larger than the moon, and that the radius of the sun is more than six times larger than the radius of the Earth. Aristarchus' geometry was perfect but unfortunately his measurements were rather inaccurate. His value for the angle between the sun, the Earth and the moon was off by a few degrees, and the width of the Earth's shadow cone at the moon is actually about three rather than two moon diameters. Today, using the correct values, we can easily show that the sun is about 400 times further from the Earth than the moon, and its diameter is approximately 109 times greater than that of the Earth. The universe is even larger than Aristarchus thought.

Centuries later the Roman historian Plutarch wrote about Aristarchus' ideas in his *De Facie in Orbe Lunae* or 'On the face of the moon's orb'. He tells us that Aristarchus' contemporaries were unimpressed. The general opinion was that of a certain Dercyllides, who said:

> we must suppose the Earth, the Hearth of the House of the Gods according to Plato, to remain fixed, and the planets with the whole embracing heaven to move, and reject with abhorrence the view of those who have brought to rest the things which move and set in motion the things which by their nature and position are unmoved, such a supposition being contrary to the hypotheses of mathematics.

Aristarchus' model was not accepted, not even his suggestion that the Earth rotates about its axis every twenty-four hours. His was a lonely voice that is heard more clearly today than it ever was during his lifetime. He had no followers in his generation, nor in the generation after.

It is the Greek Hipparchus (c. 190–125 BC) who is considered by some to be the greatest astronomer of antiquity. He rejected Aristarchus' view that the Earth went around the sun not because his mind was closed to the idea, but for the valid reason that it did not fit the observations, or rather the observations as he knew them. His charts and measurements showed quite clearly that the planets could not orbit the sun in circular paths because their apparent movement across the sky did not fit this pattern. Hipparchus created the first well-known star map and although the scale of space eluded him he accurately measured the circumference of the Earth, obtaining a figure better than that used by medieval explorers who set sail from Europe to look for new trade routes to India. Like Aristarchus, Hipparchus appreciated the value of an eclipse; it was a special moment when the geometry of the cosmos was laid out before him. He used an eclipse of the sun, probably in 129 BC, to estimate how far away the moon was.

That eclipse was total at the Hellespont, part of the narrow strait that separates the European and Asian parts of Turkey. But only four-fifths of the sun was covered by the moon when seen from Alexandria in Egypt which was further to the south. Hipparchus argued that when the sun was eclipsed, it and the moon occupied the same spot in the heavens. The reason, he assumed, was that the moon passed between the sun and us. Because the sun was more distant than the moon, as Aristarchus of Samos had shown, he believed the time of the eclipse would be the same at both locations. Now it was time for geometry to take over.

Viewed from the Hellespont, the moon overlapped the sun, but seen from Alexandria at the same moment it was one-fifth of a solar diameter short of the edge – which was why the eclipse there was not total. One-fifth of the sun's diameter covers about 0.1 degrees in the sky. That angle is the parallax of the edge of the moon, viewed from the two locations. Hipparchus knew the latitudes of the Hellespont and Alexandria because he knew the altitude of the celestial pole above their horizons. During his time the pole of the heavens was not near Polaris as it is today but Hipparchus, who had mapped the positions of about 850 stars, must have known its position quite well. The Greek astronomer estimated that the moon was between 62 and 73 Earth radii away. Today we know the average distance is about 60 radii, varying by a few Earth radii either way because of the ellipticity of the moon's orbit.

History has repeated itself. The total eclipse of the sun seen by millions on 11 August 1999 passed just a few hundred kilometres north of the one that Hipparchus used to calculate the distance to the moon. Its path of totality extended from the ocean off New England, through England and central Europe, all the way across India. It crossed the Black Sea around 11.15 a.m. about 300 km north-east of the Hellespont. And in Alexandria 71 per cent of the sun's diameter was covered (rather than 80 per cent as in the Hipparchus eclipse) at around 11.35 a.m. It is not that difficult to follow in Hipparchus' footsteps and use this modern eclipse to duplicate his calculation.

For the Romans the moon god was Diana, the huntress, whose twin brother was Apollo, the sun god. The Romans knew her as the queen of heaven and helper of women in childbirth.

The Roman historian Plutarch (46–120 BC) took a keen interest in the natural world and saw a solar eclipse on 20 March 71 BC. He wrote that it 'tempered the air in the manner of twilight' and went on to give an extremely accurate description of the so-called 'Baily's beads' which are beads of light scattered around the lunar limb caused by sunlight shining through valleys. Uniquely among classical authors describing a solar eclipse, he mentions the sun's outer atmosphere, the corona. In the next 1,500 years there were only two other accounts of the corona.

He wrote: 'The effects of the moon are similar to the effects of reason and wisdom, whereas that of the sun appear to be brought about by physical force and violence.' According to Plutarch, the moon has 'the light which makes moist and pregnant, is promotive of the generation of living beings and the fructification of plants'.

Aristotle's idea that the moon was perfect was very influential in the ancient world but Plutarch did not believe it. He suggested that the moon had deep recesses on its surface into which the light of the sun could reach and that the spots were the shadows of rivers or deep chasms. He also believed that the moon was inhabited. In the second century AD, the Greek rhetorician Lucian of Samosata (120–180) pulled together the ideas of Pythagoras and Plutarch and wrote a satirical account of a journey to the moon. In his *Vera Historia* ('True History') the heroes are whisked to the moon in a whirlwind and caught up in a war between the sun and the moon. They meet moonmen riding on giant three-headed vultures, while soldiers ride into battle on fleas ten times the size of elephants. The moonmen live on roast frogs and occasionally borrow each other's eyes!

At Alexandria, with his own observations of the stars and planets and the vast library to work with, Claudius Ptolemy (85–165) refined and improved the work of Hipparchus and produced a description of the universe that held sway until the Renaissance. The Earth was the centre and the moon and planets circled it with a motion that consisted of circles of various sizes superimposed on one another. He explained the theory in a mighty thirteen-volume work that later came to be known as the *Almagest* or 'Greatest'. Ptolemy also did what many writers of deep scientific works have done since then, he wrote a popular account of his work under the title *Planetary Hypothesis*.

When sailors entered the port of Alexandria their boats were searched for books. Copies were made and stored in the great Library of Alexandria. Most of this library has been lost. It must have included books that mentioned the moon. What, I wonder, did they say?

The *Almagest* not only explained astronomy, it came to define it and to cast in stone the world-view of Aristotle. The heavens were perfection; below the moon was decay; and all in the cosmos moved in circles or combinations thereof. This world-view lasted over a thousand years. It fettered and hampered man's thinking because it was all so logical, so plausible and so wrong.

CHAPTER FOUR

The Temple of Sin

For countless ages the full moon has risen over Harran, a village in south-east Turkey. Today it is a collection of mud brick houses and historic ruins. Its inhabitants, just over two thousand of them, sit around in the evening gloom. They are better off now than in living memory because of the economic benefits of a new dam across the Euphrates. The men watch TV, smoke, gather to drink, the women cook and clean; the children play among the ancient ruins. The sound of western pop music can be heard, and young men speed away on their motor scooters in search of entertainment. No one would think that this place had once been chosen over fabled Babylon as a seat of royal power.

Few of the present inhabitants look at the full moon hanging in the sky over the strange beehive houses made of bricks plundered from the ruins of temples older than most nations. Yet there was a time when the life of this place was intimately connected with the moon, when its cold light had a power that was feared and courted by the 20,000 people who lived here. There is nowhere else on Earth (with the possible exception of Cape Canaveral in the United States) that has such a strong connection with the moon. For three thousand years, this was the sacred city of Sin, the Mesopotamian moon god. It was the place where the moon touched the Earth; the epicentre of its influence on all the people, plants, animals and waters of the world.

Harran – the name means journey or crossroads in some ancient tongue – once stood at the crossroads of history. There was a settlement here, a merchant outpost of Ur, in 2000 BC and probably much earlier than that. It was strategically positioned at the junction of two major trade routes linking the Persian Gulf and the Far East with the Mediterranean, and the route linking the Anatolian plateau with Syria and Palestine to the south. Strange people, with their strange ideas and beliefs, were always passing through Harran. It was an important place during the time of the Old Testament patriarchs in the fourteenth century BC. Abraham and his family lived here for a while. Some even believe that our seven-day week originated with the thinkers of ancient Harran. The Egyptians had a week of ten days and a month of thirty but by at least 500 BC the seven-day week was in use, with each day named after the sun or moon or the planets.

An inscription carved in stone at Harran concerns King Nabonidus of Babylon (555–539 BC). His father was the governor of Harran and his mother a priestess in the Temple of Sin. In the carving Nabonidus can be seen in the company of Ishtar (Venus), Shamash (the sun) and Sin (the moon) and he addresses the moon as 'the Divine Crescent'. Such was the power of the moon that, after a dream, Nabonidus abandoned Babylon and reigned from Harran where he rebuilt the Temple. The moon rewarded him for such devotion, peace returned and his empire prospered for a while. Thanks be to Sin.

Sin was a God depicted with a long crescent for a crown and a beard of gleaming blue lapis lazuli. His power was demonstrated every month as his changing face and silver light was not only able to illuminate heaven but also to crush the nether world. Not even the sun could do that. Sin, or Nannar as he is sometimes called, is often described as a young bull, the fabled strong bull of heaven, perfect in every part. The connection between the moon and bulls, seen earlier in the Lascaux frescoes, continued at Harran.

After the fall of Nabonidus, Harran was ruled by the Persians until the coming of Alexander the Great and by the first century

BC the Romans. They called it Carrhae. Although they recognized its strategic importance they did not pay due homage to the moon so it was not kind to them. In 53 BC it was the scene of a disastrous defeat and the death of the Roman governor Crassus, he who had put down the revolt of the Thracian gladiator Spartacus. Later, the Emperor Galerius was defeated nearby by the Persian king Narses. Then, when Emperor Caracalla was assassinated after paying a visit to the temple of the moon god, it was rebuilt by Emperor Julian, only to be torn down by Emperor Theodosius in AD 382. The Romans appear to have paid a heavy price for offending the moon god.

In 717 the Caliph Umar II founded the first Muslim university here but although Harran stood as an island between the triumph of Christianity and the ever-expanding sea of Islam, the moon god's power over the world of men was declining; the traders and Bedouins moved along other routes. Edessa, now known as Urfa, some 40 km away, came to dominate the area as it became Christian, and the moon-worshipping pagans were forgotten. In 1271 the Mongols came and decided that Harran was too much trouble. But instead of destroying the city they relocated all its inhabitants and sealed the gates, allowing it to be filled with sand and wind-blown dirt. Much of it is still partly buried.

Today, the most conspicuous ruin in Harran is the fortress said to be on the exact spot of the Temple of Sin. You can still climb over its wrecked bulk and watch the moon rise over its ramparts. Nowhere on Earth is moonrise quite the same. Never destroyed, never sacked, never fully excavated, there are still secrets beneath its sands. Perhaps the moon god has been watching over this place after all.

Science lingered in Harran after it turned its back on the moon. Long after the Romans had departed and their empire had splintered between east and west, a great mathematician lived here dividing his days between Harran and the university at Baghdad, a unique seat of learning at the time because of the range and depth of its studies and its large numbers of students. Underneath Harran's moon Al-Sabi Thabit ibn Quarra al-Harrani, known as Thebit, pondered the mystery of numbers and even travelled to Cordoba in Spain to translate the great texts of the ancient Greeks into Arabic and perhaps occasionally ponder on what the Greeks said about the moon.

Some accounts of the history of astronomy relate that speculation about the moon, and indeed about the whole of the sky, ended with the fall of Rome, only to be revived again during the Renaissance a thousand years later. This is not so. During the Dark Ages there was much thought and discussion about the moon, much of which came from the Middle and Far East. The West frequently overlooks Arabic astronomers who made the leap from Ptolemy and his Earth-centred universe of cycles and epicycles directly to Copernicus and his heliocentric or sun-centred cosmos. There are others in between who had great insights, many far ahead of their time.

For example, Abu Abdullah Al-Battani (858–929) was one of the greatest astronomers of any age. He improved upon Ptolemy's calculations of the moon's orbit, fixed the position of the ecliptic (the band of sky traversed by the sun), and measured, to within a few minutes, the length of the year. Hundreds of years later, the astronomer Hevelius, who will feature in our story later, used his work to determine the motion of the moon. If he is not very often given due credit in astronomy textbooks, Abu Abdullah Al-Battani at least has his place on the moon. The moon mappers of later centuries were well aware of his contribution and two German astronomers, Beer and Mädler, named one of the largest and most imposing central craters after him using the Latin form of his name, Albategnius, though personally I prefer Abu Abdullah Al-Battani.

By the ninth century the Arabs developed the astrolabe, an instrument that would be the astronomer's basic tool for hundreds of years until the invention of the telescope. It was, in effect, a replica of the stars in the sky along which sightings could be made and angles read off. Often on its reverse it had a series of gear wheels which could be used to place the sun and moon in any position. Soon Harran was the centre of astrolabe production.

The Arabs were now moving west across North Africa and into Spain, taking their religion and knowledge with them. In the tenth century the library of Cordoba in Muslim-controlled Spain contained more than 600,000 manuscripts, more than could be found at that time in England and France combined. Many of the books were translations of Greek masterpieces and when the libraries eventually fell to the West it was knowledge that Europe, recovering from centuries of confusion, was ready to accept. Some of the ancient texts in Cordoba had been translated by Thebit. He was known for his work on mechanics, astronomy, mathematics and geometry, and his formulae for computing the surface area and volume of solids was the basis of what later became integral calculus. He was also one of the first to criticize the Ptolemaic view of the cosmos and he analysed several problems concerning the moon's motion. He translated many Greek and Syrian works into Arabic, including Ptolemy's *Almagest* and Euclid's *Elements*.

But the only true book written about the moon between the time of Plutarch and the Renaissance, a period of some 1,400 years, was by the remarkable Al-Hasan ibn al-Haytham (965–1039), whom we call Alhazen.

Alhazen gave up a lucrative but dull civil service job in Basra and travelled to Egypt about the year 980 to devote himself to science. The ruler of the time, Al-Hakim, was a cruel Caliph and somewhat eccentric. After the sacking of the city of al-Fustat he ordered the killing of all its dogs since their barking annoyed him, and he banned certain vegetables and shellfish because he did not like them either. But he did surround himself with scientists and astronomers, including a shabby, careless, absent-minded stargazer called Ibn Yunis. Yunis is most famous for his many trigonometrical and astronomical tables. The Muslim religion required considerable knowledge of the moon and the sun to determine times of prayer during the year and it was Yunis's task to search the evening sky each month for the first sight of the crescent moon. He also described forty close approaches of the planets to one another (so-called planetary conjunctions) as well as thirty lunar eclipses. Centuries later they were used by English astronomer Simon Newcomb in his lunar studies. Ibn Yunis met a strange end. He predicted the date of his own death to be in seven days' time even though he was in good health. He then settled his business affairs, locked himself in his house and recited the *Qur'an* until he died on the predicted day.

Meanwhile Al-Haytham was charged with controlling the flood of the Nile, the Nile that the ancient Egyptians said obeyed the moon. When he failed, as he inevitably did, he had to find a way to placate the vengeful Caliph. He feigned madness until his master's death and then returned to his homeland where he wrote two works about the moon, *On the Light of the Moon* and *On the Nature of the Marks Seen on the Surface of the Moon*. He writes: 'If one were to carefully observe and consider the surface markings, one finds them to be of constant disposition, revealing no changes in themselves, neither in their form, their position and size, nor in their respective types of darkness.'

He continues:

Certain people hold that the spots belong to the lunar body itself: Others believe that they exist apart from it, namely between the lunar body and the eye of the observer, still others conceive that they offer an inverted image [of the

Earth], since the lunar surface is smooth and reflecting. There are also those who maintain that the form of the Earthly oceans can be seen there, in mirror image, while others say that it is mountains and mountain ranges of our Earth that are reflected.

Al-Haytham did not believe the spots on the moon were caused by vapours because he could see they were constant in shape and size but he did not believe that they were caused by mountains either. He was partially correct in thinking that the moon's light was reflected from the sun but he believed that the moon could hold back some of the sun's light and give it off later. The spots were simply regions where this process was less efficient.

Ibn Sina (981–1037), known in the West as Avicenna, read Ptolemy's *Almagest* as a teenager before turning his attention to medicine. Like Leonardo da Vinci, he lived during a time of political instability and wandered around seeking the patronage of the powerful. He gathered about him a band of students who followed his teachings on medicine, astrology and astronomy and he wrote about 450 books, of which 240 survive. One was the *Qanun*, said to contain a million words and to be the most comprehensive book on medicine ever written. He observed a transit of Venus across the sun and correctly deduced that Venus was closer to the sun than the Earth. He also tried to calculate the difference in longitude between Baghdad and Gurgan by observing the meridian transit of the moon. He believed the speed of light to be finite, though we do not know why he held this view. He designed machines and musical instruments and said he wanted to unify all knowledge into one grand vision that reflected the pure intellect of God. All very much like Leonardo. He once said, 'I prefer a short life with width to a narrow one with length.' He died at the age of fifty-eight and was buried in

Hamadan where his grave can still be seen.

Concerning the moon, he wrote: 'If what we perceive in the lunar surface is only reflected light then it can be maintained that the spots on the moon represent nothing other than the physical irregularities in this surface, which hinder the reflection of light.'

Abu Ishaq ibn Yahya al-Zarquali (1028–1087), also known as Arzachel, was a Spanish Arab. Observing from Toledo, he compiled what became known as the Toledan tables. Copernicus thanks him, along with Albategnius, in his *De revolutionibus Orbium Celestium*; the book that started the astronomical revolution in the sixteenth century. The lunar crater named after him is magnificent, more than 105 km across.

Although intellectually the West was sleeping there were some in the twelfth and thirteenth centuries who did ponder the nature of the moon. Alexander of Neckam (1157–1217), said by some to be foster brother of King Richard the Lionheart, wrote a book called *De naturis rerum* ('On the nature of things'). In it he wrote that some thinkers believed the moon to be covered in mountains and depressions but that he did not believe it. True to the spirit of his time, he thought the markings on the face of the moon were a sign from God who had allowed original sin to stain its face. Some day, when all sin was gone, the moon and the Church would be spotless before the Lamb.

In April 1453 Mohammed and the Turks laid siege to Constantinople but, despite their heavy bombardment of the walls, the inhabitants of the city were able to repair them every night. The Byzantines were exhausted but took solace in the old legend that Constantinople would never fall while the moon was waxing. But on the night of 22 May the moon rose in eclipse and their morale was crushed. Mohammed knew of the legend and waited a few days before starting a fresh attack, when the moon was waning. During the battle a small gate was left open by accident – it was all the Turks needed. The sack of Constantinople lasted three days, as the moon waned.

But by now the mist of the Dark Ages was slowly clearing, wafted away by the breeze from the pages of the rediscovered Greek texts. And the world beyond the mists, at first glimpsed only in fragments, was not what man had thought it would be.

CHAPTER FIVE

The Shrine of Hecate

Miyako Island is halfway between the Japanese mainland and Taiwan, part of the ridge that defines the Pacific Rim, on the boundary between the East China Sea and the Pacific Ocean. It is warm, fragrant, colourful and unspoilt. A paradise.

There is a legend that when the first settlers arrived on the island the sun and the moon were friends and one New Year's Eve they decided to grant mankind the gift of immortality. They sent a messenger to the island who carried across his shoulders a yoke – on one side was the water of life and on the other the water of death. The servant rested on his journey to Miyako and did not notice a serpent upset one of the buckets and become drenched in the water of immortality. In a panic, after realizing what had happened, the messenger poured some of the water of death into the other bucket so that both appeared equally full. He arrived at Miyako and mankind drank from the waters of death and remained mortal. The sun was angry at this and sentenced the messenger to stand upon the moon, bearing his yoke and buckets, for as long as man lived on the island of Miyako. They say this is how the moon got its spots and, judging by Miyako's beauty, the hapless messenger will not be reprieved soon.

We have all looked up at the spots on the moon and tried to make out a recognizable shape. We are programmed at birth to see faces in patterns so it is not surprising that some have seen a face on the moon. But what *is* surprising is what else has been made of these spots. In many parts of the world the spots are a rabbit, or a tree or a three-legged toad; to the Maoris they are an old woman under a tree.

The rabbit-in-the-moon crops up in many cultures. In India the image is Chandra, god of the moon, holding a rabbit. According to the Hottentots of southern Africa the moon sent a rabbit to Earth to tell humans that she had died but rose from the dead after three days, and because she had done so then humans could do the same. But the rabbit got the message wrong and only told humans that the moon was dead. The furious moon struck out at the rabbit splitting his upper lip, and the rabbit scratched out at the moon leaving the marks we see today.

Perhaps the first person to mention names for the features on the moon that are visible to the unaided eye was Plutarch in his *De Facie in Orbe Lunae*:

Just as our Earth has deep and great gulfs, one of which flows to us through the Pillars of Hercules, another outside is that of the Caspian Sea, and also that of the Red Sea (known as the Arabian Sea), so on the moon there are hollows and deeps; they call the greatest of these the Shrine of Hecate, where souls endure or exact retribution for all the things they have suffered or done ever since they became spirits. Two of them are long, through which the souls pass, first to the parts of the moon which are turned towards Heaven, then back to the side next to Earth. The parts of the moon towards heaven are called 'The Elysian Plain', those towards Earth are called 'The Plain of Persephone Antichthon'.

It is believed that the Shrine of Hecate may be Mare Imbrium.

The lunar features are often described as a man carrying a bundle of twigs on his back. Shakespeare says in his *Midsummer Night's Dream*: 'This Man with lantern, dog and bush of thorns, presenteth moonshine.' In another version the man was caught stealing cabbages and his neighbours sent him to the moon where the cabbages can still be seen. In another version it was the moon who was doing the thieving and had a cabbage thrown in his face where it remains still. In other tales, the man in the moon is Judas, exiled for the betrayal of Jesus, or Cain carrying thorns. However, the spots do not always signify a man.

The woman in the moon is less well known but many groups have seen her. The Samoans see Sina and her child on the moon. One evening Sina looked at the rising moon and as there was a severe famine said to the moon that it should come to Earth so that her children could eat it. The indignant moon did come down and swept her and her children up and they now live there. The Shawnee Indians of North America also see a woman crouching over a cooking pot; in the Cook Islands a girl weaving cloth is seen. One group in the Pacific said that an immortal woman lived on the moon, making a sail of white clouds to propel herself across the sky. One day she fell in love with a mortal man whom she brought to the moon. But, unlike her, he grew old and she had to send him back to Earth lest the moon be defiled with death.

There is an intriguing Zambesi myth that the moon was pale and envious of the brilliant sun and once, when the sun was on the other side of the Earth and not looking, the moon stole some of her fire feathers. The sun found out and splattered her face with mud, causing the spots. But that is not the end of this myth. It becomes even more remarkable. Every ten years, when the sun's attention is distracted, the moon gets her revenge and splatters him with mud. Curiously every ten years or so the sun does go through a cycle of activity that results in more sunspots appearing on its surface and occasionally these spots can be seen by the unaided eye. Did the tribes of the Zambesi notice this solar cycle and link it to the moon?

In art, from the twelfth to the fourteenth century, a less stylized and more naturalistic approach was beginning to emerge. By the

1300s the natural world was no longer a storehouse of symbols reflecting the glory of God. For more than 800 years, from the beginning of the Dark Ages to the start of the Renaissance, not a single figure was painted that cast a shadow. Soon that was to change. Writers such as Hugh St Victor said that it was the visual world that was the source of true knowledge. To appreciate the realities of God's creation one had to look at the world, describe it, and paint what one could actually see and not its deeper symbolic and spiritual meaning. But few looked towards the moon in this way.

The frescoes in the Arena Chapel in Padua are considered the finest work of the greatest and most influential painter before the Renaissance, Giotto di Bondone (1277–1337). Here God, surrounded by angels, is sitting in judgement. The golden sun hovers to the left and to the right is an ashen moon. The sun is radiant but the moon is grey as if they were painted from real life, the first time it had ever been done. I wonder, did a mathematics professor later stare up at Giotto's masterwork and ponder upon the grey disc above him? Did Galileo Galilei realize that the moon had not yet finished with Padua?

Into this climate came Jan van Eyck (1390–1441), undoubtedly the most famous and innovative Flemish painter of the fifteenth century. For many years he was wrongly credited with being the first to paint in oils. In fact oil painting was already in use when he came to it and it was the medium that set painters free. Oils gave them a brilliance, translucence and intensity of colour they had never had before. The flat dullness of egg-based tempera was transformed into a jewel-like medium perfectly suited to the representation of precious metals and gems and, significantly, to the vivid and convincing depiction of natural light. Van Eyck's inspired observations of light and its effects, using this new type of paint, enabled him to represent a new kind of reality.

His *Crucifixion* is a masterpiece painted some time around

1420–25. Christ crucified is obviously the centre of the painting but hanging in the sky is the moon. Not a stylized moon nor a symbolic crescent, but a real-life moon below an arm of the cross of one of the two thieves, gibbous just as it would appear in the late afternoon. The shapes of the dark spots on its surface can be clearly seen. It was the first time anyone had painted it this way.

There is another lunar connection with the crucifixion. In various places in the Bible allusions are made to an eclipse that took place on the evening after the crucifixion of Jesus Christ. Did the moon turn to blood? It is straightforward to calculate the dates of lunar eclipses around the time we think Jesus was crucified. One occurred on 3 April 33 AD, just after the moon rose.

Leonardo da Vinci understood Van Eyck's motivation. In his only book (which was about painting) he wrote: '. . . you cannot be a good one if you are not the universal master of representing by your art every kind of form produced by nature'. For Leonardo, art was a pathway to science and that is all too apparent in his sole surviving sketch of the moon. It is so different from Van Eyck's, not so much a drawing as a study.

Of the moon he wrote: 'That part of the moon that shines consists of water, which mirrors the body of the sun and reflects the radiance it receives from it.'

He continued:

If you keep the detail of the spots of the moon under observation you will often find great variation in them and this myself I have proved by drawing them. And this is caused by the clouds that rise from the waters in the moon, which come between the sun and those waters, and by their shadow deprive these waters of the sun's rays. Thus those waters remain dark, not being able to reflect the solar body.

Leonardo's drawing looks very much like something drawn by someone with keen eyesight but there are hints elsewhere in his works that he might have used some form of optical aid. He had a habit of starting projects and not completing them; those who commissioned paintings were often exasperated as he started well but lost interest as other projects and ideas took over. So it was with his study of mirrors. Practically all we know is that they kept him busy for a long time and were a source of trouble. In the 1490s he had begun thinking of building a mirror-making machine to make mirrors that would use the sun's rays to boil water for producing and colouring clothes. The fortunes of his patrons the Medici family and indeed of Florence itself, depended in great measure on the textile industry.

But did Leonardo dream of building a telescope to look at the moon?

He certainly seems to have considered the possibility of constructing a telescope and in notes later assembled as the *Codex Atlanticus*, written around 1490, he talks of '. . . making glasses to see the moon enlarged'. He may even have invented some kind of telescope – we know he experimented with lenses. In statements made around 1510 he clearly describes the principle of the telescope: 'It is possible to find means by which the eye shall not see remote objects as much diminished as in natural perspective.' But we do not know whether he ever built such an instrument, and many scholars doubt that he did. In the *Codex Arundul*, written about 1513, he says: 'In order to observe the nature of the planets, open the roof and bring the image of a single planet onto the base [of a concave mirror]. Then the image of the planet reflected by the base will show the surface of the planet much magnified.'

So Leonardo's telescope, if there ever was one, is a mystery. A mystery that deepened in 1938 when a researcher called Domenico Argentieri was looking at one of Leonardo's scripts, now called manuscript F. There was a drawing that had been overlooked. Looking at it, you realize that it could be a crude diagram of a telescope. Elsewhere on the page, in Leonardo's mirror writing, are descriptions of lenses. Was it just in his imagination or was it real? A typical Leonardo question.

When da Vinci died in April 1519 at Cloux in France his many notebooks were placed in the care of his assistant Francesco Melzi. They comprised some 13,000 pages of notes on just about everything. Melzi took them to his home at Vaprio near Milan but did not catalogue or order them. When he died in 1570 his son showed no interest whatsoever in Leonardo and the precious notes slowly began to disperse. Today about half of Leonardo's notebooks have been lost and I wonder what they contained. Somewhere in his lost notebooks, might there be other drawings of the moon?

For someone whose thoughts took him so far Leonardo never suspected that the planets went around the sun. But he did believe that the Earth was not unique in the cosmos and that the stars were suns like our own. He understood that the moon shone with reflected light from the sun and he correctly explained the 'old moon in the new moon's arms' (or ashen light) as the moon's surface being illuminated by light reflected from the Earth. He thought of the moon as being similar to the Earth, with seas and areas of solid ground. And he left us that accurate sketch of the spots on the moon, and many questions.

In 1504, when Leonardo was thinking about lenses, Christopher Columbus was in trouble in the Caribbean. He had been stranded in a bay called Santa Gloria for six months, had abandoned two ships, his remaining two were riddled with marine worms and the natives were becoming unfriendly. Some men were sent in canoes to Hispaniola for help but did not return. Others mutinied and left when the natives stopped providing food. Columbus was facing disaster but he knew that a lunar eclipse would take place on the night of 29 February and he decided to use it to his advantage.

He called the natives on board his ship and explained that he worshipped a powerful god who had been angered by their actions. They could have one last chance after he had provided a sign in heaven. The natives were unimpressed and went home. But later that night the moon passed into the shadow of the Earth and they were terrified. The next morning they began supplying food once more until a rescue ship arrived.

In 1532 a poet called Ludovico Ariosto, the great satirist of the Renaissance, wrote a strange epic poem 'Orlando furioso'. The hero Astolpho is disgusted with life on Earth, with its injustice and corruption. In the poem Astolpho finds that everything lost on the Earth finds its way to the moon. There are countless prayers, vows, tears and sighs. There are bribes hanging on gold and silver hooks, flattery is trapped in snares, greedy locusts burst with empty praise, the handcuffs of lost love sparkle with jewels, while wasted kindness drips off plates. Most of all there are bottles that contain a thin, light liquid called Common Sense. It has been lost from the Earth but can be found on the moon.

It was the common sense of the time that most astronomers were convinced that there was life on the moon; one of them was Johannes Kepler (1571–1630), a German astronomer who formulated the laws of planetary motion. Kepler wrote a remarkable book called *Somnium* ('The Dream'), which was published posthumously in 1634. In this science fiction fantasy, Kepler describes an imaginary journey to the moon.

The story begins with the discovery of a bridge between the Earth and the moon, a bridge built of the shadow cast by the Earth into the celestial void. When the top of the shadow reached the moon (which happened every time there was a lunar eclipse), it formed a link between the Earth and the moon. In 'The Dream' all you had to do to reach the moon was to glide along this shadow. When the moon cast its shadow on the Earth (which occurred every time there was a solar eclipse), you could make the return trip to Earth.

The moon was a dark world inhabited by creatures who lived in caves, sheltering against the scorching heat of the sun during the day and the icy cold at night. It was a world teeming with life: strange animals glided eerily around the exotic foliage. There were snakelike monsters weighing more than humans, many of them with wings. Most animals rested during the long lunar day and came to life only at night. This book was certainly a fantastic flight of the imagination. But when Kepler acquired a telescope and turned it towards the moon what he saw only served to confirm that the moon's craters had indeed been built by moon creatures. This from a man who had solved the mathematical riddle of planetary motion by discarding preconceptions and appealing but fanciful ideas.

Also at the beginning of the seventeenth century, the English bishop Francis Goodwin wrote an exotic tale of travel to the moon. *The Man in the Moon: Or a Discourse of a Voyage Thither* was about a Spanish sailor named Domingo Gonzales. After being marooned on an uninhabited island, he was determined to get back home. He captured and trained some wild swans to carry heavy weights and, once they had managed that, he added a chair. First, he tied a lamb to the chair and the swans flew the lamb over the island. So, in the hope that the swans would fly him back to Spain, Gonzales climbed into the chair, and the swans carried him aloft. Unfortunately, they flew him to the moon.

A few years later the French poet Cyrano de Bergerac also described a trip to the moon. Cyrano assumed that, at dawn, dew was sucked upwards by the sun. He reasoned that a man wearing vials full of dew would likewise be drawn upwards. It worked, at least in the story, and he rose so fast that he had to break a couple of bottles to keep from flying past the moon. However, he broke too many of them, and slipped back to Earth. In a way, the same thing happened to the first spacecraft that tried to reach the moon in the 1950s.

Undaunted, he planned a second attempt, this time using a flying chariot. But again things did not go entirely to plan. Soldiers attached firecrackers to his spaceship and Cyrano came along just as they were lighting the fuses. He leapt aboard to put them out but was too late. He was propelled to the moon in a blaze of fireworks. To his surprise, the moon was inhabited and whom should he bump into but Domingo Gonzales, the Spanish sailor from Goodwin's story.

Until the seventeenth century western science had lagged behind that of rival cultures but this was about to change because of the impetus provided by the Renaissance. Christendom was to spread around the globe and onto the moon as well. Dutch conquerors and explorers wrested control of the world's most valuable spices and one Dutchman wanted to take control of the moon.

In retrospect it is clear that, as the sixteenth century drew to a close, nothing much more would be discovered about the moon. Its orbit was known with rough accuracy and its eclipses could be predicted, but as to the nature of the surface all was speculation. It would take a new invention to reveal, for the first time, the moon as it truly was.

CHAPTER SIX

'. . . A Tarte That My Cook Made'

Whoever did invent the telescope it was not the Dutch spectacle-maker Hans Lippershey who is given the credit for it in many books. He certainly had one in 1608 but others had been using them before. Lippershey was preceded by someone called Pierre Janssen, of whom we know little, who may have had a hand in its development and there is the Italian architect Giacomo della Porta who died in 1602. Some believe he was the person who engraved the date 1590 on a telescope taken from Italy to Holland. Others contend that the date is a fake. Knowledge of the magnifying properties of precious stones dates back to antiquity. It has been suggested that the genesis of the telescope lies hundreds if not thousands of years before its appearance in Europe in the first years of the seventeenth century.

In Room 55 of the British Museum, in Case 9 of the Lower Mesopotamian Gallery, lies the oldest known lens in the world. Looking at it evokes mystery and wonder. It is a lens made of rock crystal, fascinating to look through, even though little can be seen. Called the Nimrud lens, it was found in 1850 by the legendary archaeologist Sir John Layard, during an epic series of excavations at the palace of Nimrud in what is now Iraq. Upon his return to England, Layard showed it to physicist Sir David Brewer who thought it could have been used as a magnifying glass or to concentrate the sun's rays. Used as a magnifying glass, it could have been useful to ancient Assyrian craftsmen who often made intricate seals and produced minuscule texts on clay tablets using a wedge-shaped script. It is a theory many scientists might be prepared to accept, but the idea that the rock crystal was part of a telescope is something else. To get from a lens to a telescope, they say, is an enormous leap. Where is the evidence?

The ancient Assyrians regarded the planet Saturn as a god surrounded by a ring of serpents. Today we know Saturn to be the planet surrounded by rings and they can only be seen with a telescope. Could they have seen Saturn's rings through their crude telescope and interpreted them as serpents? On its own it is an unconvincing argument; the Assyrians saw serpents every-where. A more pertinent question is: why do their many astro-nomical reports on clay tablets contain no mention of such a device? What is more, the Nimrud lens may not be unique. Another, possibly fifth-century BC, lens was found in a sacred cave on Mount Ida on Crete. It was more powerful and of far better quality than the Nimrud lens.

Consider a scene from Aristophanes' play *The Clouds*:

Strepsiades: You have seen at the druggist that fine transpar-ent stone with which fires are kindled?
Socrates: You mean glass, do you not?
Strepsiades: Just so.
Socrates: What will you do with it?
Strepsiades: When a summons is sent to me, I will take this stone, and placing myself in the sun, I will though at a distance, melt all the writings off the summons.

The Roman writers Pliny and Seneca refer to a lens used by an engraver in Pompeii. There seems little doubt that the ancients knew of lenses, and there are also curious references in Japanese folklore. In one story giant ogres with blond and red hair come to rape and plunder Japan with the aid of a tube 'through which you can see a thousand miles'. Stories are one thing, good evidence is another. Nevertheless, food for thought, if not convincing evidence, is to be found in some museums. Many trinkets on display as jewellery or ornaments may in fact be something else.

In 1997 a team of scientists went to Gotland Museum to take a close look at what were thought to be ornaments but which turned out to be ten lenses ground with remarkable precision by the Vikings. When put through their paces they passed a series of tests almost as well as modern optics, also made from rock crystal. The lenses have an accurate shape that betrays the work of a master craftsman. Indeed the Gotland crystals – found on the isle of the lunar grooves – provide the first evidence that sophisticated lens-making techniques were being used by craftsmen over a thousand years ago.

We also know that in 1267 Friar Roger Bacon, in his *Opus Majus*, wrote of the 'wonders of refractive vision' and commented that 'we might read the smallest letters and grains of dust and sand owing to the magnitude of the angle under which we viewed them'.

But a telescope? For that you need the right type of lens, held at the right distance in front of another, also of just the right type. Did nobody ever do that? It seems unlikely that a telescope would have been invented and then forgotten, given its obvious military applications.

In the 1570s Thomas Digges wrote that he, 'hath by proportional glasses duely situate in convenient angles, not onely discovered things farre off, read letters, numbered peeces or money and the very coin and superscription thereof'. William Bourne, in a book called *Inventions or Devices* published in 1578, wrote: 'For to see any small thing a great distance from you, it requireith the ayde of two glasses', and 'to see a man four or five miles from you'.

Whatever their origin, in 1608 telescopes suddenly started appearing everywhere in Europe. That autumn the fair in Frankfurt had a trader (we do not know his name) who was selling one with a cracked lens for an outrageous sum. On 2 October Hans Lippershey, from Middleberg in Flemish Zeeland, applied for a patent on the device. Soon there were two other applications placed before officials in the Hague requesting a patent for the same thing. By then it was clear that the secret of the telescope was out and the patent requests were turned down. A few months later 'spyglasses' had reached Paris, London, Milan, Venice and Naples.

It was not long before the professor of mathematics at the University of Padua heard about them. Galileo Galilei (1564–1642) said he was 'seized with a desire for the beautiful thing'. Forty-five-year-old Galileo knew an opportunity when he saw one and he reasoned that the device, two lenses and a tube, could not be all that difficult to construct. If he could present one quickly enough to the Venetian Senate a rich reward or a pension would be his and he certainly needed the money. There was no time to lose. Spyglass salesmen were in Padua and some had plans to go to Venice. He sent word to the Venetian Senate not to accept any rival claims for the instrument and a few weeks later he had made one.

On 25 August 1609 Galileo led a procession of Venetian senators across the Piazza San Marco and up a tower so that they could look across Venice and out to sea where they saw ships several hours before they could be picked up by the unaided eye. He got his reward, a fivefold increase in salary for life. Giovanno Battista della Porta protested and said he had done such a thing twenty years earlier in a book he had written on concaves and convexes, but he had failed to see the potential of the telescope. However, even Galileo failed to realize just how revolutionary it was.

In October 1609 on a visit to Florence he showed his telescope to his former pupil Cosimo de Medici, now the grand duke, and together they looked at the moon. But the view was poor and

Galileo thought the telescope could be improved. By November it had been and, with a telescope now capable of magnifying up to twenty times tucked under his arm, Galileo walked into his garden in Padua and pointed his so-called perspicillum towards the moon.

It was one of those rare moments when the universe changed, when the speculations and prejudices of antiquity fell away. Through Galileo's telescope, the one that he would call the 'old discoverer' that can still be seen at Arcetri near Florence (as indeed can Galileo's preserved finger that pointed the way towards the new heavens), the modern face of the moon first emerged in the early evening of 30 November 1609. Galileo saw irregularities on its crescent face, and made a drawing, adding at least five more over the next eighteen days. He knew what he was seeing was revolutionary and he rushed into preparing a book. He produced watercolours for it and the *Sidereus Nuncius* (or 'The Starry Messenger') appeared the following March to 'unfold great and wonderful sights . . . to the gaze of everyone'.

Galileo looked at the dark spots that had for so long intrigued mankind, the 'great or ancient spots', as he called them. 'Just like the surface of the Earth itself which is varied everywhere by lofty mountains and deep valleys.' He could not actually see deep valleys through his crude telescope but he was convinced they were there, given the pockmarked nature of the surface. The dark spots, he said, were 'rather even and uniform'.

He adds: '. . . if anyone wishes to revive the old opinion of the Pythagoreans, that the moon is another Earth, so to say, the brighter portion may very fitly represent the surface of the land and the darker the expanse of water.' He believed that if you could look back at the Earth from the moon's distance the land would appear bright and the seas dark. Although he was careful not to say there was water on the moon he certainly hinted at it, saying that the spots were 'more depressed'.

He continued:

> It is most beautiful and pleasing to look upon the lunar
> body . . . from so near . . . the moon is by no means
> endowed with a smooth and polished surface, but is rough
> and uneven and, just as the face of the Earth itself, crowded
> everywhere with vast prominences, deep chasms, and convo-
> lutions.

Galileo had once wanted to be a painter but his father forbade it.
Now, as one of the first truly modern scientists, he returned to his
first desire, perhaps unconsciously. He was the first to paint a
series of moon portraits and what magnificent paintings they are.
Here is the modern moon, a planet stripped of symbolism and
myth, a stark world awaiting exploration and discovery. Galileo
wrote down all his observations of the lunar landscape emerging
from darkness. So it was, in more ways than one.

Several lunar features are quite recognizable in the drawings. In
the second in the series, based on a sketch made on 3 December
1609, we can see the mountains east of the Mare Imbrium (Sea of
Rains) and the sizeable crater at the bottom is probably Albategnius, drawn quite a bit larger than life, undoubtedly conveying
the impression it made on Galileo. He wrote: 'And it is like the
face of the Earth itself which is marked here and there with chains
of mountains and depths of valleys.' Aristotle was wrong, the
moon was not perfect. Democritus and Plutarch were right after
all.

Many rose to defend the perfection of the heavens. Jesuit priest
Christopher Clavius (whose large and imposing lunar crater we
have looked at) wrote to Cardinal Bellarmine in April 1611,
saying: 'it appears more probable that the surface is not uneven,
but rather that the lunar body is not of uniform density and has
denser and rarer parts, as are the ordinary spots seen with the

natural sight.' It was an old idea that was doomed in the face of the observations. A few years later a pope and a cardinal inquisitor wrote to Galileo suggesting that he curtail his celestial observations.

Within hours of the publication of the *Sidereus Nuncius* on 12 March 1610 the British Ambassador Sir Henry Wotton had obtained a copy and sent it post haste to the court of King James. Galileo's sensational pamphlet also quickly reached Germany, where it was reissued in a pirated edition in Frankfurt. In the rush little time or expense was devoted to copying Galileo's careful lunar engravings. Consequently, the Frankfurt edition contains woodcuts, not engravings, that are much less skilfully prepared than the originals. What is more, they are oriented incorrectly and identified wrongly. The Frankfurt woodcuts were the source for the illustrations in most of the later editions of the *Sidereus Nuncius*, leading unwary scholars to unfairly criticize the Galileo images as crude and unrealistic.

Galileo wrote: 'I render infinite thanks to God for being so kind to make me alone the first observer of marvels kept hidden in obscurity for all previous centuries.' But what he did not know was that the face of the moon had not been hidden until then. Someone else had been first to look at the moon through a telescope. An Englishman.

In the British Library is a simple sketch of the moon made in 1600 by William Gilbert (1544–1603). Gilbert was physician to Queen Elizabeth I and author of the famous book *De Magnete*. In this remarkable work he proposed, for the first time, that the planets circled the sun because they were attracted by some invisible force; he had magnetism in mind. In his studies of static electricity in amber he also invented the word 'electric'. Later Galileo would call Gilbert 'great to a degree that is enviable'. Even more than Francis Bacon, Gilbert was the father of experimental science, yet today he is largely forgotten.

Gilbert's crude sketch was included in his posthumous book *De Mundo Nostro Sublunari Philosophia Nova* ('New Philosophy Concerning Our Sublunar World'). Like Leonardo, he believed the light areas represented seas and the dark regions land. He gave some of the features he saw names: the Northern Island, the Southern Continent, the Middlemoon Sea. Gilbert possessed a large library of books, as well as many globes of the Earth and of the heavens, all sadly destroyed in the Great Fire of London in 1666.

Today, Syon House, to the west of London, is an oasis of relative calm amid the noisy suburbs. Often on Sunday afternoons my family and I stroll through its Capability Brown designed gardens or dally in the great conservatory. The peace is disturbed by aircraft from nearby Heathrow airport but after a while you pay them no heed. In summer, Emily, my youngest daughter, clambers aboard the miniature railway that winds around the grounds, persuading me to join her. As it rounds a bend, whistle blowing, I look across the water to the corner of Syon House, to where Thomas Harriot lived four hundred years ago. The story of Thomas Harriot is a little-known one, though he was one of the finest scientists the world has ever produced and if only he had published his discoveries he would have been known as the English Galileo. He travelled to the New World and was a peripheral character in the Gunpowder Plot.

Four hundred years ago the great house was already here, set among the undrained marshes. Travellers used to halt a while at Syon House before they headed west to Windsor or through the heathlands that barred the way to Winchester. It was a good place to be – the centre of London was only three hours away, by boat along the Thames. Catherine Howard, wife of Henry VIII, was held here before her beheading and the equally ill-fated Lady Jane Grey also stayed here.

And it was from here, through the chilly mists that rose from the marshes and not from a warm Paduan garden, that mankind first looked at the moon through a telescope.

I am standing within a few feet of where those first telescopic observations were made, in the bedroom of a flat built into an extension of the grand and imposing house. I am told the view east has changed little in the past four hundred years. I can see the flood plain of the Thames and one of the last remaining water meadows on the river. Beyond it are the large trees that border Kew Gardens. Across to the right I can just make out the rose garden that has the 'King's meridian' running through it. In the days before the Greenwich meridian the King had his own, which ran through his observatory at Kew and across the Thames to Syon.

Thomas Harriot, whose home this was so long ago, was a mathematician and astronomer who founded the English school of algebra. He has been described as the greatest mathematician Oxford has ever produced and that may well be true. We know very little of his youth. All we do know is that on Friday 20 December 1577 he matriculated at the University of Oxford, with an entry in the official records giving his age as seventeen, his father as a plebeian, and his birthplace Oxfordshire. Despite extensive searches of the Oxfordshire records, no further information concerning his birth or parentage has been found. According to Harriot, as a youth he was often punished by his teachers for asking awkward questions.

He entered the service of Sir Walter Raleigh in London, and spent his spare time roaming the docks talking to sailors. Soon he became acquainted with the longitude problem. 'Sailing west by compass is simple, for you just sail due west following a line of latitude. But sailing north, or in a north-westerly direction is treacherous, for there is no way of calculating longitude.' The moon was to play a role in the solution of this problem.

Harriot stayed at Raleigh's lodgings in the Strand and gave

lectures to admirals on navigation. He wrote a book called *Arcticon*, which was never published and of which no copies have ever been found. His lectures were to seamen preparing to explore the new world, and his usefulness extended into other areas. He was involved with the design and construction of the ships for Raleigh's expeditions, as well as selecting the seamen. He was also Raleigh's accountant.

On 9 April 1585 he left Plymouth for the new settlement in Virginia and his observations of a solar eclipse on 19 April allow us to compute the exact position of the ship on that day. He stayed in Virginia for a year and was particularly interested in the language and customs of the native inhabitants. When many of them died, due to diseases brought by the Europeans, he wrote of 'invisible bullets' striking down the natives. On his return he wrote *A Briefe and True Report of the New Found Land of Virginia*, a book in which he recommends the smoking of tobacco which he started in Virginia. He was later to become one of the first in the West to die of tobacco-induced cancer.

When Raleigh came back to England his situation changed in a way that had dramatic consequences for Harriot. Raleigh secretly married a maid at court and thus incurred Elizabeth's displeasure. There were also allegations of atheism against Raleigh and against 'the conjurer that is master thereof', meaning Harriot. He was probably not an atheist and on his death described himself as a loyal Christian but he was part of a circle of free thinkers and Harriot's scientific approach to the world was, to say the least, viewed with great suspicion by the Church.

Harriot moved and began working for Henry Percy, Earl of Northumberland, known as the 'wizard earl' because of his eclectic interests. In 1595 the Earl gave him some property in Durham and he moved up the social ladder. Harriot also held estates in Cornwall and Norfolk. Not long after, the Earl gave him the use of a house on the estate at Syon. He was widely known, friendly with Christopher Marlowe and probably knew Shakespeare. It was at Syon that he did his finest scientific work.

When Elizabeth I died on 24 March 1603, it was clear that Raleigh's fortunes would change. James I became king and he quickly saw Raleigh as someone who opposed his claim to the throne. Henry Percy had been more astute and had taken care to put himself on a good footing with James, sending a letter of support only days before Elizabeth died. In July plots were discovered against James, and Raleigh was arrested and charged with high treason. Raleigh attempted suicide but failed. He then sought Harriot's help in obtaining evidence on his behalf but Raleigh was convicted and sentenced to death by hanging. Harriot was singled out in the judgement as being an atheist and an evil influence. Raleigh received a last-minute reprieve and was imprisoned in the Tower of London. Harriot was to become well acquainted with the Tower; one of his masters was already in it while the other was soon to join him.

Further trouble was on the way. On 4 November 1604 Guy Fawkes and others were arrested for attempting to blow up the Houses of Parliament. Four others, including Thomas Percy, the grandson of Henry Percy, were also arrested as the main conspirators. Harriot was held on suspicion of being involved and was imprisoned for a while. He was interrogated on the charge that he had cast a horoscope of King James in an attempt to use magical powers to influence the king's future. Then on 27 November Henry Percy, Harriot's patron, was sent to the Tower where he remained for seventeen years.

Harriot was released and because of Raleigh and Percy had more than enough money to do what he wished. As well as scurrying between the Tower and Syon, managing the Earl's affairs, he now devoted himself to science. He employed Christopher Tooke, whom he called 'Kit', as a lens grinder, began investigating the dispersion of light into colours, and began to develop a theory for the rainbow, treading a path that many years later would see the footsteps of the great Isaac Newton. His work with lenses and glass led him to discover the law of refraction that today we call Snell's Law, which every schoolchild knows. It was later discovered by Dutch professor Willebrord Snell though his work was not published until 1703. Snell's Law should be called Harriot's Law.

In September 1607 Harriot saw a comet which turned his mind towards astronomy. Later the comet would be named after the astronomer Edmund Halley. Harriot's observations were valuable in helping Halley to calculate its orbit and predict its return.

On 26 July 1609 at 9 p.m., seated at the window of the first floor of his house, with a crude telescope in his hand, he sketched the five-day-old moon. His telescope gave him a magnification of 6. Kit was at his side taking notes.

So I stand within a few feet of that place, looking out in the same direction, wondering what it was like in that small attic in the half-light. What was said? What was written down? But there were other aspects of astronomy that attracted Harriot and the moon was forgotten, for a while.

We do not know what went through Harriot's mind when he saw a copy of Galileo's *Sidereus Nuncius* the following summer. But whatever regrets he might have had about not publishing, Galileo's book spurred him to look at the moon again and start drawing, but he was not a good draughtsman and Galileo's drawings were superb. His simple pen-and-ink drawings of the moon were only rediscovered in 1965 but we can see that Harriot did not have anything like the same artistic ability as Galileo. He sketched the moon again on 17 July 1610, when he had a telescope giving him a magnification of 10. Soon he had constructed a telescope with a magnification of 20. And by April 1611 he had one that magnified 32 times.

Harriot sent his friend Sir William Lower, who had married Percy's daughter, one of his telescopes. From his Pembrokeshire home Lower also looked at the moon through it and his description is charming:

> . . . as you wished I have observed the moon in all his changes . . . the brimme of the gibbous part towards the upper corner appeare luminous parts like stares, much brighter than the rest, and the whole brimme along looks unto the appearance of coasts, in the Dutch bookes of voyages. In the full she appeares like a tarte that my cook made me the last weeke. Here a vaine of bright stuff, and there of darke, and so confusedlie al over.

Like Galileo, Harriot also turned his telescope elsewhere in the sky. In the early morning, through the thick mist that still sometimes hangs over the water meadows of the Thames, he observed the sun with his crude telescope and discovered sun spots. In October 1610 he first saw the satellites surrounding Jupiter; two years later he calculated the distances of the moons from the planet and computed the periods of their revolution.

But soon afterwards his scientific work came to an end. In 1618 Raleigh was put to death with Harriot present to witness. By this time he was suffering from cancer of the nose, almost certainly the result of tobacco. At the time he was, according to his doctor: '. . . a man somewhat melancholy . . . A cancerous ulcer in the left nostril eats up the septum of his nose and in proportion to its size holds the lips hard and turned upwards. It has gradually crept well into the nose. This evil the patient has suffered the last two years.'

I am in the president's room of Trinity College, Oxford, and in front of me is a portrait of a bearded man holding a pomander. Some have suggested that I am looking into the face of Thomas Harriot. It may be so but it cannot be proven. At the moment Harriot, unlike the moon, has no face.

Why is Harriot not one of England's most celebrated scientists?

The answer is all too apparent. He had enough money to study the things that interested him and no incentive to publish what he discovered; he simply lacked the ambition of a Galileo.

He has been called the most original and fluent algebraist of his time; it was he who invented the equation. The idea of placing terms on either side of an equals sign appears first in Harriot's notes. He thought that the binary system of numbers, with its 1s and 0s, would make computing simple, but couldn't think of a way to put it into practical use. He was also by all accounts an excellent card player, able to compute the odds of winning and losing. It was said that only Raleigh himself could take him on, as he would bluff his way through a game of cards irrespective of the odds, much like his approach to life at court.

In Italy there are many monuments to Galileo, trumpeting his use of the telescope and his influence on the development of human thought. But in Britain, for the man who was the first to look at the moon through a telescope, there is, as yet, only one place you can go to see Thomas Harriot's name. In the last years of his life he had lost many of his friends. In 1612 his student Prince Henry, the heir to the throne, died suddenly. Sir John Harington, a fellow observer of the stars, had also suddenly died, as had his friend Sir William Lower. Then, in October 1618, he witnessed the beheading of his former master Sir Walter Raleigh. In his will he bequeathed a 'perspective trunke' to his patron, the Earl of Northumberland. His faithful servant, Christopher Tooke, who was at his side when he became the first person to look at the moon through a telescope, received the rest of the telescopes and £100.

On 1 July 1621 Tom Buckner wrote: 'Today my old friend Thomas Harriot died. At last he is in peace.' He was buried in St Christopher's in London and his grave was lost in the Great Fire of 1666. It is now believed to be somewhere underneath the Bank of England. Today there is a brass plaque in the entrance hall of

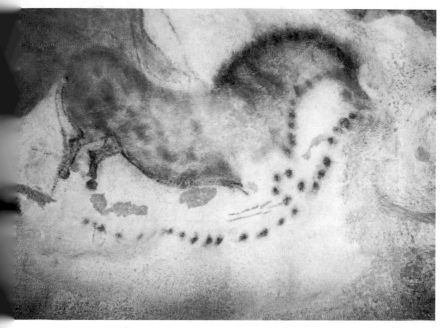

The oldest lunar calendar? The markings in the Cave of Lascaux said to depict the moon's monthly cycle (*David Whitehouse*).

The moon stone in the central chamber of the Knowth neolithic mound in central Ireland. Carved about 5,000 years ago, it is possibly the oldest known map of the moon (*David Whitehouse*).

The markings on the moon stone superimposed over a map of the moon drawn to the same scale: the line up is impressive (*Phillip Stooke*).

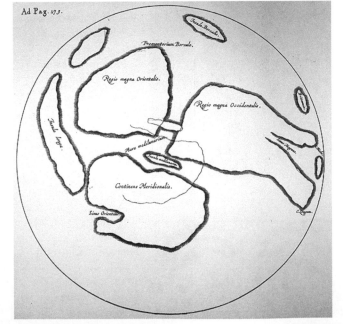

Leonardo da Vinci's sketch of the moon, circa 1512.

The map of the moon drawn by William Gilbert circa 1600 (*The British Library Board*).

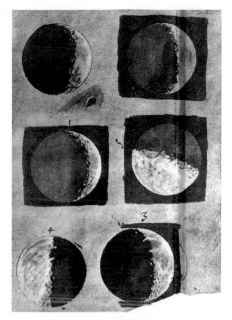

Galileo's drawings of the moon, 1610.

The moon map by Langrenus, completed in 1645, is remarkably accurate considering the telescopes used to compile it. Only three of his names for lunar features are still used (*Royal Observatory, Edinburgh*).

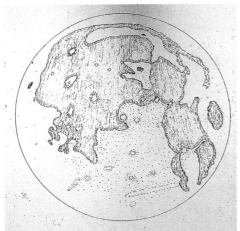

Thomas Harriot's map of the moon, 1611 (*Lord Egremont*).

Is this the face of Thomas Harriot? Some scholars have suggested it is but there is no solid evidence (*Trinity College, Oxford*).

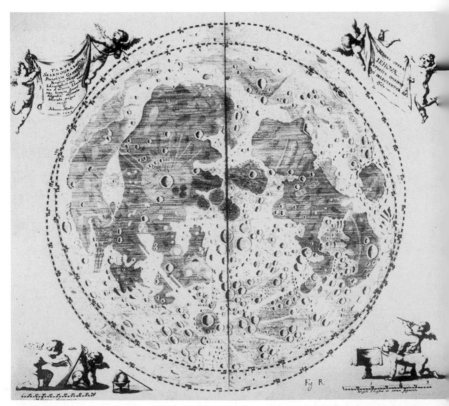

The mighty moon map made by Hevelius, completed in 1647 (*Royal Astronomical Society*).

the Bank of England dedicated to his memory. It makes no mention of the moon.

After Harriot died the moon moved away from Syon House and only returned once. Many years later the poet Percy Shelley was partly educated at Syon. In his poem 'The Moon', Shelley likens it to a '. . . dying lady lean and pale, who totters forth, wrapp'd in a gauzy veil . . . arose up in the murky east, a white and shapeless mass.' The moon did indeed rise up in the east at Syon and Harriot turned it from a shapeless mass into the world we know today.

Only now has Harriot's achievement started to be appreciated. He stands, a key figure, at a time when the new science of logic, reason, mathematics and experiment was coming into being. A man who, like Bacon, took all knowledge for his province, Harriot was a true Renaissance scientist. He has a crater on the moon named after him, on the far side, awarded in 1970.

But if Harriot was the first (by several months) to observe the moon, it was Galileo who was the swiftest to make his observations known. Galileo's telescope was the best available in 1609 but his crude 'optik tube' was not able to see the entire moon at one time because of its confined field of view. It has been said that using it was like looking down the barrel of a Colt revolver held at arm's length. It is not surprising therefore that today we have difficulty in matching some of the craters he drew with actual features. One can imagine him, sometimes observing from the tower at Nona with his telescope and its small crude unstable mounting, peering up at the night sky above the torches and campfires of the town. Wax from a candle would drip onto the ledge where he rested his telescope, with its small, quaking silver image, ringed with the rainbow colours of aberration.

Galileo sent a copy of his book to Prague, to Johannes Kepler, Royal Mathematician to the Hapsburgs. Kepler was impressed and, from the tone of his letter, perhaps a little miffed and jealous.

He wrote back praising Galileo but pointing out that he had come to many of Galileo's conclusions about the moon being an Earth-like body himself years previously and that the telescope was described in a book called *Natural Magic* by none other than Giovanno Battista della Porta in 1558. This was Kepler staking a claim on the moon. Writing as much for posterity as for Galileo, he said that he, Kepler, would take on the task of mapping the moon and Galileo would do the same for Jupiter! He also said other things that, for his day, were extraordinary.

When writing of the moon as an Earth-like world he said that 'settlers from our species of man will not be lacking'. He also said, 'let us create vessels and sails adjusted to the heavenly ether, there will be plenty of people unafraid of the empty wastes'. These comments show that the moon was now a place, as real and as physical as the Earth, and that some day men would explore it.

But first they had to map it.

CHAPTER SEVEN

The First Moon Race

Following the sensational publication of *Sidereus Nuncius*, many astronomers procured telescopes and turned their attention towards the moon. Crude maps were produced in the next few years by the astronomers Scheiner, Malapert, Biancani and Borri but they did not have any real merit. Perhaps the best of the bunch was by Francesco Fontana, a Neopolitan lawyer who made copperplate engravings of two of his drawings. The maps were poor partly because of the poor quality of telescopes available at the time. That was about to change.

News of the moon spread throughout educated circles. In England Ben Jonson wrote a little-known play called *Newes from the New World Discover'd in the Moone*. It was a parody of news reporters and journalists. In the play it is said that the moon is inhabited and a journalist asks, 'What inns or alehouses are there?' Nearly 400 years later I was at the BBC, covering the discovery of ice on the moon, when an editor of a TV news bulletin stopped me in a corridor and asked why there could not be a pub (alehouse) on the moon? Before I could think he burst out, 'Because it would have no atmosphere!' As he disappeared down the corridor, chuckling to himself, I thought of Ben Jonson's satire.

Times were changing, politically and scientifically. By 1620 the political situation in Europe was very tense. The Thirty Years War was about to begin, animosity between Catholics and Protestants was growing as power and influence shifted northwards. For thirty years the telescope had improved little but by about 1640 there was some progress. Galileo's telescopes were feeble things with object glasses barely more than an inch in diameter that produced weak, badly distorted images. Until they improved, accurate moon maps were clearly out of the question. The first great moon race was about to begin.

To map the moon would be to claim all the features that could be seen for posterity. They would sail the skies long after earthly empires had passed away. But who would be first?

Gilbert had given some names to the features he had mapped with his unaided eye in 1600. Mare Crisium was called Britannia. Harriot's map had some, but not many, names; in his case Mare Crisium was 'the Caspian'. But the prize of naming the moon would go to the person who produced the first accurate map, or so they thought.

In 1628 a 28-year-old heir to a Dutch mapmaking family decided that the moon would be his fortune. Michael van Langren had first sketched the moon the year before and the idea of a grand lunar map was born. A few years later he was in Madrid as 'Royal Mathematician and Cosmographer' to King Félipe IV of Spain. He was looking for some grand adventure, some big project that would make his fortune and place his family at the forefront of European mapmakers. He dreamed of producing a grand globe of the moon, complete with latitude and longitude circles, and at the same time solving the vexed problem of determining longitude on the Earth's surface. If he succeeded he would become one of the most famous men in Europe and fabulously wealthy. So, as he travelled between Holland and Spain, van Langren (or Langrenus as we know him) had his gaze fixed on the heavens. It had been said that the moon looked like a Dutch map; it was Langrenus who wanted to turn that statement into a reality.

Maps held an intense fascination in the late sixteenth and early seventeenth centuries. They encompassed all that was known about the Earth and its newly discovered, little-explored territories. As one *terra incognita* after another was explored the narrow horizons of the old world were being widened. Maps would guide the way for the pursuit of trade, the spread of religion and the rise of political power. England's defeat of the Spanish Armada in 1588 lessened Spain's sea power but it was the Dutch, until then dominated by the Spanish emperors, who finally broke that power. With the aid of maps the Dutch rose to become the world's foremost naval and commercial nation, penetrating all known oceans.

But maps were not only records of geographical information, they also contained and communicated ideas and legends. Until this time maps were based on myths and literary sources rather than observation and experience. God's world had been shown as a circle, within which the three continents outlined a T-shape reminiscent of the cross. But now, more accurate maps of many far-flung parts of the world, as well as sea charts, were appearing. Many were available as pocket atlases: a world to carry around.

In the fifteenth century the rediscovered works of Ptolemy translated into Latin had a powerful impact on Renaissance cartographers. Gradually, with increasing accuracy and confidence, maps emerged from the mythic mists and came to represent geographic reality. Ptolemy's writings, coming near the close of nearly six centuries of Greek speculation about the shape and size of the Earth and the extent of its habitation, were the starting point for this new phase of discovery. Ptolemy knew the Earth was spherical and was aware of the problems of depicting a spherical Earth on a flat surface. He developed several solutions, or projections, but within a century of his death, his work was virtually forgotten.

It was not until the fourteenth century that his manuscripts, preserved for over a thousand years in places like Constantinople and Toledo, were distributed throughout Europe. Here was a way of mapping space that Renaissance cartographers eagerly adopted. Early in the sixteenth century, editions of Ptolemy's *Geography* began to include maps that reflected the new discoveries being made. The world was changing, growing beyond the bounds of its ancient confines, and each year it was growing larger.

Some consider Abraham Ortelius, cartographer, map collector and businessman, to be the father of the atlas because of his great work, *Theatrum Orbis Terrarum*, published in Antwerp in 1570, thirty years before Langrenus was born.

Geography, Ortelius said, was 'the eye of History'. Now the eye of history was about to turn its gaze upon the moon.

Although Ortelius was the first to publish a modern atlas, it was Gerardus Mercator who was the first to use the word 'atlas' when referring to a collection of maps bound in a volume. Mercator's world map of 1569, drawn on the projection that bears his name, was one of the most important ever made. Soon the production of globes was a lucrative business and, given the pace of discovery, Mercator's globes became dated, allowing others into the market.

In 1586 globe production began in Amsterdam under Jacob Floris van Langren. It was a busy time. In 1597 the first ships set sail for India; between 1598 and 1603 nearly ninety more followed. Soon globe production in Amsterdam was in the hands of three independent publishers. But the brothers Arnold and Hendrik van Langren, sons of Jacob, were unable to face the competition of Jodocus Hondius and the Blaeu family. So for Michael van Langren the moon held the key to the family fortune. We can only imagine what an impression Mercator's map must have made on the young Langrenus. Mercator had devoted the last twenty-five years of his life to making a great atlas which was still incomplete when he died. Langrenus did not want the same fate to befall his moon map ambitions.

Like all educated men of his time, Langrenus knew of the longitude problem. Since man had first sailed the seas he had suffered because of his inability to determine longitude. Determining latitude at sea was easy. All one had to do was to measure the height of the pole star above the horizon and that angle was your latitude. But longitude, east or west around the globe, was a different matter. Many tales were told of many ships, fleets and sailors who perished because they could not find their longitude as they sailed out of sight of land. A fortune awaited the conqueror of this problem and many solutions had been suggested.

It was known that a precise clock would solve it but clocks carried to sea were not accurate enough, nor would they be until a hundred years after Langrenus' death. So it was that some looked to the moon for a solution. Perhaps the apparent position of the moon against the background stars, which would appear slightly different when observed from different sides of the globe, could be used. That would require an accurate star map and an accurate knowledge of the moon's motions through the stars, neither of which was available. However, the passage of the Earth's shadow across the face of the moon during a lunar eclipse might also solve the problem, as it would provide a kind of standard celestial clock that could be used to determine local time and hence longitude. Langrenus thought about this and came up with what he considered an even better idea. He would observe the moon itself and would time sunrises and sunsets on: '. . . islands and the peaks of mountains most often isolated from the main continuum which in an instant appear on the face of the waxing moon, and also those which suddenly vanish on the waning moon.' And for that he would need a map of the moon.

He explained his idea to King Félipe who was interested. A solution to the longitude problem would undoubtedly be of great value to his fleet and would help Spain regain some control of the high seas. He was especially impressed by Langrenus' idea of naming the lunar features he mapped after 'illustrious men'. He wrote to his aunt, Princess Isabella, asking her to find money for the project. His letter speaks of the task: '. . . to have the names of illustrious men applied to the luminous and resplendent mountains and islands of the lunar globe which might be used in the future in astronomical and hydrographical observations and corrections.'

All seemed to be set fair and Langrenus began making plans to map the moon. But while he was returning to Holland in 1634 to commence his project, Isabella died. Now Langrenus ran out of money and had to face the possibility that others might achieve the goal before him. But he did not allow it to be more than a temporary setback. Soon he was observing the moon as often as he could and learning how to draw it in Dutch cartographic style.

In 1637, while he was immersed in his great project, there were many others looking towards the moon. Among them was an Englishman, one Jeremiah Horrocks, who was observing the moon from the tiny village of Much Hoole in Lancashire. One night he observed an occultation of the Pleiades (or the 'Seven Sisters' star cluster) by the dark side of the moon. They winked out instantly and Horrocks correctly deduced that the moon had no atmosphere. In his brief life Horrocks walked on many of the intellectual foothills that in later years Isaac Newton would use to reach spectacular heights. How high, one wonders, would Jeremiah Horrocks himself have climbed had he not died aged only twenty-two?

For nine years Langrenus stuck to his task, producing some thirty drawings of the moon. In 1643 he became aware that others were close to producing a moon map of their own, in particular the astronomers Caramuel and Hevelius. Hevelius had a great reputation, so he accelerated his efforts and by 1645 he had his *Plenilunii Lumina Austriaca Philippica*, showing 322 names, engraved in copper. He named the dark spots 'Mare' or 'Oceanus'. Under the map he wrote: 'There was even the danger that since the work was being divulged abroad to a growing extent, some other person would appropriate it as his own and publicise it in his own name.'

There are only four known original copies in existence and all seem to be slightly different. The one in the Leiden Observatory is probably the earliest; those in the Crawford Library Royal Observatory, Edinburgh, at the National Library in Paris and at the Observatorio de Marina, San Fernando, seem to be a little later.

When I look at it now I am lost in admiration. Here is the moon I recognize but with unfamiliar names attached to familiar landmarks. Although simple by today's standards it is nonetheless magnificent. Considering the telescopes of the time, it was quite an achievement. Craters are shaded as if illuminated by the morning sun, a technique still used today. It is adorned with the names of European royalty, philosophers, scientists, mathematicians, explorers, religious leaders, saints. Here we have Mare Venetum (the Venetian Sea), Sinus Geometricus (the Geometric Bay), as well as oceans, lakes, straits and rivers, capes and mountain ranges. Langrenus had been true to his cartographic heritage.

The prominent crater we call Tycho today is here labelled Vladislav and the mighty Copernicus is naturally Félipe IV. The Medici are there and the astronomers are clustered near Mare Astronomicum, with the Greek and Arabic astronomers positioned towards the limb. Mare Langrenreni, the Sea of Langrenus, can be seen, as well as Mare Belgium and the largest 'sea' on the moon, Oceanus Philippicus. Near the Langrenus Sea can be seen the magnificent crater he named Langrenus.

There is another Langrenus map, a shoddy forgery in the library of the University of Strasbourg, on which some of the names have been replaced with others. Langrenus was aware that this would happen and was clearly desperate to keep his names on the moon. On his map he wrote: 'By Royal Decree changes in the names of this map are forbidden under pain of indignation, and copies and other forgeries are forbidden under pain of confiscation and a fine of three florins.'

Elsewhere he adds: 'We have freely communicated to the whole world the great bounty of these plans, by which we now venerate those men famous for these studies and their defenders and promoters. For this grave reason with total submission we produce this image of the moon, dedicated to the Kings, Princes and most famous lovers of the arts . . .'

Langrenus had done just what Galileo had done when he saw the four major moons of Jupiter and named them after the rich and influential Medici family. But, as was the case with Galileo, the names did not stick. Of the 325 names on the map, some sixty-eight are still in use but only three in the same location. Only Endymion, Pythagoras and, fittingly, Langrenus remain. Langrenus' names might have lasted had if not been for the other moon maps that were being published. His moon, a place of patronage and homage to powerful men, did not stand the test of time. In a way Langrenus tried to preserve an image of a Catholic Europe on the moon and failed because on Earth a Catholic Europe was in the throes of defeat. Looking carefully at the map, it is true that many of the craters are not exactly in their correct position but it is not to be judged by the more accurate maps of later years. It is a remarkable document, the starting point for all other maps to emulate and follow. With it the moon had been mapped in Dutch style and with it the science of selenography was born.

One of the people Langrenus was to honour with a crater would prove to be his most ardent rival. Pierre Gassendi was a professor of mathematics in Paris and one of the leading astronomical thinkers of his day. As Langrenus began his mapping, a lunar eclipse of 20 January 1628 was used by Gassendi and his friend Nicolas de Peiresc (who 'discovered' the great nebula in Orion) to determine the longitude difference between Paris and Aix-en-Provence. It was a technique that could in principle be used to determine the longitude of any place on Earth. They, like

Langrenus, realized that they needed an accurate map of the moon to make the idea work.

They made sketches of the moon and found an artist called Claude Melan who was a skilled engraver. The drawings they produced together are remarkable and far better than anything produced before 1637, even though the telescopes they used were no better than those used by Galileo. Gassendi worked on a naming scheme but with the death of Peiresc when the project was just a year old it progressed no further than his notebooks.

A few years after the engravings were produced Gassendi learned that the German astronomer Hevelius was planning a lunar map made from observations carried out from his observatory in Danzig. Some people have said that Hevelius wanted to leave the task to the senior astronomer but when Gassendi saw Hevelius' first drawings he was overwhelmed and recognized the younger man's keen eye and superior draughtsmanship. He urged Hevelius to carry on and even suppressed the publication of some of Melan's drawings and sent them to Hevelius. Gassendi wrote to his friend Juan Caramuel y Lobkowitz saying that he was pleased that someone else had taken up the task of mapping and naming the moon. His friend replied that in all future naming schemes 'All our friends will be there. You yourself and Peiresc', and so they were, but not yet.

Danzig (before and afterwards called Gdansk) was a typical northern German town, with narrow streets and tall houses with steep-pitched roofs to prevent the accumulation of snow. If you could have looked across the rooftops in the mid-seventeenth century you would have seen that built across four of them was a platform with strange spindly scaffolding carrying lenses and measuring rods towards the sky. Welcome to the observatory of Johannes Hevelius (1611–1687), a prosperous merchant and city official. Probably the foremost observational astronomer of his time, he also had a passionate desire to produce a lunar map.

As the eldest son of a wealthy brewer, Hevelius inherited the family business and this gave him the financial freedom to follow his calling. Unlike so many other scientists of his day, Hevelius did not have to find a patron. His interest in astronomy was kindled by his tutor and later friend, Peter Kruger. Kruger was a modern scientist who believed that observation, not philosophy, was the key to understanding the universe. He believed you had to build top-quality telescopes and then push them to their limits to find out how things really were, not what you thought they should be like. But Kruger could not do this himself because his eyesight was poor. So the young, impressionable Hevelius became his eyes.

In 1630, when he was nineteen, Hevelius went to Leiden University. He had the means to travel widely, intending to meet many of the leading astronomers and scientists of his day, absorbing their words and studying their methods. But before he could get to Italy to meet Galileo (surely the highlight of his tour), he was called back home to Danzig. It must have been a bitter blow. A secure place in his father's firm beckoned, a safe and loyal occupation but dull. He managed to put astronomy aside for several years and tried to be satisfied with brewing and the social life of Danzig but he was always looking for the right time to turn his attention away from vats and towards the skies. Soon he was sitting at Peter Kruger's deathbed. With his dying words, Kruger urged Hevelius to take up astronomy once again before it was too late. So Hevelius' observatory, built in the 1640s, was one of the finest in Europe and the envy of every astronomer who saw it.

Hevelius did not think much of Galileo's drawings, saying that he 'lacked a sufficiently good telescope', and was 'ignorant of the art of picturing and drawing'. In Hevelius it seemed that all the skills and talents necessary to produce an accurate map of the moon came together: drawing, engraving, telescope-making, printing, as well as the all-important time and money. His observatory contained not only one of the largest telescopes in existence but also a workshop, and engraving and printing facilities.

He commenced serious observations of the moon in the late autumn of 1643 and soon discovered that one of the astronomers he had met years previously as he travelled around Europe, Pierre Gassendi, was also mapping the moon. He also saw the work of Francesco Fontana (1602–1656) who had begun drawing the moon in 1630 and had published a book of his lunar engravings that could be described as the earliest lunar atlas, because it included woodcuts of the moon at different phases. Hevelius decided he could do better.

Hevelius modelled himself on his great hero Tycho Brahe who, almost a century earlier, had charted the heavens with great accuracy, before the advent of the telescope, from his island observatory of Uraniborg. Hevelius named his rooftop observatory 'Sternenburg' and had copies made of many of Tycho's sighting instruments. At that time telescopes had been forced to grow to gargantuan lengths because of the poor quality of the objective lenses. Hevelius built a telescope 12 feet long, with the main lens and the eyepiece supported by ropes and pulleys. It magnified 50 times, yet its main lens was probably no more than 2 inches across – tiny by today's standards. He followed that with a telescope 150 feet long, which must have been a strange and puzzling sight to the citizens of Danzig. With its aid he produced his 1647 *Selenographia*, a magnificent work including 275 named lunar features. He went straight into a dispute with Langrenus.

Hevelius had already written, '. . . I have taken on an arduous task, hitherto unheard of, of applying certain names to parts of a remote heavenly body, which has not been done by anyone to this day, as far as I know . . .'

When he heard of this Langrenus was incensed. In a letter to a friend he wrote, '. . . who [Hevelius], in my opinion, was wrong not to mention my work which he saw fully two years before he produced his selenographic production.'

Selenographia is an astounding work, undoubtedly one of the top five books ever written about the moon. Looking at Hevelius' map I can see the dedication, count the hours and feel the attention to detail. He was the first to produce a true lunar atlas as well as a consistent series of drawings showing lunar features emerging from and then retreating into shadow. The frontispiece unashamedly sets the work in its historical context. Al-Haytham and Galileo hold the title banner (Hevelius had no small ego). Pope Innocent X was to read it, no doubt fully aware of the trouble his church had had with observers of the moon in the recent past. He said of the Protestant Hevelius, 'such a book would have no equal were it not written by a heretic'.

With poems written by friends extolling his abundant virtues and talents, one gets an almost overpowering sense that Hevelius felt his *Selenographia* entitled him to be counted among the greatest astronomers of any age: Hipparchus, Ptolemy, Copernicus, Tycho, Galileo and now Hevelius. Conceited perhaps; realistic, probably. Years later, in his final work, called the *Astronomical Catalog*, there is an engraving showing Hevelius presenting his work to a council of the greatest astronomers of the past as well as Urania, the muse of astronomy. In an age when astronomy made some remarkable progress, his lunar drawings were not bettered for 100 years. His atlas was produced in the same style as atlases of the Earth. It included something almost like a flip-chart to show the moon changing over its lunation. It was a homage to astronomy and an indication of what it might achieve in the future with refinements in the telescope. Strange then that, after *Selenographia*, he abandoned the telescope.

Naming the features he mapped, he wrote that, 'the nature of our work, necessarily makes inroads on the perogatives of God'. So, never shy in the face of such a task, he decreed the Ocean of Copernicus, the Sea of Kepler, the Lake of Galileo, the Peninsula of Gassendi. On the moon he paid homage to the great astronomers of the past that he so desperately wanted to join. He took a swipe at Langrenus, saying that he 'could have preferred one or other person because of friendship of faith or some less worthy reason'.

Was Hevelius' motivation more noble? In his observations Hevelius was helped by his second wife Elisabetha about whom we do not know very much. She is present in the corner of one engraving from one of his star maps, operating a measuring instrument with an air of experience. Hevelius has a crater on the moon named after him but Elisabetha does not. This injustice was remedied when a crater on Venus was named after her some three hundred years later.

Curiously, he perceived that if the moon was turned on its side the distribution of highland and lowland was faintly reminiscent of the classical world as known by the Greeks and Romans (the mirror moon). So we have again the Mediterranean Sea, the Adriatic, the Black and Caspian Sea, Africa, Arabia, the Alps, the Caucasus. The crater we now call Copernicus was called Etna and Plato was the 'greater Black Lake'. But, like Langrenus' names, his did not last; only four are still in use. In his book the moon was like the Earth, there were islands and active volcanoes, and inhabitants. 'Just because we do not perceive any beings there, it does not follow there are none. Would a man raised in a forest, in the midst of birds and quadrupeds, be able to form the idea of the ocean, and the animals which live there,' he wrote.

How strange that, as someone so driven to reach an exalted place among the great astronomers, Hevelius did not include his own name on the face of the moon. When it came to observing the stars Hevelius was never convinced that the telescope was more accurate than the unaided eye. Because of this the English astronomer Robert Hooke charged Hevelius with ignoring progress in practical astronomy. Another English astronomer John Flamsteed, likewise, doubted whether Hevelius, for all his work, was actually improving on the accuracy of Tycho's observations without the aid of a telescope. Edmund Halley travelled to Danzig to settle the matter and concluded that Hevelius, with his unaided eye, was as accurate as any of the telescopes of the time in obtaining the positions of stars.

The Dutch astronomer Christian Huygens (1629–1695) who had done so much to improve the telescope in 1654, wrote in 1657: 'the moon has no air or atmosphere surrounding it as we have', and he could not 'imagine how any plants or animals whose whole nourishment comes from fluid bodies, can thrive in a dry, waterless, parched soil'.

He added:

What, then, shall this great ball be made for; nothing, but to give us a little weak light in the night time, or to raise our tides in the sea? Shall we not plant some people there that they may have the pleasure of seeing our earth turn upon its axis, presenting them sometimes with a prospect of Europe and Africa, and then of Asia and America; sometimes half and sometimes full.

Copies of Hevelius' maps still exist but not the original copper-plate. In a story that probably comes from Edmund Halley, who came to know Hevelius quite well in his old age, it was said to have been melted down after his death into a teapot!

Two great maps, those of Langrenus and of Hevelius, had been produced and many lunar features had names. But those names would not last. The names we use today were invented by an Italian monk who did not believe that the Earth went around the sun at all.

CHAPTER EIGHT

The Anguish of Riccioli

That man was Giovanni Battista Riccioli (1598–1671). He was a Jesuit priest and professor, first at Padua and then at Bologna, a man of many talents, teaching philosophy, mathematics and astronomy and a man on a doomed mission.

He joined the order in 1614, aged sixteen, at a time when the Jesuits regarded themselves as the intellectual defenders of a church increasingly under siege by the recent discoveries of science, especially astronomy. They wanted to use that very science and its advances to prove that Aristotle was right, and to take Copernicus' own tools and logic and use them to destroy his works. But, as the heavens revealed their secrets to a growing number of telescopes whose observations were described and confirmed in an increasing number of books, this stance became more and more difficult to maintain. Typical of their approach was a story written by one of the Jesuits, Athanasius Kircher, about a voyage to the moon. The hero, Theodidactus, was escorted by the angel Cosmiel, who said, 'There are no plants, nor people, nor animals, nor any such living thing on the moon.'

For what he intended to be a decisive contribution to the battle, Riccioli wanted to write the most influential and authoritative book on astronomy that had ever been produced. He called it the *Almagestum novum* (or the 'New Almagest') and he clearly saw it as a successor to Ptolemy's great and enduring work. As he gathered his arguments he had no inkling that the cosmic battle he would win was not the one he was preparing to fight. While writing his refutation he even refused to read the works of Galileo and so failed to follow the first rule of military conflict: know your enemy. Perhaps he knew that if he looked too closely at Galileo's arguments and observations he would begin to be swayed. But, as he marshalled his evidence, he felt a nagging doubt grow louder within him. So loud in fact that he soon reached a crisis in the book when his changing personal doubts and beliefs fundamentally threatened his ability to proceed. He was beginning to be seduced by the enemy, to believe the heretics. He was racked by inner turmoil, tempted by the very thing he had sworn to destroy.

But he had to produce the book and, as one reads it, it is all too obvious that his attacks on Galileo, Kepler and Copernicus are weak and half-hearted. His proposed alternative explanations for the apparent motions of the planets – explanations that are supposed to be in accordance with the scriptures, that Mercury, Venus, Mars, Jupiter and Saturn orbit the sun with the sun orbiting the Earth – are absurd. It was later said that without his cowl Riccioli would have been a Copernican. He must have known it.

The 'New Almagest' took him only three years to write and it was published in 1651 with a frontispiece showing the sun with a face, the moon cratered with the planets, the sun and a comet carried by cherubs. Here again is Urania, the muse of astronomy, and she holds a balance weighing the system of Copernicus against that of Tycho who did not believe all the planets circled the sun. The Tycho system is heavier but the muse says, 'It will not be tipped for all time.' It is a book riven with tension and strain, a conflict between science, faith and the inevitable; the cusp of the moon was the cusp between the classical and the modern world. It is a work of many voices shouting at each other that could perhaps have been written at no other time. That it had been written by a Jesuit priest should have been a clear sign to the Church that the battle for the immobile Earth was lost.

When it came to naming the features on the moon Riccioli's book was revolutionary. The only pictures in the New Almagest are those of the moon drawn by Riccioli's friend and fellow Jesuit Francisco Maria Grimaldi. Grimaldi took the best from the previous maps. In naming the features on the moon Riccioli had a stroke of genius. The 'seas', continents, lakes and peninsulas were named after effects and influences. From fecundity we have Mare Fecunditatis; serenity, Mare Serenitatis; madness, Mare Crisium; storminess, Oceanus Procellarum; rain, Mare Imbrium; cold, Mare Figoris. Today we have lost some of Riccioli's names for the upland regions. He wanted to name some of them after: heat, Terra Caloris; sterility, Terra Sterilitatis; cheerfulness, Terra Vigoris.

In naming the craters Riccioli was at his most logical. He divided the moon into eight regions and sub-divided them among astronomers and philosophers. There is the ancient Greek region, with Rome nearby, a region for medieval Europe, and one for Arabic thinkers. There is also a sector allocated for modern astronomers. Perhaps as divine judgement, or maybe reflecting his inner turmoil, Riccioli placed many of his adversaries who believed in a sun-centred cosmos near the Ocean of Storms. Copernicus is in the region of storms, Aristotle near the frigid sea and the reviled Galileo as far away from the venerable ancients as possible. Just beyond Galileo, Hevelius was granted a sizeable crater in Terra Caloris, again on the margin of true astronomy. Around the Sea of Nectar are a cluster of holy saints, Catherine, Theophilus, Cyril, and to the west of the saints in the land of Healthfulness (Terra Sanitatis) are the Arabic and Jewish thinkers, Azophi, Albategnius and Arzachel. But where is Aristotle? The great thinker who dominated western thought about the moon and the heavens for two thousand years, whom Riccioli had been attempting to defend? Curiously, he can be found near Mare Figoris (the Sea of Cold), below Hevelius. Riccioli undoubtedly knew which theory would stand the test of time. As for himself, his crater is the last feature along the moon's western edge, on the limb, showing allegiance to no one.

This is Riccioli's greatest achievement, not his half-hearted and doomed book, but his claiming of the moon for science. Gone were the clumsy long-winded names used by Hevelius and the wealthy patrons' names given by the fawning Langrenus. On the moon Riccioli established the tradition of placing not only the great minds of religion and philosophy but also the ever-growing, ever more powerful force that would overwhelm the future: science itself. He could not resist it, personally or professionally. But Riccioli did not stop there. He also paid homage to the moon's superstitious past. Long associated with fertility, birth, growth, the harvest and the weather, he anointed its face with all these things for all time. His nomenclature was revolutionary but would others accept it?

Crucial to its acceptance was the decision by Jean Dominique Cassini, the first director of the Paris Observatory (who took the job after Hevelius declined it), to choose the Riccioli–Grimaldi naming scheme for one of his maps. It was not long thereafter that Hevelius' map started appearing in many books but with the Riccioli–Grimaldi scheme. When, over 300 years later, the crew of Apollo 11 touched down on the moon they did so on a sea named by a Jesuit priest who never came to terms with his inner conflict when the tides of his faith and his logic pulled him in opposite directions.

In the final years of his life Langrenus must have felt bitter that Hevelius had deliberately shunned his work and that Riccioli had superseded him. Only three of the names he suggested survive on modern maps. Perhaps Langrenus took solace in the fact that most of the names proposed by Hevelius did not last either.

The moon is a fickle mistress and it takes its light where it will with no warning or explanation. It once shone over Greece and then moved its light to the Middle East, before returning to the Mediterranean with Galileo. But now the moonbeams were moving again, heading northwards, where they would linger for only a short while before moving on.

★ ★ ★

When Riccioli was thirty-seven, before he had started work on his *New Almagest*, the remarkable Robert Hooke (1635–1703) was born in England. He was to become one of the world's foremost scientists, with a greater range of studies than Sir Isaac Newton. His pathfinding work on microscopy, *Micrographia*, contains magnificent engravings of magnified insects but a surprise is in store: as you pass the microscopic creatures you come across a drawing of a crater on the moon. The book contains the very first attempt to draw in great detail a particular lunar feature, in this case the crater Hipparchus, just south of the centre of the moon. To make the drawing, Hooke used a 30-foot long telescope and observed just before the first quarter, when the shadows were long and the terminator jagged with relief. His drawing is a considerable improvement on the undefined circles that appear on the maps of Hevelius or Riccioli, and Hooke even suggested that, since the floor of Hipparchus reflected less light than the mountaintops, it was perhaps covered with vegetation and might be, in his words, a 'fruitful place'.

But Hooke went further. He was not content just to observe and record, he had to experiment. So, one day he packed wet clay into a box and dropped balls into it to see what shape the impact craters would be. To his eye they did not look like lunar craters so he tried a different approach. He heated pans of alabaster until they bubbled and boiled like small volcanoes. From what he saw, he thought the moon more closely resembled the pock-marked alabaster. He wrote: '. . . it would be difficult to imagine whence those bodies [the projectiles] should come; and next, how the substance of the moon should be so soft.'

Hooke made other important astronomical observations showing how Jupiter revolves on its axis, and his drawings of Mars were later also used to determine its period of rotation. He held the post of City Surveyor of London, was a competent architect and was chief assistant to Sir Christopher Wren (also an astronomer), in the rebuilding of London after the Great Fire of 1666. He argued bitterly with Sir Isaac Newton, claiming that he had postulated the inverse square law of gravity first. Consequently, the sour Newton removed all references to Hooke from his great work, the *Principia*.

No portrait of Hooke is known to exist. A possible reason for this is that he has been described as a lean, bent and ugly man and so he may not have been willing to sit for a painting. But there is another theory. We know there was a portrait of him at the Royal Society in 1710, because it was seen by a visiting German scientist. Where did it go? The informed guess is that shortly after Sir Isaac Newton became president of the Royal Society he took the portrait up to his quarters where he threw it into the fireplace!

Although not the most important map of the moon drawn in the seventeenth century, that made by Jean Dominique Cassini (1625–1712) is perhaps one of the most beautiful. Cassini published an engraved map in 1679 that at 21 inches across was twice as large as those made by Hevelius and Riccioli. It was undoubtedly superior in detail to its predecessors but it was only printed as a broadsheet and was soon very scarce. Smaller versions of it quickly appeared in various optical and astronomical treatises but minus much of the detail of the original map that made it so charming. One of its most delightful features was the portrayal of Cape Heraclides on the Sinus Iridum (Bay of Rainbows) as a 'moon maiden', with face and flowing hair.

By 1700 the moon had been mapped in broad detail and on Earth the shapes of the main continents were pretty well known. Only the outlines of Australia and northern Siberia, the far American North-west and the Bering Strait were not yet known.

As the seventeenth century drew to a close, the moon was to show another of its many sides and play a prominent role in the most important scientific question of the age, the problem of 'fixing the longitude'.

Until the end of the fifteenth century, sailors rarely ventured out of sight of land. In the Mediterranean it was difficult to go very far astray. In western and north-west Europe most navigation was coastal so ships hugged the shore from Gibraltar to Norway and the Baltic. The only exception was the trade between Scandinavia, Iceland, and occasionally Greenland, routes the Vikings had discovered around 1000 AD. During the Portuguese voyages of discovery in the fifteenth century ships followed the coast of Africa closely as they explored the contours of the continent. But with the voyages of Diaz, who rounded the Cape of Good Hope in 1486, Columbus in 1492, and da Gama in 1498, sailors were out of sight of land for weeks.

Ships were equipped with instruments such as astrolabes and devices like cross-staffs to measure the altitudes of stars or the sun. It was not difficult to determine one's latitude to within about a degree by this method but longitude was a different matter. World maps prepared in the sixteenth century were widely wrong in the longitudes of places. The east–west length of the Mediterranean was in error by 19 degrees – about 1000 miles! The longitudes of China and Japan were off by much larger margins. For nations engaged in trade with the Far East and the West Indies, finding longitude at sea was a matter of great national and economic importance.

Soon after the discovery of the satellites of Jupiter by Galileo it was realized that they acted as a kind of clock whose face could be seen from every vantage point on Earth. In 1612 Nicolas de Peiresc in Aix-en-Provence sent an assistant to the eastern part of the Mediterranean to observe Jupiter's satellites while he did the same from home. The plan was to compare the satellite positions observed at the same time and deduce the difference in local time between the two locations. It was a good idea in theory but the results were disappointing.

That same year Galileo observed an eclipse of a satellite of Jupiter – when a satellite enters the shadow behind the planet it disappears very quickly. Such eclipses were, for all practical purposes, instantaneous events. Perhaps they could be used as a celestial time marker? If a sailor of the high seas could note the local time of such an eclipse and compare it with the local time at which it was predicted to happen at a reference location then the difference in times could be converted into a difference in longitude. Galileo began negotiations with the Spanish Crown to provide Spanish navigators with eclipse tables for the satellites and telescopes to make the observations. He worked for many years on this plan but never published his results. The eclipse predictions were not sufficiently accurate and at the time it was not feasible to make observations from the deck of a rolling ship. Later the English went so far as to install gimballed seats that were independent of the motion of the ship.

In the 1670s French astronomers, led by Cassini, began making observations of Jupiter's satellites from many locations to produce an accurate map of France. The resulting map, finished in 1679, showed that the west coast of France was too far west by an entire degree; similar adjustments had to be made to the Mediterranean coast. Upon seeing this map, King Louis XIV remarked that he was losing more territory to his astronomers than to his enemies.

Eventually the chronometer was developed in England and the rest is history. But before the clock conquered the longitude problem there were many who hoped the moon would come to the rescue. One of these was John Flamsteed, born near Derby in England and – like Hevelius – the son of a prosperous brewer.

Because of ill-health he did not go to university and, against the wishes of his father, studied astronomy by himself at home.

Flamsteed believed that if the exact position of the moon relative to the stars could be predicted then the longitude problem would be solved. So the English astronomers began to use the moon as their main means of attack on the longitude problem, the French worked largely on the moons of Jupiter method, and clockmaker John Harrison (who eventually triumphed) worked mostly alone. Flamsteed had an audience with the king and told him it was a matter of national pride that England have its own Royal Observatory as the French already had one. The king moved swiftly and on 4 March 1675 appointed Flamsteed his Astronomical Observer by Royal Warrant or the first Astronomer Royal. From his salary of £100 a year he had to pay £10 taxes and also provide all his own instruments so that he might: '. . . apply himself with the most exact care and diligence to rectifying the tables of the motions of the heavens, and the places of the fixed stars, so as to find the so-much-desired longitude of places for perfecting the art of navigation.' Unlike Hevelius, Flamsteed felt that the telescope could be the workhorse of positional astronomy.

From the new Royal Greenwich Observatory Flamsteed was to spend the next fifteen years, from 1689 to 1704, compiling tables of the moon's motion to use for the lunar distance method of finding the longitude. Sir Isaac Newton also required information from him in order to perfect his understanding of the moon's orbit in terms of his new theory of gravity but Flamsteed refused to hand them over. By 1712 Newton and Halley could stand it no more and, claiming that all work by the Astronomer Royal was public property, they seized his observations and published them. Flamsteed was incensed, tracked down most of the books and burned them. When Flamsteed died in 1718 his widow was swift to pounce on the Observatory (the telescopes were legally hers) and the next Astronomer Royal, Edmund Halley, had to start from scratch.

Solving the longitude problem was becoming an increasingly urgent task. Between 1690 and 1710 there were many incidents in which English naval ships were lost at sea. In 1707 over 2000 men were drowned when four ships ran aground on the Scilly Islands while returning to England. Pressure was mounting for a solution.

The English were convinced that the lunar method would solve it. In 1742 James Bradley, the third Astronomer Royal, and Tobias Mayer, a self-taught mathematician who worked as a cartographer, were certain that they were on the right track. Tobias Mayer had sent his own lunar tables to the Board of Longitude, the panel established to assess proposed solutions, in 1756. But the Seven Years War with France had prevented a proper test of the method. In 1761 Nevil Maskelyne, another strong believer in the lunar method, was dispatched to St Helena in the South Atlantic to test Tobias Mayer's tables.

In the first issue of the *Nautical Almanac* Maskelyne wrote of Mayer's tables:

> The Tables of the moon had been brought by the late Professor Mayer of Göttingen to a sufficient exactness to determine the Longitude at Sea to within a Degree, as appeared by the Trials of several Persons who made use of them. The Difficulty and Length of the necessary Calculations seemed the only obstacles to hinder them from becoming of general Use.

Bradley claimed that he and Tobias Mayer would have shared the £10,000 longitude prize but for Harrison's blasted watch.

Hevelius' *Selenographia* had reigned supreme for 140 years, along with Cassini's imposing map of 1679, but the map made by Tobias

Mayer was more accurate. In producing his map of the moon Mayer had introduced the idea of using a micrometer within the telescope to determine the exact positions of the lunar features. He began his lunar studies in 1748 and made at least forty detailed drawings of various regions, from which he planned to construct both a lunar map and a lunar globe. In 1750 the Cosmographical Society of Nuremberg issued a prospectus for the globe, which included two plates, made from Mayer's drawings, to demonstrate the quality of his observations. The lunar globe was never produced as the publisher almost went bankrupt.

Tobias Mayer's map of the moon was not published until 1775 but it was more accurate than anything that preceded it. It was the first map to be gridded with lines of latitude and longitude. One unusual feature is that it has north at the top, contrary to the tradition inaugurated by Cassini and continued by every other lunar map until 1960. When Schröter incorporated Mayer's map in his own moon book he had the map re-engraved with south up.

Nobody had ever seen anything change on the moon, until now.

CHAPTER NINE

Where Unicorns Roamed

Friedrich Wilhelm Herschel was the first man in recorded history to discover a planet. He was born in Hanover on 15 November 1738, one of ten children, four of whom died young. His father was a military musician who not only taught him music but also astronomy. Soon, after leaving school, Wilhelm was playing in the same military orchestra as his father. After a battle in Germany Friedrich Wilhelm and his brother Jakob went to Hamburg to embark as passengers on a ship to England, where they planned to earn a living as musicians; only Wilhelm (now called William) stayed. After spending some time in Richmond and Leeds, he moved to Bath, lived as a musician, and pursued his love of astronomy. In the summer of 1772 he went back to Hanover to fetch his sister Caroline. They lived at various addresses in Bath and for a while ended up at 5 River Street. They had no garden so one evening, when a man passing by asked to have a view of the moon, William placed his telescope on the street right beside the house.

On the evening of 13 March 1781 his life was to change forever. He was working on compiling a catalogue of all the 'double stars' in the sky when he found a bright object in an area near the star H Geminorum where the charts showed none. Herschel suspected a comet but observations made the following night showed a slow-moving object. His friend Nevil Maskelyne was sure it was a new planet, and so it was. Soon Herschel was elected a Fellow of the Royal Society and became a full-time astronomer. King George III, after whom he had tried to name the new world (other astronomers thought Uranus was a better name), offered him the position of court astronomer at Windsor for a salary of 200 pounds per annum (a vast sum at the time). His sister was paid 50 pounds for assisting him. Nobody had ever discovered a new planet before.

In 1787 Herschel published a remarkable paper in the Philosophical Transactions of the Royal Society entitled 'An Account of three volcanoes in the moon'.

He wrote:

It will be necessary to say a few words by way of introduction to the account I have to give of some appearances upon the moon, which I perceived the 19th and 20th of this month. The phenomena of nature, especially those that fall under the inspection of the astronomer, are to be viewed, not only with the usual attention to facts as they occur, but with the eye of reason and experience . . . we see, on the surface of the moon, a great number of elevations, from half a mile to a mile and an half in height, we are strictly intitled [sic] to call them mountains; but, when we attend to their particular shape, in which many of them resemble the craters of our volcanoes.

April 19, 1787, 10h. 36' sidereal time. I perceive three volcanoes in different places of the dark part of the new moon. Two of them are either already nearly extinct, or otherwise in a state of going to break out; which perhaps may be decided next lunation. The third shows an actual eruption of fire, or luminous matter.

[. . .]

April 20, 1787, 10h. 2' sidereal time. The volcano burns with greater violence than last night . . . as Jupiter was near at hand, I turned the telescope to his third satellite, and estimated the diameter of the burning part of the volcano to be equal to at least twice that of the satellite. Hence we may compute that the shining or burning matter must be above three miles in diameter. It is of an irregular round figure, and very sharply defined on the edges. The other two volcanoes are much farther towards the centre of the moon, and resemble large, pretty faint nebulae, that are gradually much brighter in the middle; but no well defined luminous spot can be discerned in them. These three spots are plainly to be distinguished from the rest of the marks upon the moon; for the reflection of the sun's rays from the earth is, in its present situation, sufficiently bright, with a ten-feet reflector, to show the moon's spots, even the darkest of them: nor did I perceive any similar phenomena last lunation, though I then viewed the same places with the same instrument.

The appearance of what I have called the actual fire or eruption of a volcano, exactly resembled a small piece of burning charcoal, when it is covered by a very thin coat of white ashes, which frequently adhere to it when it has been some time ignited; and it had a degree of brightness, about as strong as that with which such a coal would be seen to glow in faint daylight.

All the adjacent parts of the volcanic mountain seemed to be faintly illuminated by the eruption, and were gradually more obscure as they lay at a greater distance from the crater.

This eruption resembled much that which I saw on the 4th of May, in the year 1783; an account of which, with many remarkable particulars relating to volcanic mountains in the moon, I shall take an early opportunity of communicating to this Society. It differed, however, considerably in magnitude and brightness; for the volcano of the year 1783, though much brighter than that which is now burning, was not nearly so large in the dimensions of its eruption: the former seen in the telescope resembles a star of the fourth magnitude as it appears to the natural eye; this, on the contrary, shows a visible disc of luminous matter, very different from the sparkling brightness of star-light.

WILLIAM HERSCHEL

Slough, near Windsor

April 21, 1787

What it was that Herschel saw we do not know. His observations cannot be dismissed – he was an experienced and keen-eyed observer. But it has to be said that there is nothing that can be seen on the moon today that could be the result of what he observed, another moon mystery. He says that the phenomena of nature, especially those that fall under the inspection of the astronomer, are to be viewed, not only with the usual attention to facts as they occur, but with the eye of reason and experience. Nobody has an experience of volcanoes on the moon to draw upon when judging what he described. The puzzle of the volcanoes remains, but the moon was not yet finished with the Herschel family by any means, as we shall see shortly.

Among many others, Hershel and the young William Wilberforce had their portraits painted by John Russell (1745–1806), portrait-ist to King George III. Russell was also taken with the moon's beauty. In a letter dated 9 Feb 1789 he wrote: '. . . how much struck a young man conversant with light and shade must be with the moon in this [first quarter] state; especially, as I was not taught to expect such clearness and expression, as to be found near and upon the indented edge.' He looked for the maps that were available, those by Hevelius and Riccioli, but what he saw disappointed him. They were accurate and scientific certainly but he paid no worship to the moon of science; he wanted an artist's moon. He was more impressed with the large Cassini map but was sure he could produce a better one. So he began a series of observations in 1764 that continued for more than forty years.

William Herschel had told him: 'seeing is in some respect an art which must be learnt'. Russell strove for a more artistic but still accurate representation of the moon that corresponded to the way he saw it, asserting that:

> . . . the moon requires much attention to be well understood, being composed of so many parts, of different characters, so much similitude in each class of forms, and of such a variety in the minutae composing these forms and this difficulty also most considerably increased by the various effects caused by the different situations of the Sun; that I am perswaded many considerable improvements may be made; in correctness of form in the spots, their situation and distinctness of parts.

On a giant artist's canvas he painted one extraordinary portrait of the moon fully 5 feet across, and on one of his drawings the moon maiden of the Bay of Rainbows reappears.

For me Russell's drawings are the first to capture the essence of the moon I see through my telescope, something that is hinted at in Galileo's portraits but lost entirely to Langrenus and Hevelius. The midnight moon hanging over frozen winter fields, the soft summer silver moon are somehow captured by this artist. His drawings are more detailed than anything before and, as 'eye to the telescope' maps of the moon, they have never been equalled. Few copies of his globe and maps were distributed; more's the pity.

But the moon is not just furrowed with craters, valleys and vast plains, it is also streaked with narrow clefts, or rilles. And the first person to chart them was Hieronymus Schröter (1745–1816), a man for whom the moon brought both joy and tragedy. He observed thousands of features on the moon, 'as many as the features identified in the heavens by our contemporary star charts,' he said, and produced a magnificent atlas, the best ever made before the photographic era.

He was chief magistrate at Lilienthal near Bremen in Germany and his self-proclaimed ambition was to observe and draw lunar features under all conditions of illumination, as well as to measure the heights and depths of craters and to look for evidence of an atmosphere and for changes on the lunar surface.

To do this he purchased two small reflectors from Herschel. Everyone who was serious about observing the moon had a Herschel telescope, and a strange 'projections-maschine' [sic], a seemingly useful device if one could get the hang of it which allowed one to view the moon through the eyepiece with one eye while at the same time using the other eye to guide a drawing on a board fixed to the telescope. Using this method, and more conventional ones, he had by 1790 gathered enough observations to write his *Selenographische Fragmente* the following year and produce a lunar map 4 feet across and for the first time use the word 'crater'. He added nearly seventy new names to the named features.

The *Selenographische Fragmente* is sumptuous and seductive, with its seventy-five engraved plates spread over two volumes. Not everyone liked it however; Schröter has been much maligned during his time and since. To be truthful he was not the world's best draughtsman. His drawings were sometimes crude and he had some strange ideas. He believed that he had found some important changes on the lunar surface and that it was inhabited by intelligent beings. But, to his credit, he never drew what he did not see – unlike many other lunar observers.

He was one of the first to make detailed drawings of small areas of interest, rather than just full disc views, and he made many measurements of mountain heights. The most famous rille he discovered, now justly called Schröter's Valley, lies just north-west of the crater Aristarchus, scene of many TLPs (Transient Lunar Phenomena). He was also the first to publish a drawing of the

Straight Wall. (We know that both the Straight Wall and Schröter's Valley were sketched a century earlier by Christian Huygens,
but those drawings were not published until 1925.)

But what happens to a man when his life's passion and work is
destroyed? Schröter was observing during the Napoleonic Wars
and in 1813 the French, under van Damme, occupied Bremen.
Lilienthal fell into their hands and one night, while the pitiless
moon looked on, 68-year-old Schröter saw his observatory
burned to the ground; his notes, manuscripts and unpublished
observations became mere sparks, floating upwards towards the
stars The smouldering wreckage contained all his telescopes, his
engravings, his notes and his life's passion; little could be saved.
Some of his instruments were looted by the troops who believed
the polished brass to be gold. Although he lived to see Bonaparte
beaten at Waterloo, he never recovered from the loss and died
three years later.

Then, from the sublime to the ridiculous, someone discovered
unicorns on the moon!

On 25 August 1835 an article appeared in *The Sun*, a New York
daily newspaper, 'Great Astronomical Discoveries Lately Made by
Sir John Herschel at the Cape of Good Hope'. It was written by
Richard Adams Locke (1800–1871), who was trying to make a
name for himself in America, having arrived with his wife and
daughter three years before. A distant relative of John Locke, he
soon became a reporter for the *New York Courier* and *Inquirer* and by
1835 had taken a job with the fledgling, faltering *Sun*. He was to
turn it into the world's highest-selling newspaper. This is how he
began the first of a series of articles which transformed the paper's
fortunes:

In this unusual addition to our Journal, we have the happi-
ness of making known to the British publick, and thence to

the whole civilized world, recent discoveries in Astronomy which will build an imperishable monument to the age in which we live, and confer upon the present generation of the human race a proud distinction through all future time.

The Sun reported that the English astronomer Sir John Herschel, son of Sir William, had used a 7,000 kg telescope lens, with a magnification of 42,000 to observe rocks, trees, flowers, and even intelligent winged beings of both sexes on the moon.

The article continued breathlessly:

> ... the younger Herschel, at his observatory in the Southern Hemisphere, has already made the most extraordinary discoveries in every planet of our solar system; has discovered planets in other solar systems; has obtained a distinct view of objects in the moon, fully equal to that which the naked eye commands of terrestrial objects at the distance of a hundred yards; has affirmatively settled the question whether this satellite be inhabited ...

New York was in a frenzy and after having read only one instalment. Locke could hardly believe his luck. In the first article he had relied heavily on the power of suggestion so he next did what all good journalists should do, especially when relaying an outrageous story ... he established the credibility of his sources.

Sir John Herschel (1792–1871) was the son of Sir William Herschel, the 'father of stellar astronomy' and the discoverer of the planet Uranus in 1781. In 1834, Sir John had packed up his family and his telescope and set sail on the *Mountstuart Elphinstone* to Cape Town, South Africa. After setting up the telescope, he spent several years cataloguing the stars and nebulae of the relatively unexplored southern skies.

Building on the excitement, Locke said that *The Sun* had an exclusive series of reports about Herschel's latest discoveries thanks to his faithful assistant of many years, Dr Andrew Grant. Evidently, so the *Sun* story went, Herschel had given the data to Grant to pass on to the Royal Society but Dr Grant went to the press in the form of the *Edinburgh Journal of Science*, and, by some great stroke of luck and journalistic brilliance, *The Sun* had been able to obtain an advance copy of the journal so that its readers were the first to hear this exciting news.

Locke had done his homework. He explained: 'The existence of volcanoes discovered by his father and by Schröter of Berlin, and the changes observed by the latter in the volcano in the Mare Crisium of Lucid Lake, were corroborated and illustrated, as was also the prevalence of far more extensive volcanic phenomena.'

The readers of *The Sun* certainly got their money's worth – with one spectacular lunar discovery after another. The second instalment was written as if the moon had come down to the Earth, and the readers could walk on it. It was covered with crimson flowers 'precisely similar', remarked Dr Grant, 'to the Papaver rhoeas, or rose-poppy of our sublunary cornfield'.

There was also the usual pseudo-scientific gobbledegook that even today accompanies such entertaining drivel:

After a few moments silent thought, Sir John diffidently inquired whether it would not be possible to effect a transfusion of artificial light through the focal object of vision! Sir John somewhat startled at the originality of the idea, paused awhile, and then hesitatingly referred to the refrangibility of rays, and the angle of incidence. Sir John, grown more confident, adduced the example of the Newtonian Reflector, in which the refrangibility was corrected by the second speculum, and the angle of incidence restored by the third. And, continued he, 'why cannot the illuminated microscope, say the hydro-oxygen, be applied to render distinct, and, if necessary, even to magnify the focal object?' Sir John sprang from his chair in the ecstasy of conviction, and leaping half-way to the ceiling, exclaimed, 'Thou art the man!' Each philosopher anticipated the other in presenting the prompt illustration that if the rays of the hydro-oxygen microscope, passed through a drop of water containing the larvae of a gnat and other objects invisible to the naked eye, rendered them not only keenly but firmly magnified to dimensions of many feet; so could the same artificial light, passed through the faintest focal object of a telescope, both distinctify (to coin a new word for an extraordinary occasion) and magnify its feeblest component members.

Poppies were not all the moon had to offer; it seemed there was an entire lunar forest. 'The trees,' said Dr Grant, 'for a period of ten minutes, were of one unvaried kind, and unlike any I have seen, except the largest class of yews in the English church-yards, which they in some respects resemble.' The observers also saw a green plain on which some kind of fir tree grew and then a lake of marine-blue water. In the next valley Herschel and Grant saw that groups of crystals, and amethysts rose from the ground in the shape of obelisks and pyramids. In the distance were herds of tiny bison, their shaggy pelts covering their faces to protect their eyes from the extremes of light and darkness on the moon. Then blue goatlike creatures appeared. The second article in *The Sun* ended with a description of the unicorn that lived on the moon. New Yorkers loved it.

The circulation of *The Sun* climbed from 8,000 to 19,360 overnight and it became the world's largest newspaper. Even *The Times* of London had a circulation of only 17,000. And Richard Adams Locke had barely begun. His next article reported on the discovery of intelligent life:

We were thrilled with astonishment to perceive four successive flocks of large winged creatures descend with a slow even motion from the cliffs on the western side, and alight upon the plain. We counted three parties of these creatures, walking erect towards a small wood near the base of the eastern precipices. Certainly they were like human beings, for their wings had now disappeared, and their attitude in walking was both erect and dignified. These creatures were evidently engaged in conversation; their gesticulation, more particularly the varied action of their hands and arms, appeared impassioned and emphatic. We hence inferred that they were rational beings.

Journalists, particularly newspaper editors, will always do their best to milk a good story and those at *The Sun* were no exception. Before the last instalment, *The Sun* prepared a booklet containing the entire story. In the last instalment, Locke promised that Sir John himself would comment on his discoveries. The deception was near complete.

Locke told them of the temple of the moon, constructed of sapphire, with a roof of yellow resembling gold. There were pillars 70 feet high and 6 feet thick. More man-bats were seen walking through its precincts. But by now even Locke could not continue. Readers of *The Sun* who were eagerly awaiting more astounding detail were told that the telescope had, unfortunately, been left facing the east and the sun's rays, concentrated through the lenses, burned a hole '15 feet in circumference' entirely through the reflecting chamber, putting the observatory out of commission.

Rival editors were frantic; they all wanted a piece of the action. Many of them pretended to have access to the original articles and began reprinting *The Sun*'s series with embellishments of their own. But not everyone was fooled.

Two professors from Yale University went to the offices of *The*

Sun and asked to look at the mathematical data that the editors said they had omitted from the article. Locke was in a corner but, like many journalists in his position, he reacted with guile and imagination. He told them that the extra information was at the printer's and gave them the address. The two professors went off in pursuit, but Locke was faster. He knew a short cut and because he had put obstacles in the way of the professors he got to the printers first (this was before the telephone). He bribed the printer to send them to another address. Eventually the professors gave up. They suspected they were the victims of a hoax, but they had no proof.

Because of *The Sun's* story, Edgar Allan Poe once explained that he had stopped work on the second part of his 'The Strange Adventures of Hans Pfaall' as he felt he had been outdone. And one Harriet Martineau of a Springfield, Massachusetts, missionary society resolved to send missionaries to the moon to convert and civilize the bat-men.

At this stage Locke must have begun to fear that the story was spinning out of control. The *Journal of Commerce*, another New York paper, wanted to reprint the entire story. At first Locke tried to dissuade the editors from running it. It was, after all, yesterday's news, he argued. But they persisted and Locke was eventually forced to tell the truth. The *Journal of Commerce* finally got their story by announcing that the whole story had been a fabrication, from beginning to end.

And Sir John? He was totally unaware of what had happened. He saw *The Sun* for the first time when an American visitor came to see him in Cape Town. Herschel inquired if the story had actually appeared in the *Edinburgh Journal of Science*. His visitor assured him it had not – the journal had gone out of business years before – and that the whole thing had been a hoax. Herschel treated it just as it should have been treated and laughed at it. But by now the story had spread to Europe, where many astronomers (who in my experience sometimes tend to get the media out of perspective) failed to appreciate it for what it was and got very upset.

As for *The Sun*, despite public exposure, the paper never conceded the issue. On 16 September 1835 they did publish an article in which they discussed the possibility that the story was false, but they never confessed to anything. Quite the contrary. 'Certain correspondents have been urging us to come out and confess the whole to be a hoax; but this we can by no means do, until we have the testimony of the English or Scotch papers to corroborate such a declaration.' This was the closest the paper ever came to an admission of guilt. It never lost its increased circulation.

Over a century later, in another age, when instantaneous global communications were taken for granted, Neil Armstrong stepped onto the surface of the moon. No sooner had he done so than the idea began to circulate that this momentous event was all a carefully calculated hoax. It just shows that history sometimes repeats itself and that some people will never learn!

CHAPTER TEN

No Copy of the Earth

The most important book written about the moon in the nineteenth century was produced by two Germans, Wilhelm Beer (1797–1850) and Johann Mädler (1794–1874). It was called simply *Der Mond* and what a magnificent tome it is. Beer and Mädler produced a brilliant map, determined that the moon had neither water nor air (because of its sharp and unchanging features) and said it is 'no copy of the Earth, much less a colony of the same'.

Like several other prominent lunar astronomers before him, Wilhelm Beer was the son of a wealthy brewer. His mother was also from a wealthy family – her father was in charge of the Prussian lottery. His brother became the famous composer Mayerbeer. The 'Beer Villa' with its distinctive observatory dome was a local landmark in nineteenth-century Berlin, close to the Brandenburg Gate.

Mädler, the dominant figure in the partnership, wanted to measure the position of every lunar feature. He had other astronomical interests as well. In particular he wanted to find the centre of our galaxy and the point in space towards which our sun is heading. His theories made quite an impression on Edgar Allan Poe who wrote: '. . . much has been said, latterly, of the hypothesis of Mädler – that there exists, in the centre of the Galaxy, a stupendous globe about which all the systems of the cluster revolve. The period of our own, indeed, has been stated – 117 million of years.'

Beer and Mädler's map was the result of four years work. It is in four sections and is on a scale of just over 38 inches to the moon's diameter. It was without question the most influential lunar publication of the century. Because it did not appear until 1878, it was the first large-scale moon map to be based on really precise measurements.

The book *Der Mond* has to my knowledge never been fully translated into English but it should be. Here was everything that was known about the moon: drawings and maps, details of its motion, eclipses and tides, as well as speculation about the origin of the lunar features. With *Der Mond* in hand some astronomers dared to believe that almost everything had been discovered about the moon. Had the last word been said on this lifeless world? The book had a tremendous effect on lunar studies but Mädler was unable to equal it in other areas of astronomy. He became the Director of the Dorpat Observatory in Estonia, and passed into obscurity.

Julius Schmidt (1825–1884) was fascinated by two things, the moon and earthquakes, and he convinced himself that there was a connection between the two. He completed a beautiful lunar map left unfinished in 1840 by a German called Wilhelm Lohrmann. But by the time it came out in 1878, the same year as Beer and Mädler's, it was out of date. Schmidt is one of several astronomers to be mentioned in Jules Verne's 'Round the moon', published in 1869:

This, however, is an exact description of what Barbicane and his companions saw at this height. Large patches of different colours appeared on the disc. Selenographers are not agreed upon the nature of these colours. There are several, and rather vividly marked. Julius Schmidt pretends that, if the terrestrial oceans were dried up, a Selenite observer could not distinguish on the globe a greater diversity of shades between the oceans and the continental plains than those on the moon present to a terrestrial observer. According to him, the colour common to the vast plains known by the name of 'seas' is a dark gray mixed with green and brown. Some of the large craters present the same appearance. Barbicane knew this opinion of the German selenographer, an opinion shared by Beer and Mädler. Observation has proved that right was on their side, and not on that of some astronomers who admit the existence of only gray on the moon's surface. In some parts green was very distinct, such as springs, according to Julius Schmidt, from the seas of 'Serenity and Humors'. Barbicane also noticed large craters, without any interior cones, which shed a bluish tint similar to the reflection of a sheet of steel freshly polished. These colours belonged really to the lunar disc, and did not result, as some astronomers say, either from the imperfection in the objective of the glasses or from the interposition of the terrestrial atmosphere.

With Germanic thoroughness, Schmidt depicted more craters, rilles and mountains on his own map than anyone had before. Using the techniques invented by Schröter, whose book had inspired him to take up astronomy in the first place, he probably made more estimates of peak heights and crater depths (about a thousand) than anyone else and many of his measures have yet to be replaced by modern ones. In many ways, the Schmidt map was the pinnacle of nineteenth-century selenography. There are over 33,000 craters depicted and over 3,000 mountain heights.

In 1856 he wrote:

In the early morning the mountains suddenly emerged from the night. Not from a grayish dawn, nor from the steaming mists of a valley, but from the deepest darkness. During this change from the long night to the day, during this dawn in a world alien to us, not a sound reaches our ears. On the moon, the new day does not trigger the sounds of awakening animals that we are accustomed to hearing. No birds fly. No plants grace the bare soil. A deathly silence reigns on the ground and in the sky. When a boulder falls, there is not a roar. Nor do the mountains resound with an echo. The eye searches in vain for cloud formations or shadows. The sky is an inky darkness. Only the Sun, the Earth, and the stars shine.

Schmidt's other passion was earthquakes. At the age of twenty he started to collect material for a global earthquake catalogue. Studying an earthquake in the Rhineland in 1846, he calculated the speed of the shock wave that travelled through the Earth's crust. Then in 1858 he became director of the observatory in Athens where he recorded more than 3,800 earthquakes during twenty years in the most earthquake-prone country in Europe. He had heard of the theory that the moon might actually trigger earthquakes but he did not believe it and hoped he would gather enough data to disprove the notion. Using tables of the moon's orbit for the best part of a hundred years, and when necessary extending them with his own calculations, he came to a startling conclusion.

What he found was a small increase in the frequency of earthquakes when the moon was nearest to the Earth. For the relatively short period between 1842 and 1874, for which he had records of all the moon's phases for each day, there was a clear earthquake maximum on the day after new moon, and the lowest earthquake frequency on the day of the last quarter. Although he preferred to leave it to others to work out what was going on between the moon and earthquakes he was convinced. But the moon had played a trick on him.

Seismographs were left on the moon by the Apollo astronauts and they recorded moonquakes but they are feeble compared to even the weakest earthquake. In a year the Earth releases about

100 million million times more seismic energy than does the moon. There is no evidence that earthquakes are influenced by the position of the moon. On the contrary, it seems to be the other way round. Moonquakes are clustered around the time when the moon is closest to the Earth and the effect of its pull is the strongest.

Schmidt was also responsible for a great lunar mystery. Sheet 4 of his impressive map shows the crater Linne. Lohrmann had mapped it as a typical 10 km wide crater, but Schmidt announced in 1866 that it had disappeared. This is the most famous – or infamous – case of a change on the moon. But was it real?

Mädler had named the crater in honour of Karl von Linne, the Swedish botanist. It is easy to find, being fairly near the centre of the moon in Mare Serenitatis, lying in relatively flat country. There is little distraction near it, apart from low ridges and mounds. In 1834 Lohrmann described it as 'the second most conspicuous crater on the plain with a diameter of about 6 miles, it is very deep and can be seen under all angles of illumination.' Mädler said, 'The deepness of the crater must be considerable for I have found an interior shadow when the Sun has attained 30 degrees. I have never seen a central mountain on the floor.'

Schmidt drew it between 1841 and 1843. But on 16 October 1866 when observing Mare Serenitatis he suddenly realized that Linne had disappeared. All that remained in that position was a small whitish patch. Perhaps the moon was not the dead and changeless world he had thought it was? Soon, many telescopes were turned towards Linne, making it the most studied crater in lunar history.

And here it gets more puzzling. After its change Schmidt describes it as a shallow depression but today nothing like that can be seen. Did it change? How could a mistake have been made by experienced observers such as Beer, Mädler and Lohrmann? It is not in a crowded and confusing part of the moon. Cassini's map is inconclusive. Did Lohrmann, Mädler and Schmidt make the same mistake? Mädler's telescope was small, only 3.75 inches, Lohrmann gave up observing because of failing eyesight and when he first saw Linne he was young, inexperienced and impressionable.

Today we have the view of Linne from lunar orbit and looking down over this small and unprepossessing crater you can see that it is small and deep, just a few kilometres wide with a slight dome inside it and a west wall that is higher than the east. It is certainly not what Mädler and Lohrmann described. There is no indication that it has changed. I suppose the occasional mistake is to be expected in such a grand undertaking as mapping the moon, with its face being constantly revealed and then covered up. In such a task, over many generations with many different observers and instruments, perhaps a few inconsistencies will crop up from time to time. It is just a puzzle that it should have been Linne.

By the mid-nineteenth century the age of the great amateur moon mappers was drawing to a close. With only a few excep-tions, great maps would no longer be made by painstaking measurements and drawings, peering down the eyepiece at the shining moon across the hours of midnight. Something of the intimacy between man and the moon was lost with the invention of the camera.

In 1839 François Arago described the invention of the camera in a speech to the Chamber of Deputies in Paris: 'We hope to make photographic maps of our satellite which means that we will carry out one of the most lengthy, most exacting, most delicate tasks of astronomy in a few minutes.' (Incidentally the word 'photography' was coined by John Herschel.)

Daguerre took the first photo of the moon in 1839, but no details were discernible. In 1840 J.W. Draper took a photograph of the moon through a 12-inch telescope with a 20-minute exposure. Photographic emulsions improved rapidly and within ten years W.C. Bond and others at Harvard College Observatory were taking much better photos with exposures of 'only' a minute or so. However, there was still a problem when it came to printing such images for publication. It was Warren De la Rue, an amateur British astronomer with an observatory at Cransford, who first overcame the technical difficulties.

With the assistance of Paul Pretsch, who invented the process, De la Rue succeeded in producing a copperplate map suitable for printing. This was taken from a photographic negative of the moon, by using the unusual swelling properties of gelatin after it is exposed to light. De la Rue called the print a heliotype. By the end of the century, gelatin-based plates would allow exquisite reproductions of the lunar surface, in the form of photogravures and collotypes.

Richard Proctor, the foremost nineteenth-century popularizer of astronomy, the Carl Sagan of his day, used photographs in his treatise on the moon. In addition to numerous lithographs and wood engravings, and a large folding lunar map, there are three photographic prints of the moon by the American Lewis Rutherfurd, whom Proctor called the greatest lunar photographer of the age. Ten years later Fred Whipple at Harvard obtained a series of photographs of different phases of the moon. They were shown at the Great Exhibition in London in 1851 to great interest.

But the first photographs of the moon were no good for mapping. The available emulsions were relatively insensitive to light, and the long exposures they required meant that lunar photographs were blurred and certainly not as useful as drawings. But everyone knew they would get better. The human eye was not changing, whereas cameras and the art of photography were. By 1900 better maps were being produced. Yet the eye had an advantage because it can wait for the best viewing times, when the air is exceptionally still and fine detail is visible. Whereas photographs record an average, with the best viewing times blurred out by the worst ones. Before the great photographic surveys became invaluable, there was room for one final generation of astronomers who looked at the moon with their eyes.

One of these was James Nasmyth (1808–1890), who made a fortune as a manufacturer and inventor and retired to take up astronomy at the age of thirty-four. He built his own 20-inch reflector in 1842 (inventing the Nasmyth focus in the process), and began to concentrate on lunar studies. Since photography was not yet advanced enough to take very detailed photographs of lunar features, he constructed plaster models and photographed them. The photographs were then printed by the arduous Woodburytype process, perhaps the most faithful method of photographic reproduction ever devised. It has no grain whatsoever to break up the original image because it does not use cracks or dots to reproduce tone. Instead, a relief mould is made of the image in lead, so that the areas of dark tone are deep and areas of light tone shallow. Ink suspended in gelatin is cast in the mould, and the resulting print produces contrast by the thickness or thinness of the ink. Cumbersome and time-consuming, yes. Impressive, certainly. One of his most striking models was of Archimedes and the Apennines. You can look at the deep, dark shadow cast by Mount Hadley. In that shadow, nearly one hundred years later, Apollo 15 would become the fourth manned spacecraft to land on the lunar surface.

The Germans had led the world in moon-mapping but now British astronomers were taking an increasing interest in our nearest celestial neighbour. In 1865 the British Association put down a resolution to map the moon at the finest detail possible. It was a project that was doomed from the start. But soon along came Edmund Neville (1851–1940) whose map was the first important British work of that era. Remarkably he produced it in

1876, at the age of twenty-five. He died in 1940 but seems to have paid little attention to the moon in the last sixty years of his life.

Neville, who wrote under the name Neison, produced the first observer's guide to the moon written in English, and it is still one of the best, giving information about more than 500 named features, as well as a map in twenty-two sections, to the scale of 24 to the moon's diameter. The map is not entirely original, being based on that of Beer and Mädler, but it is much easier to use. Looking at its photograph of Plato at sunrise, you can see the world of the moonshots.

In the 1870s the Selenographical Society was formed in England and for ten years or so it was very active but it faded with the death of its president William Birt and the resignation of its secretary Neison. A few years later the newly formed British Astronomical Association with its Lunar section continued its work.

The last decade of the nineteenth century saw the start of the great photographic surveys – in particular the 1896 Lick and Paris Observatory surveys which produced 6,000 photographic plates of the moon. With such coverage it seemed that the observer armed with notepad and pencil, pen and ink, charcoal and crayon, was needed no more. But that was not quite true.

Johann Krieger (1865–1902) was a gifted draughtsman who realized that it made no sense to spend hours drawing features that the camera could record in seconds far more accurately. So he had the idea of starting with a low-contrast photograph as a base and adding finer details by hand at the telescope. The resulting maps of selected craters were not equalled until the US Air Force began issuing its own series of lunar charts in the 1960s in preparation for a manned landing.

Krieger published the first volume of his drawings in 1898, containing twenty-eight plates, but due to overwork and exhaustion his health broke and he died before the second volume could be issued. This posthumous publication is almost heartbreaking to examine. Here was a man of great talent, with an eye for detail and an obvious love of the moon. It contains one of the most impressive drawings of the crater Gassendi ever made (Gassendi was always a favourite subject for observers, because of the intricate rille system on its floor).

On 4 October 1884 an eclipse of the moon took place when the moon looked exceptionally dark and red when it entered the Earth's shadow. In addition the shadow was strangely pointed. Many remarked that the Earth's shadow seemed to be tinted a 'phosphorescent green'. In August 1887 there was a similar weird shadow spectacle. The explanation probably lies in the material thrown up into the Earth's atmosphere by volcanic eruptions. Krakatoa occurred some thirteen months before the 1884 eclipse and the eruption of Tarawera in New Zealand took place in 1886. The material and dust blocked and filtered the sunlight streaming through the Earth's atmosphere and it was refracted towards the moon.

And so the moon entered the twentieth century.

CHAPTER ELEVEN

The Old Moon and the New

The modern moon revealed itself slowly at first and not to the astronomers. It was a second Gilbert, three hundred years after the first, who first saw the modern moon and transposed studies of geology on Earth to the lunar surface. Grove Karl Gilbert (1843–1918) recognized that landforms reflected a balance between the forces that act upon them and the rocks that compose them. The title of the paper he wrote for the Philosophical Society of Washington was almost exactly the same as the one used by the ancient Greeks and the Arabs, 'The moon's face, a study of the origin of its features', but his conclusions were different. It is one of the most important papers ever written about the moon, but it was almost completely overlooked until the 1960s. The reason it was important was that Gilbert was right!

In 1869 he joined the second Ohio State Geological Survey as a volunteer assistant and in 1871 was assigned to survey all land west of the hundredth meridian. During his three years with the Survey, he journeyed by boat through the lower canyons of the Colorado River, by mule train through central Arizona and down the valley of the Gila River, and again by boat down the Colorado to the Gulf of California. He was the Indiana Jones of geologists. After the success of this survey when the US Geological Survey was formed in 1879 Gilbert was a natural choice to be one of its senior geologists. He was placed in charge of the Appalachian division of geology, and in 1889 made head of the new division of geologic correlation. This temporarily tied him to a desk but he soon tired of administrative duties and passed them on so that he could get back to his first love, rocks in the landscape.

Some astronomers have dated the revolution in our perception of the moon to the time Gilbert began using the US Naval Observatory's large refracting telescope in Washington, DC. With his observations, as well as photographs from Yerkes Observatory near Chicago, he took a fresh look at the moon. What interested him was not so much the almost random distribution of features across the moon's surface but the underlying story of how they were not volcanoes and concluded, far in advance of other lunar observers, that they were formed by giant impacts. He proposed that the giant circular maria like Mare Imbrium, were impact basins that had later been flooded with lava.

Gilbert's search for evidence that our moon had been bombarded makes him one of the most important, but little known, scientists who ever took an interest in the moon. His work indicated that there was more to understanding our nearest neighbour in space than just mapping its surface; it also marked the beginning of the next stage in the moon's shifting allegiance, away from the astronomers and towards the geologists. Unfortunately, at the close of the nineteenth century, there was little interest in the moon outside a small band of enthusiasts. Gilbert's paper was published in a journal that few astronomers read and his work was hardly known or appreciated until it was rediscovered in the 1960s when researchers scoured the literature for anything written about the moon as they prepared for unmanned and manned spacecraft to visit it.

Ironically, Gilbert's recognition that impacts play a dominant role in the formation of lunar craters did not prevent him making a big blunder when studying the most impressive impact crater on Earth. His study of the Arizona feature known as Coon Butte convinced him it was a volcanic crater even though, during the first decade of the new century, many had started calling it Meteor Crater.

★ ★ ★

Not only geologists but also engineers had a part to play in man's quest to understand the moon. Perhaps the most skilled observer of the moon in the time before the moonshots was George Willis Ritchey (1864–1945) who studied mechanical design at the University of Cincinnati in the 1880s. After he graduated he obtained part-time work in the university's observatory. However, his interest in astronomy was more functional than theoretical and his skill with tools and anything mechanical drew him towards the construction of astronomical instruments. By 1890 he was head of the woodwork department at the Chicago Manual Training School where he met the redoubtable George Ellery Hale. Hale, more than anyone else, was responsible for the construction of large telescopes that not only industrialized astronomy but also gave the United States a pre-eminent position in the subject.

In 1896 Ritchey was hired by Hale as an optician. One of his first tasks was to negotiate the purchase of a 60-inch mirror which Hale planned to use in a large reflecting telescope in the grounds of Yerkes Observatory near Chicago. This mirror would occupy Ritchey for a decade and it did not end up at Yerkes but at the Mount Wilson Solar Observatory in Pasadena, California. Yerkes had a troublesome 40-inch refractor, the biggest in the world, and Ritchey soon turned his talents to eliminating its problems, thereby enhancing his reputation as a master telescope maker and optician. Soon he had complete control over the Yerkes instruments. His ability to translate Hale's theoretical genius into practical instruments and equipment made them a world-beating team. And he excelled as an observer because of his ability to coax the best out of a camera and telescope.

So it was natural that when Hale left Yerkes in 1905, to establish another observatory in California, Ritchey went with him. Ritchey was to grind a 100-inch mirror. But Hale had a darker side. He jealously guarded his financial backers and when

Ritchey privately approached one of them to help fund a venture of his own Hale was incensed. Just as the 100-inch mirror was completed, the mirror that could justifiably be said to have been the heart of the most important telescope built since that of Galileo, Ritchey was fired. And such was Hale's influence that he could not get another job in astronomy. He lost all his savings after he tried to make a living growing lemons and oranges. Then the French offered him the chance to build a new kind of telescope but after seven years in France he could not make his ideas work. So he returned to the United States in 1930, where he watched his 100-inch mirror change our understanding of the universe by showing that it was expanding. Eventually he got a job at the US Naval Observatory in Washington DC but by now his health, strength and confidence were gone. He lost the job after he dropped a mirror he had been working on. Although it suffered only minor cracks, the Navy was embarrassed and lost confidence in him. Ritchey retired to his ranch and died in 1945.

His new optical design, developed jointly with Henri Chretien, became known as the Ritchey–Chretien design. Hale had refused to consider it for the 100-inch telescope. Although Ritchey did not live to see its success, today the Ritchey–Chretien is the choice of nearly every professional observatory. Every large telescope built or designed since Hale's 200-inch reflector in 1948 has used the Ritchey–Chretien design.

Ritchey's contribution to the study of the moon was made mainly with the 40-inch refractor at Yerkes. He was able to capture details in his negatives that were beyond the abilities of astronomers at other observatories. His photographs were so good that, over sixty years later, when Gerard Kuiper and his colleagues were assembling the monumental *Photographic Lunar Atlas*, and had thousands of more recent photographs to choose from, they still used some of Ritchey's.

★　★　★

Now the moon turns away from geologists and instrument-makers and back to its earliest devotees, astronomers. It would be hard to beat the story of William Henry Pickering (1858–1938) as an example of how one can become so bound up in the moon that one loses an earthly perspective.

Born in Boston, Pickering was to become one of the foremost lunar and planetary observers of his day. In 1887 he became professor of astronomy at Harvard, and became interested in astrophotography, showing in one spectacular project that the entire constellation of Orion is immersed in wispy gas clouds. In 1891 he and his brother Edward travelled to Peru to establish an out-station of the Harvard Observatory to explore the rich southern skies. A few years later he helped design and build the observatory at Flagstaff, in Arizona, for Percival Lowell, another rich Bostonian who used the observatory to chart what he believed were canals on Mars constructed by intelligent beings. Back at Harvard, Pickering predicted the existence of, and gave a position for, the planet Pluto which was found in 1930 not far from his estimate.

His book, *The Moon*, was published in 1903. He believed he had proof that the moon had an atmosphere. One night he was observing an occultation of Jupiter when the giant planet passes behind the limb of the moon. Moments before it did, Pickering thought he saw Jupiter change as if turned dusky by a thin lunar atmosphere. He was convinced of this but others could not see it.

For five years from 1919 he observed from the clear skies of Jamaica. One evening he noticed strange dark patches inside the 4900 m deep, 61 km wide crater Erasosthenes situated at one end of the Apennine mountain chain. The dark patches seemed to change during the lunar day and for William Pickering there was only one explanation, insects! Imagine, he wrote, if an observer from the moon was looking down on North America a century previously. They would have seen moving dark patches as herds of buffalo roamed across the prairie. Pickering's lunar patches moved at a few metres a minute. So, he concluded, they had to be made of smaller animals, hence insects. He said they would emerge from eggs with the lunar dawn and then trudge across the surface looking for food. But what could they live on? Pickering believed that some colours he saw on the moon were moss and algae. Despite evidence to the contrary and the disbelief of other astronomers, he never changed his mind and died in 1938. But let us forgive him his fantasies about insects because he did leave an enduring lunar legacy.

When Pickering began his work, three photographic atlases of the moon had been attempted and all of them had encountered difficulties: the Lick atlas had been abandoned; the Paris atlas was a mess with no logical structure or even scale; and the Weineck atlas was just too expensive and unwieldy. Pickering decided to produce an affordable atlas, with every feature covered five times under different angles of illumination and all the photographs to the same scale. They were taken in 1901 in Jamaica and, although the final work may not be as impressive as its competitors, it was much more useful and it established the standards which most later atlases would follow.

Until Pickering's *Atlas* it was generally agreed that photographs were still inferior to the human eye in seeing fine detail. That was to change when, in September of 1919, the mighty 100-inch Hooker telescope, with its Ritchey influence, opened at the Mount Wilson Observatory. In a remarkable series of photographs taken by Francis Pease on 12–15 September, the moon appeared clearer and sharper than ever before.

Walter Goodacre, another astronomer, was to say, of a particular series of photos of the southern highlands: 'These photographs reveal details which do not appear on any chart or previous photograph, and probably are now rendered visible to the human eye for the first time in the history of the race.'

Philipp Fauth (1867–1941) has a small but prominent crater on the flanks of mighty Copernicus named after him. He was a schoolteacher from Kaiserslautern who managed to alienate most other observers of the moon during his lifetime with his intolerant criticism of them and his unshakeable belief that the moon was covered with ice. But, despite this, there is no denying that Fauth was a skilled observer and perhaps the last in the line of astronomers stretching back to Galileo who mapped the moon by eye.

Born into a family of potters, his great passion was astronomy and by 1898 he had published a book about his observations of Mars and Jupiter, followed in 1906 by *What We Know About the Moon* (translated into English in 1909 as 'The Moon in Modern Astronomy'). But Fauth became an advocate of the crank Hörbiger who believed that the moon was entirely covered with a layer of ice. Sadly, his allegiance to this crackpot idea effectively destroyed his reputation as a serious scientist, even though for those who could appreciate it his moon observations were admirable. His major work *Unser Mond* ('Our Moon') was published in 1936 but had little influence and copies of the book are very rare today. He was also a consultant for some of the earliest science-fiction films, such as *Mondlicht* (*At Moon's Light*, 1932) at a time when man's thoughts were turning away from drawing and photographing the moon to visiting it.

The drive for rationalization continued. In 1919 the International Astronomical Union was formed, with thirty-two commissions to deal with many aspects of modern astronomy at a time when the number of professional astronomers was steadily increasing. Commission 17, responsible for lunar nomenclature, had as members William Pickering and one Mary Blagg. By this time, with so many maps being compiled and surveys being carried out by observers who were giving their own names to lunar features, it was clear that some rationalization had to take place and that was up to Mary Blagg (1858–1944) from England. She compared the maps of Mädler, Schmidt and Neison as well as taking into account the many new names that had crept onto the moon over the years. Her *Collated list of Lunar Formations* is a work of undaunted enthusiasm. After several years' effort the list of named lunar formations was published. Blagg also produced a map that must win the prize for being the ugliest map of the moon ever drawn!

But for some the work of centuries was ending. The great work that had started with Galileo's portraits of the moon, and perhaps with crude sketches that were even older, was nearing its natural completion. It was time to bring everything together and produce the definitive lunar map, the first to be based on accurate positions from photographs. Walter Goodacre (1856–1938) took on this task.

Goodacre, a London businessman, became the second Director of the Lunar Section of the British Astronomical Association (which had been established in 1890). In 1931 he produced one of the most prized and sought-after books about the moon, privately printed and today extremely valuable. Each section is replete with the influence of those who helped pave the way for it. In its review the *Journal of the British Astronomical Association* commented:

> It is earnestly to be hoped that all amateur astronomers will immediately possess themselves of the new volume and that many of them will find themselves driven to examine one topic or another in the literature and on the surface of the moon. That, one believes, is the recompense which would best please its author.

Goodacre's map is a magnificent study but it was produced at a time when lunar science was changing. The day of the talented amateur armed with only a smallish telescope was ending; lunar science was moving beyond just describing the surface features.

Thinking back to 1647, when Hevelius was presenting his works to a council of the great astronomers for approval, I have a dream that I could show Goodacre's map to those whose story I have told. What would Galileo and Harriot have made of it? What would they have said to each other? Langrenus would have criticized its non-Dutch style and Hevelius would have asked how Goodacre allowed for the libration of the moon. Schröter would have looked for the rilles and Russell would have tutt-tutted at its lack of artistic inspiration. But, whatever one imagines the high council of moon mappers saying, they would probably all have agreed that the moon had been mapped, defined and in a way conquered. How wrong they would have been.

To my mind, the most important book about the science of the moon since Beer and Mädler's *Der Mond* (in 1837) was written by Ralph Baldwin (b. 1912). A physicist by training and a business-man by profession, he was never an academic; the moon was his spare-time fascination. His book was called *The Face of the Moon* and in it there is a remarkable graph that contributed more to the understanding of how the craters were formed than anything that came before, including Robert Hooke's boiling pans of alabaster. Baldwin drew a graph showing the relationship between a crater's depth and its diameter. He plotted craters made by bombs, the larger terrestrial craters and lunar craters, and he showed that the lunar ones were not volcanic but had been caused by impacts. Baldwin also used meteor data to estimate the size distribution of meteors in space and showed that they matched the size range of craters on the moon. He also correctly explained that the maria were formed by lava flows filling giant impact basins. In almost every aspect Baldwin got it right. But, although he presented a logical and believable case, it was not until the first samples of moon rock were returned that he was finally believed.

★ ★ ★

For most of the twentieth century, interest in the moon had been confined to a small number of enthusiasts. The great preoccupations of astronomy were the desire to understand how stars generate the energy to shine, how they live their lives and, in the realm beyond the stars, to understand how large the cosmos was and how fast it was expanding. The lifeless pock-marked world close at hand seemed almost irrelevant to more than one generation of astronomers who contemplated these grand questions. At one stage it was said that there was only one full-time American astronomer whose interests covered the moon. That was Gerard Kuiper, whom we shall meet shortly.

But it was Nobel prize-winning scientist Harold Urey who started to make the study of the planets and the moon fashionable again, a task that became complete when the first space probes were launched. In 1952 he published a book called *The Planets – Their Origin and Development*, based on a series of lectures he had given at Yale University. Although much of what he wrote about the moon was wrong, it didn't matter. His book asked questions and woke up astronomers – just in time for the space age.

Impatient and demanding, Urey worked on the theory of atomic structure with the great Niels Bohr in Copenhagen before joining Columbia University. He won the 1934 Nobel Prize in chemistry for separating the isotope deuterium from hydrogen but, instead of attending the prize ceremony, stayed at home for the birth of his third daughter. During the war he was involved in the Manhattan project to build an atomic weapon and afterwards took the lead in questioning the ethics of nuclear weapons. In the 1950s, he worked with biochemist Stanley Miller on a now famous experiment which demonstrated that the crude building blocks of life could be synthesized in a glass jar inside which the conditions of the primitive Earth were simulated.

The other major planetary and lunar scientist of the time was

Gerard Peter Kuiper (1905–1973) and he definitely did not get on with Urey; in fact they hated each other. The origin of the feud has been lost in the mists of time but probably had something to do with Kuiper resenting Urey's intrusion into his field and Urey resenting Kuiper's not referring to Urey's research when he believed he should have done so.

Kuiper, a Dutch-born American, made important contributions to solar system science and to the United States space programme. When he was young he had worked with Percival Lowell, of Martian canals fame. Although Lowell was discredited, Kuiper said he learned much from him. He published a research paper, in the *Proceedings of the National Academy of Science in the United States*, entitled, 'On the origin of lunar surface features'. It was based on visual observations made with the MacDonald Observatory 82-inch telescope in Texas. In the paper he suggested that the entire surface of the early moon had melted, forming a low-density crust that solidified on top of a magma ocean. Urey scoffed, saying that the moon was formed by an accumulation of cold bodies.

By the early 1940s experiments in rocketry were being carried out and the Second World War had given added impetus to rocket development.

In the late 1950s the United States military was taking an interest in space exploration (this was before the creation of NASA) and at the time they believed they could control America's direction and destiny in space. They gave Kuiper lots of money, which in turn gave him power, and influence, his use of which was at times questionable. (Kuiper was by all accounts difficult to deal with and was always playing politics of one sort or another.) But his contribution to planetary science cannot be questioned. His achievements include measuring the diameter of Pluto, discovering satellites of Uranus and Neptune, detecting carbon dioxide on Mars, and discovering that Saturn's major moon, Titan, had an atmosphere. Kuiper also suggested that there was a belt of comet-like debris at the edge of our solar system, a theory that was proved true twenty years after his death. In the 1960s he was the chief scientist for the Ranger spacecraft crash-landing probes of the moon. By analysing Ranger photographs, he confirmed that manned landings on the moon would be safe and he helped pinpoint the first landing sites.

Kuiper undertook his *Photographic Atlas of the Moon*, the last great photographic lunar atlas based on images taken from the ground. The complete atlas has 281 photographs, prepared with the help of his colleague Ewen Whittaker, and covers forty-four fields under different angles of illumination. The photographs, printed four to a sheet, were folded so that they might be used at the telescope. One of the photographs shows sunset over the Bay of Rainbows. The Heraclides promontory, where the moon maiden looked out across the waterless sea, juts out just right of centre. The photograph also reveals the existence of a second, shyer, moon maiden at its lower left, as the east wall of the crater Maupertuis captures the last rays of the setting sun.

Finally, no summary of man's efforts to map the moon would be complete without reference to the remarkable work that is *The Moon* by Henry Percy Wilkins and Patrick Moore. This was published in 1955, just before Patrick Moore began his BBC television series *The Sky at Night* which has continued for over forty years. It was the apex of the British school of lunar mapping, and I have fond memories of it. When I was a youngster the copy owned by the Birmingham Central Library was on semi-permanent loan in my bedroom. But, despite my affection for it, much of the intricate mass of detail that can be seen in the lunar highlands is virtually undecipherable; it is a deeply confusing moon. Wilkins and Moore also took the liberty of introducing almost a hundred new names of their own. But the book's main contribution to lunar science are its charts of the limb regions drawn under favourable libration. They were the best charts of

Riccioli's names on the map of the moon made by Grimaldi, 1651. The names Riccioli chose are those that we use today (*Royal Greenwich Observatory*).

The frontispiece of the *Almagestum novum* (the New Almagest) by Giovanni Battista Riccioli (1651). The abandoned Ptolemaic system of the stars and planets lies on the ground and in the hand of Urania, the muse of astronomy, lies a balance in which the Tychonic system outweighs the Copernican sun-centred system.

The map of the moon produced by John Russell showing an artist's approach to moon mapping (*Museum of the History of Science*).

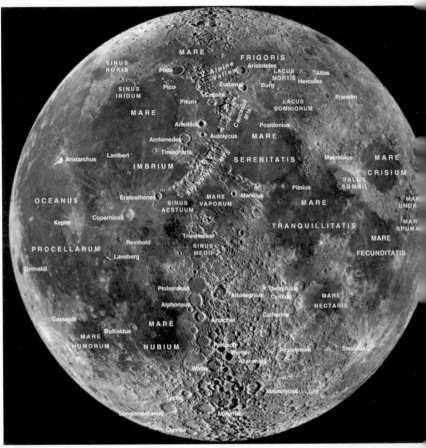

The moon with its main features (*Sky Publishing Corp*).

One of the first photographs of the moon taken by Warren de la Rue from his observatory in Oxford, England circa 1875.

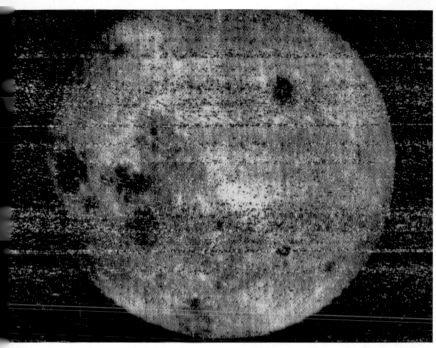

The first ever image of the moon's previously hidden far side. Luna 3, 7 October 1959. The lack of dark mare regions on the far side is evident even in this poor quality image.

The first ever photograph taken on the surface of the moon of Oceanus Procellarum, taken 3 February 1966 by the Soviet Luna 9 spacecraft. The Jodrell Bank Radio Observatory intercepted the image.

The 'picture of the century'. An oblique view of the crater Copernicus taken by Lunar Orbiter 2 in November 1966 (*NASA*).

A magnificent view of the third quarter moon showing the heavily cratered southe highlands and the near-circular Mare Imbrium in the north. The straight gash o: the Alpine Valley can be seen in its northe flanks (*Peter Armstrong*).

The full moon showing the division of the surface into two regions: light-coloured mountainous regions and darker lowland consisting of plains of solidified lava. The brilliant rayed crater Tycho is prominent (*Lick Observatory*).

these regions that were available at the time and when the Soviets came to send a space probe over the limb to photograph the unseen far side it was to Wilkins and Moore's map that they turned for guidance.

But things were changing. No longer would man merely dream of going to the moon, no longer study it from afar. For the first time he was to walk upon the Shrine of Hecate.

CHAPTER TWELVE

The Dark Side of the Moon

Perhaps it is impossible, after millennia of observation and superstition, to unravel the scientific reality of the moon's influence from the myths that have grown up about it. There has never been a time when the moon has not been in our sky, when it has not been part of the rhythm of human life. When our distant ancestors tried to make sense of a harsh world they took some comfort in the things that were predictable – the cycle of the days, the march of the seasons, the phases of the moon. The sun ruled the day but the influence of the moon was subtler, as it often waited for the sun to leave before it occupied the sky.

To the early civilizations, it seemed that the moon regulated life, the tides and all moisture. Pliny the Elder, the first-century Roman naturalist, wrote, 'when she approaches, she fills all bodies, when she recedes she empties them'. He also wrote of the stars and planets that, 'the blood of man is increased or diminished in proportion to the quantity of their light'.

Today the legacy of the Swedish scientist Jons Jacob Berzelius (1779–1848) is all around us. One of the founders of modern chemistry, he was the first to establish a chart of accurate atomic weights and symbols. He was also the first to use familiar words for chemical compounds, such as *methyl* (Greek for 'wine') and *hyle* (Greek for 'wood'). Wood alcohol is now called methyl alcohol.

He was both brilliant and irascible; he glowers at us from an 1844 Daguerreotype photograph, proudly displaying his medals of achievement. By all accounts he was driven and passionate about his science and he persuaded authorities in Sweden to introduce science in schools. But he was also a bully. In 1836 a young French scientist called Auguste Laurent proposed theories about molecules containing carbon that conflicted with the great man's views. Berzelius used his influence to destroy the young scientist's career. From then on Laurent had to work in poor laboratories that exacerbated his tuberculosis and he died prematurely in obscurity. But he was eventually proved right.

Meanwhile Berzelius isolated the elements silicon (a major constituent of the moon's and the Earth's crust), thorium, zirconium and cerium. He also isolated an element that in its most stable form is a metallic grey and not unlike the colour of the moon; he called it selenium, after the moon goddess. It is found in foods such as mushrooms, broccoli, onions and tomatoes. In our bodies it helps to convert fats and proteins into energy and it boosts our immune system. It has industrial uses as well in light meters, solar cells and photocopiers, and is an additive to stainless steel. Viruses are more virulent where selenium is deficient. In Zaire, where HIV and the Ebola virus are thought to have originated, there are widespread deficiencies of selenium. But Berzelius' connection with the moon does not solely rest with his naming an element after it.

Perhaps it was justice for his treatment of poor Laurent but during his later life he saw his theories and the very structure of his chemistry begin to crumble and he became depressed and withdrawn. Maybe that is what made his headaches worse but he maintained that they were more than headaches. He was convinced that the debilitating migraines, which he had had, off and on, since he was twenty-three were brought on by the new and full moon. They would begin in the morning of the day of a new or full moon and last until near the end of the day. He said he had reached this conclusion after careful observation but his friends refused to believe that his migraines had anything to do with the moon.

In the winter of 1818–19 he visited his friend the famous mathematician and astronomer Pierre Laplace (1749–1827). Laplace had proposed that the solar system had been born in a vast contracting cloud of gas. Laplace assured Berzelius that his migraines could have no possible connection with the moon. But once when Berzelius was having a particularly bad attack and had lain down in a dark room he received a letter form Laplace inviting him to dinner. He declined and a few days later saw his friend who admitted that it had been a ruse. Laplace had seen that it was the time of the full moon and he guessed that his friend would be aware of it. Berzelius said he had indeed forgotten that the moon was approaching full, until, that is, he started having a severe migraine. He found no cure and took his belief, and possibly his bitterness, to his grave.

In Berzelius' day the journal *Science* was not published weekly in the United States. Along with the British journal *Nature*, it is the premier place for scientists to publish their work. In a lifetime some scientists can expect a handful of their papers to be published in these journals, if they are lucky. To get a research paper published in *Science* you have to pass the most exacting scientific standards so we should take seriously its 1977 report by a team of researchers from Stanford University and the Veterans Administration Hospital in Palo Alto, California. They reported the case of a healthy 28-year-old man who was a postgraduate student at a 'major university'. He was identified only as JX.

For years JX had been having difficulty sleeping at night and was excessively drowsy during the day. His doctors had given him drugs and he had tried hypnosis to overcome his affliction which was interfering with his studies and his social life. But nothing seemed to work and he was eventually admitted to hospital for observation. There he worked as normally as was possible while his condition was monitored. After a while it was noticed that his temperature, hormone levels and alertness were following a 24.9 hour pattern. JX, it seemed, was tied to the rhythm of the tides. So the doctors tried a change of plan. They allowed him to live according to his own schedule. Left alone, JX went to bed about 50 minutes later each night and rose about 50 minutes later each morning. He immediately started to feel better. The researchers noted that there seemed to be a 'remarkable coincidence' between his sleep and the local high tide. Soon JX was feeling well enough to go home and he tried to return to a normal life, but after being forced to follow a 24-hour day, he was soon feeling awful again.

What was happening to JX? Could he have seen the moon in the sky and reacted to it, playing out some deep psychological disturbance to the rhythm of its daily passage? Definitely not. JX was unaware of the position and motions of the moon because he was blind. To check their results the researchers looked at the sleeping patterns of fifty other blind people and claimed evidence of a similar lunar effect in thirty-eight of them.

The 'lunar effect' is taken for granted by many people. The idea that many aspects of our lives, from madness (lunacy) to birth times, from suicides to the best times for planting crops, are influenced by the phases of the moon has a strong emotional appeal for many. The sixteenth-century physician Paracelsus said that the moon had the power, 'to tear reason out of a man's head by depriving him of humors and cerebral virtues'. But is it true? Does the moon really affect us this way? What is the evidence? The evidence comes in two forms: personal tales of individuals affected in some way by the moon, and scientific studies that go looking for an effect. Be warned. Some readers will not like what I am about to say in this chapter.

Consider the story of Charles Hyde, a manual worker in St Coloumb Minor in Cornwall with a sideline in burglary. In 1952 he was caught in the act and sent for trial. His barrister argued that it wasn't poor Charles' fault. He was a faithful and honest father, husband and employee; it was the moon that made him do it. 'He suffers from a kind of moon madness. He seems to go off the rails when the moon is full.' It must have been a convincing argument because the judge let him off with probation.

The link between madness and the moon had already been established in English law. Sir William Hale, who was later to become chief justice, wrote in the 1600s, 'The moon has a great influence in all diseases of the brain especially dementia; such persons commonly in full and change of the moon are at the height of their distemper.' The Lunacy Act of 1842 built on this logic and as recently as 1940 a soldier who was charged with murder pleaded moon madness. Benjamin Rush, one of the signatories of the American Declaration of Independence, wrote, 'the moon when full increases the rarity of air and the quantity of light, each of which acts upon people with various diseases, and among others, in madness.' This is probably the most widely believed myth about the full moon, that it is associated with madness. But there is no reliable evidence for this at all.

The best-known examples of such lunatics (a word derived from *luna*, from the Latin, for 'moon') are Christopher Gore who, in 1992, began a sentence at Broadmoor in England for killing his parents and two others on full moon nights, and New York's infamous murderer 'Son of Sam', David Berkowitz, who killed eight times, five times during a full moon. Charles Hyde's (another one) chilling series of full moon murders in the late 1880s inspired Robert Louis Stevenson to write *Dr Jekyll and Mr Hyde*. But is this evidence of a lunar effect? Such is the nature of deep psychological disturbance that a fixation on the moon is bound to be a factor in some examples of extreme or abnormal behaviour. But that is different from the moon *causing* such behaviour in a more direct way. Meanwhile back in Cornwall, the other Charles Hyde was trying to behave himself, but the night of the full moon was approaching.

After the next full moon or two he once again found himself in court, accused of breaking the terms of his probation. In the interim he had left England and joined the French Foreign Legion. When he returned, disenchanted with his new desert life, he was again put on probation. Until, you guessed it, the next full moon.

The night after the very next full moon he broke into his brother-in-law's house and stole some money. This time the judge would have no moon-madness pleas and Charles Hyde went off to prison.

Stories concerning individuals are interesting but present an unpersuasive case for the moon's effects, if there are any. A good case must rest on hard evidence rather than anecdotal reports. If the data shows an effect that can be shown to be statistically significant then something must be going on. One does not have to look far for scientific papers describing research into the 'lunar effect'. There are hundreds of them, of varying quality, and there are also many popular accounts describing the effect of the moon on our lives, some of them interesting, some trivial. But, as I have said, to be published in a respected scientific journal a piece of work must have a framework of respectable science. As one studies many of the reports of a lunar effect, one is struck firstly by the small number that detect such an effect, and secondly by the far larger number of similar reports that show no such thing. Something odd is clearly going on.

Many policemen go to work a little nervously on the night of a full moon. One told me that there was definitely 'something in the air', something that pushed some people a little too far, and he knew it, and expected it, as he clocked on for his shift on the night of the full moon. Does the full moon bring a certain tension to the air that can spill over into violence?

Consider just a handful of the many studies that have been carried out. For example, researchers at Baden-Württemberg in Germany studied police records of drunk-drivers over a period of fifty full and new moon cycles (a total of 16,495 people). They found that, on average, 175 drink-drivers were caught in the two days leading up to full moon. Afterwards it dropped to 120 per day. They were so impressed by the data that they said that people should 'leave their car keys at home when the moon is out', and that 'the results show there is a definite correlation between new and full moons and the amount of alcohol consumed.' Is this something real or perhaps just evidence that German police can see boozy drivers better at night when there is a bright, full moon?

A study in Dade County, a region that contains Miami in Florida, found that the murder rate over a fifteen-year period was much higher during the full moon. (We will return to this study later.) Another study showed that New York robbery and car theft were higher during the full moon. The American Institute of Medical Climatology has said that 'crimes such as arson, destructive driving and alcoholism all showed peaks when the moon is full and cloudy nights offer no protection against this trend.'

A study carried out at the University Department of Psychiatry of the Royal Liverpool University Hospital, UK, looked at the influence of the moon on patient consultations for anxiety or depression, recording data from 782 patients registered in a general practice in Beckenham, South London, between 1971 and 1988. No statistically significant lunar effect was found.

A 1983 United States survey of 361,580 calls for police assistance in a three-year period showed no relationship with the phase of the moon.

An analysis of 1,289 aggressive 'incidents' by psychiatric patients in hospital in a 105-week period showed no significant relationship between the severity or the amount of violence or aggression and the phase of the moon.

The rate of agitation in twenty-four nursing home residents over a three-month period was studied: no significant relationship to moon phase was found.

In the admission records of 18,495 patients to a psychiatric hospital over an eleven-year period, admissions for psychosis were highest during the new moon and lowest during the full moon.

In an analysis of 897 suicides committed in Spain in a three-year period there was no relationship to the phase of the moon.

A particularly detailed study, carried out at the University of Sydney's Department of Psychological Medicine, looked at the possibility that the full moon exerts an influence on violence and aggression in psychiatric settings. They found no significant relationship between total violence and aggression or level of violence and aggression and any phase of the moon.

Prison Officer Claire Smith carried out a psychological study of 1,200 inmates in Armley Jail in Leeds, northern England. Prisoners were asked to keep track of their moods and Miss Smith recorded every violent incident in the prison over a four-month period. To her surprise, the research linked the moon and behaviour. During the first and last quarter of each lunar month there was a marked increase in violent incidents. Miss Smith said that during the days just before and after the full moon as many as five violent incidents (ranging from breaking equipment to fights and woundings) were recorded every day. But during the other period of every lunar month, there were far fewer incidents and none at all on some days. She said: 'I think this has proved that there is definitely a link between the moon and behaviour.'

One of the first things that you will notice about these studies is that they are inconsistent. Some studies show that a particular behaviour will occur more often during the full moon, other studies will highlight a different phase, while most studies show no relationship at all. It is often not easy to compare studies because of the differing techniques and assumptions they employ. For example, some studies define a 'full moon' behaviour as anything that occurs a few days before and after the full moon; other studies include only those behaviours that take place within a single day of the full moon.

The fact that most studies have failed to uncover anything resembling support for the lunar hypothesis surely tells us that if there is an effect it must be small. What is more, some of the studies that claim to find a link fail to stand up to scrutiny. Take the claims of a 'lunar effect' for homicides in Dade County. Close inspection of this work reveals it to be very shoddy indeed. The data used spanned the years between 1956 and 1970 and the conclusion drawn from it rests on very shaky statistics presented in a very misleading way. Three tests showed a lunar effect and are discussed in the report. But look a little deeper and you will see that another forty-five tests showed no lunar effect and so they are not mentioned in any detail. This is like a gambler proclaiming triumphantly that he has achieved three heads in three tosses of a coin but failing to tell us how many times a coin was tossed before the three heads came up. If all the studies were honest and used standard techniques, with agreed levels of statistical significance, then in any collection of studies there would be, by chance alone, a small number that would show the results the researchers were seeking. The fact that the studies use all sorts of data and analysis techniques, and that some of them lack rigour, only adds to the confusion. If there was an effect it would emerge. The moon is therefore acquitted, almost.

Suicides show no lunar effect. They vary by month and day of the week, but not by lunar phase. A study from California, which gathered suicide statistics over fifty-eight years, showed that its occurrence varied substantially by time of day; for both sexes and for those under sixty-five. The fewest suicide deaths occurred during the early morning hours, from 0401 to 0800. For the more recent years of the study, suicides occurred most frequently on Monday for both males and females and for most age groups. As for the phase of the moon, there was no effect. It is the same for a study of 897 Spanish suicides. But if the moon has no influence over death perhaps it influences birth?

A man called Eugene Jonas once said that he could tell the gender of a child by the phases of the moon. He told 8,000 women at what time of the moon they should conceive if they wanted a child of a particular gender. If at the time, the moon was in a 'male' sign of the zodiac (Aries), the woman would have a boy. Conversely, if the zodiac pointed to a 'female' symbol (Taurus surprisingly), the woman would have a girl. He claimed that 95 per cent of his predictions were correct. I doubt it. Actually, I have a better way to make money out of predicting the sex of a baby that is guaranteed to make a profit. Just say to prospective clients that if you are wrong you will refund their money and then make your male/female decision by tossing a coin!

There is a widespread belief that births occur more commonly around the time of a full moon. As we have seen, the 'great midwife' has always been associated with reproduction and birth. The duration of the lunation is the same as the menstrual period and the ancients took the moon's blood-red colour during an eclipse as a sign of menstruation when complex life-giving forces were abroad. Indeed the earliest known word for 'time' was probably the Acadian word *ittum*, which originally meant 'a momentous event', such as an eclipse of the moon or a monstrous birth.

It is therefore somewhat disappointing to find that the purported link between the time of birth and the full moon is not supported by evidence. Of twenty-seven studies published since

1938 (reviewed in the journal *Psychological Reports*), most have shown no relation between birth rate and the time of the month, and, in those that have, the relationship was weak and inconsistent between studies. In the largest study, of over 12 million births in France during the fifteen years between 1968 and 1982 the ratio between maximum and minimum birth rates ordered by time of the month was only 1.01. In contrast, similar studies have consistently shown that the birth rate does vary during the day, with 60 per cent of births occurring during the twelve hours between 0600 and 1800. Births are also more frequent during weekdays than at weekends. In the French study the peak ratio of births by month was the ratio May:November which was 1.22. So it seems that there are variations in birth rates but the moon has little effect on them.

Advocates of a direct lunar effect on humans will often quote the 'biological tides theory'. This theory maintains that, since the moon's (along with the sun's) gravity pulls on vast bodies of water causing the ocean tides and since the human body is 90 per cent water, the moon's gravitational pull must also cause tides (albeit somewhat reduced) in the human body. Some believe that certain people behave irrationally when their water balance is upset, due to the conflicting tides within them when they are out of harmony. This is a common view but it is a nonsense, lacking even the kernal of truth that can be found in many superstitions. The moon's gravitational effect on the Earth is considerable but it acts because of the difference in its gravitational pull at distances. In humans those differences are tiny, in fact equivalent to less than the weight of a mosquito. The tides within us are swamped by the beating of our hearts and the breathing of our lungs. In fact the moon's pull is less than that of a wall 6 inches away, and a mother holding her child will exert 12 million times more tidal force on that child than the moon will.

This makes a nonsense of astrology. The gravitational influence of the moon and distant planets is far, far less than that of ordinary objects around us. To classify people into broad personality types on the basis of the positions of celestial bodies at the time of their birth is a prejudice from our ancient past that we should have grown out of. The number of people in the delivery room would have a far greater (but still negligible) gravitational influence on the newborn. So what about an astrology that classifies people's personalities and future prospects in life that way?! Today, astrology's only use is to sell newspapers and make fortunes for the misguided and sometimes unscrupulous. It is sad that in recent years some world leaders have even timed meetings and made decisions according to astrological advice. They should have known better. Astrology is a hoax.

In many legends the moon is female and many medieval drawings show the moon associated in some way with a woman's womb or genitals. The female menstrual cycle is on average twenty-eight days, very close to the duration of the lunation. Could this be a coincidence? Some say it is not and suggest that it is a relic of our long human prehistory.

It is estimated that behind every person alive today there stand about twenty ghosts. Since early mankind evolved about five million years ago, and more recently into *homo sapiens sapiens*, about a hundred billion people have lived on Earth. Most of them never knew electricity or any other light except sunlight, moonlight, starlight and fire. Most of them never knew what it was like to be with more than a handful of people. Most depended for their existence on an intimate relationship with and knowledge of nature; most died young and led lives full of danger; and most of them stared up at the moon not knowing what it was. During this time the men would frequently leave the settlement to hunt at the time of the full moon, when its extra light gave them an advantage. Over a long period evolution produced women who were infertile at this time when the menfolk were away, or so the story goes.

Some mythmakers believe that long ago all women bled in sync with the moon, but civilization has intervened and destroyed this rhythmic cycle. This theory may seem plausible but remember that there are quite a few other mammals on the planet who have not been affected by civilization's indoor lighting and, with the exception of the opposum, their menstrual cycles are not in harmony with the moon. Is there anything significant about this? Possibly. Some modern experiments have cast light on these speculations.

Not all women have menstrual cycles of the same length, and they can vary considerably between women and even between cycles. But it has been clearly shown that women whose cycles approach the 29.5 day period have the highest likelihood of fertile cycles. Women whose cycles are longer or shorter have a proportionately diminishing incidence of fertile cycles. About 28 per cent of reproductively mature women show a 29.5 + 1 day cycle length.

That the most fertile female reproductive cycle is the same length as the lunar cycle is intriguing. But what is also fascinating is that some studies suggest that when those women with a 29.5 day cycle (about a third of those who have periods) are studied they have an increased likelihood of menstruation beginning in the week either side of full moon (that is, the light time of the month). This study, which needs repeating, shows a relationship between the changing phases of the moon and menstrual onset in some women. I wonder if this is a coincidence. According to an ancient Assyrian fragment, 'a woman is fertile according to the moon'.

In India there are surgeons who will only operate when the moon is waning, to prevent scarring. The vast majority of western surgeons I have spoken to say they have no evidence that this is a factor and do their operations when they can. If the moon does have an effect then it poses an interesting question: if you had to have an operation to treat cancer would you want it as soon as possible or would you be willing to wait a few weeks for a better time according to the phase of the moon? I know what I would do.

In 1500 a petition was sent to the Lieutenant-General of the Languedoc in France complaining about the coopers who were cutting down the Cevennes Forest. The plaintiff's outrage was not at the felling of the forest but at the time it was being cut, 'during the improper phase of the moon'. Later, in 1562, an English farmer wrote: 'Sow peason and beanes in the wane of the moone, who soweth them sooner, he soweth too soone.' Over a thousand years earlier Paracelsus gave this advice: 'Picking medicinal herbs must be done when the moon is in the sign of the virgin, and not when Jupiter is in the ascendant, for then the herb loses its virtue.'

The Maoris also believed that the moon protected crops. One of the names they had for the moon was a female name Hina or Sina (remember the ancient Mesopotamian name for the moon, Sin). They always planted sweet potatoes on the eleventh, twenty-seventh and twenty-eighth days of the lunar month because they believed that they grew larger. Their main agricultural tools were long spades with crescents carved into the handles.

Likewise, the Miskito Indians of Eastern Nicaragua believed that crops would spoil or the harvest would be light if they were harvested at new moon. They also believed that above ground plants should be planted between the first quarter and the full moon, and below ground plants should be planted between the full moon and the last quarter.

Today many gardeners continue this ancient tradition of

'moonplanting', believing that planting vegetables during specific phases of the moon is beneficial. Some almanacs are published especially for this purpose. The *Old Farmer's Almanac* says, 'Plant flowers and vegetables during the height of the moon.' Historically, farmers often planted by moon phase. It was considered inappropriate to plant tubers any time other than by the full moon. Gardeners disagree on the exact details, but it is widely believed that planting when the moon is waxing ensures rapid germination and growth. Potatoes are planted by the dark of the moon and pasture can be improved if cattle graze on it during the first and second quarters of the moon. Violets, rosemary and lavender are best sown when the moon is new. It seems that vital energies are commanded by the waxing and the waning of the moon to be either rising or falling. Some people still believe, like the medieval farmers of the Languedoc, that timber should be cut when the moon is waning, the sap is falling and the wood is dryer.

The main environmental factor that triggers flowering is the length of the night. The same chemical reactions in some plants are capable of responding to light levels much lower than those experienced at full moon, so perhaps some plants could respond to the phases of the moon. And perhaps this could go a little way towards explaining the distinction between above and below ground plants. In the case of onions and carrots ('below ground plants') flowering is usually undesirable, as it removes energy and nutrients from the tuber. But this is not the case with many 'above ground crops' such as beans and sweetcorn.

According to one team of scientists, some intriguing changes in the diameter of a tree stem seem to occur with the rhythm of the tides. Dr Ernst Zurcher of the Swiss Federal Institute of Technology in Zurich and Stephen Pallardy of the University of Missouri found that the maximum effect happens at full and new moon when an enhancement of the germination process and the initial growth of trees takes place. They maintain that they have taken into account the effects of temperature, humidity and light. Personally, I would like to see more data and the experiment repeated at various longitudes around the Earth to compare the rhythms.

The spruce trees they studied displayed a daily lunar rhythm of about three-tenths of a millimetre that was not confined just to young trees. Douglas Firs 29 metres tall varied in diameter by 0.1 – 0.2 mm in accordance with the lunar rhythm said the researchers. Is this effect, not yet confirmed by other teams of scientists, due to a 'biological tide' in plants? I do not believe so. If it is real at all it may be the result of an internal biological clock inside the plants.

Almost every living thing on Earth synchronizes with the rhythms in its environment, and natural selection will favour the survival of those organisms who detect rhythms that give them some small advantage. Perhaps, long before there were trees, cellular organisms living on the margins of the sea learned the rhythms of the tides. Evolution selected those that used these cycles in their behaviour and bequeathed their molecular time-keeping to the future.

Many creatures spawn, gather or die by the changing phase of the moon. In the fourth century Aristotle noticed that the ovaries of the sea urchin were bigger and fuller at the time of the full moon. Later Cicero and Pliny remarked on the same thing. The sea worm, *Eunice viridis*, is a delicacy found on several coral islands in the South Pacific, especially near Samoa. The adult sea worms reproduce by swarming during the last quarter of the moon in October and November. The terminal parts of their bodies drop off and float over the surface of the water, releasing sperm and eggs. This event is so important to the inhabitants of the Banks Islands that it features in their lunar calendar. A similar species is found in the Atlantic, but here swarming takes place in June or July, during the first quarter of the moon.

The light of the full moon sends a signal to millions of species on Earth. On the Great Barrier Reef of eastern Australia coral spores on the night of the November full moon. At full moon sea turtles lumber on shore to lay their eggs and some French wine-growers like to harvest their crop at full moon. They rack it at new moon when its ability to stir up the sediment is reduced.

The breeding behaviour of the Malayan black rice bug, a serious pest in the Far East, also seems to be synchronized with the phases of the moon. More young male rice bugs are caught in light traps at full moon than at any other time. They navigate by the light of the full moon, so when they encounter other bright lights they fly around them in circles.

There are many more examples of the moon acting as a visual cue for animal behaviour. It tells us what we already know, that the moon is an integral part of the night-time and serves as a useful nocturnal light source, in the same way as the sun does in the daytime.

It is said that a halo around the moon signifies wet weather and that if the lower horn of the moon is dusky it will rain before the full moon. In Scotland there is a traditional rhyme:

> If the old moon shoes like a silver shield,
> You need not be afraid to reap your field,
> But if she rises haloed round,
> Soon we'll be standing on deluged ground.

The moon has always been seen as an omen of the weather. But in reality the moon's effect on the weather is very subtle.

A study published in *Science* in 1995 concluded that the phase of the moon did influence daily global temperature but not by much, with the warmest days coinciding with the full moon. The analysis involved newly available data obtained from satellites measuring the temperature of the atmosphere. The results revealed that the lunar phase produces a 0.02–0.03 degree modulation in lower tropospheric temperatures between the new and full moon. We do not know how it happens but several possibilities have been mentioned, including the fact that the full moon reflects more solar radiation onto the Earth. 'Most important,' say the scientists, 'lunar influence is identified as another potential forcing mechanism to consider in the analysis of the variability in the short-term global temperature record.' But it isn't much.

Undoubtedly the biggest effect the moon has is in the action of tides. The ancient Greeks knew little of tides for the simple reason that there are practically none in the confined Mediterranean. Elsewhere the tides can be large, and harmony with them is essential for those communities that live off the sea. It was Sir Isaac Newton who came up with the first proper explanation of tides: the moon tugs at the water closest to it the most, and tugs least at the water furthest away from it on the other side of the globe. The result is a bulge in the oceans that travels around the world as it rotates, giving two high and two low tides a day. Another effect the moon's pull has on the Earth is that some things actually shift their places each day. Moscow, for example, is pulled up by 50 cm twice a day. Because of tides raised on the moon by the Earth the moon is egg-shaped, bulging 1,000 m in the direction of the Earth.

The sun and the moon both have a tidal effect on the Earth but the moon has the strongest influence. Tides have a big impact on sea life; many creatures who live in the intertidal zone (and the creatures who feed on them) base their life rhythms on the ebb and flow. Some crabs change colour at high tide.

In 1997 scientists at CERN, the international centre for particle physics based just outside Geneva, were operating their Large Electron Positron collider (LEP). It accelerates a beam of electrons at almost the speed of light one way around a 27 km underground circular ring and a beam of their anti-particles (positrons) around the other way. When they collide they annihilate each other in a brief microscopic burst that recreates, on a tiny scale, the fireball at the birth of the universe. But the scientists' experiments were not working. There was an influence on the tight beam of sub-atomic particles that they could not explain.

The researchers were used to seeking out tiny effects. The level of water in the nearby Lac Leman had an effect on their beam, as did the arrival and departure of the TGV at Geneva Station. Then somebody looked at a list of tables showing the moon's position in the sky and saw that it was related to the deflection of the beam. Problem solved!

Why do people believe there is a 'lunar effect'? It could be what is often called a 'selection effect'. For example, if you are in the Accident and Emergency room at a hospital and it's a busy night, it's just a busy night. But if there is a full moon outside and it's a busy night many people think it's the effect of the moon. If it's not a busy night it does not count; as we have seen, most animals are pattern-seeking, especially humans.

Regardless of studies showing that the full moon has little or no connection with people's behaviour, most nurses and policemen believe they have witnessed the lunar influence. Questionnaires sent to 325 people indicated that 140 of them believed that the moon altered individual behaviour. Do we believe these notions, elevating them to the status of 'scientific facts'? Or do we really know that these ideas come from our superstitious past that lingers on in our minds and hearts? Myths, Carl Jung said, bring us back in touch with ourselves and can never be replaced by science.

In Shakespeare's *Antony and Cleopatra*, when the Egyptian queen is about to kill herself she signals her firm resolve by saying, 'I am marble-constant; now the fleeting moon/No planet is of mine.' These lines gain their power from the fact that the moon has always been associated, in myth and folklore, with change and mutability. But Shakespeare little knew that scientists would one day discover that the fickle moon really was changing – subtly shifting its position in relation to the Earth. The moon's pull on the waters of the Earth is dissipating energy from the Earth–moon system, some 3 billion kilowatts as a rough estimate. The result of this loss of energy is that the moon's orbit is expanding by a few cm a year. It has actually been measured. Laser beams aimed at the moon through large telescopes have struck reflectors deployed on the lunar surface by the Apollo astronauts or built into the roof of Lunokhod rovers. The recession of the moon shows up in its measured distance.

The other effect of this tidal dissipation is that the rotation rate of the Earth is slowing down by 2.2 seconds every 100,000 years.

A recent analysis of rocks from South Africa showed that the Earth's oceans were tugged by tides more than 3 billion years ago. In the sandstone and shale deposits of the Moodies group of hills geologists found tell-tale markings, technically known as tidal rhythmites, made by the ebb and flow of waters moving over an ancient continental shoreline. This shows that the moon really was in orbit around the Earth 3 billion years ago.

The markings were found on rocks exposed on the banks of the Sheba River in Mpumalanga province. They were laid down some 3,225 billion years ago while the moon was nearing the end of its volcanic period, as lava welled up from beneath its surface and flooded the low-lying basins. Had there been creatures to see it, the 'man in the moon' would have looked different in those somewhat shorter days. The tidal patterns on the rocks shows that the length of the lunar month was only 20 days back then.

Tidal rhythmites can be found in many places throughout the world, such as the Pokegama Formation in Minnesota. This is a sedimentary sequence of silts and muds laid down by tidal currents along the margins of the Animikie Sea – a long-vanished ocean that two billion years ago lapped the shores of what was to become North America. The layers indicate that, back then, there were thirty high tides per month and that the moon cannot have been less than 20 Earth radii distant. Today it is 60 Earth radii away. Research on deposits laid down in the Proterozoic era, 900 million years ago, suggests that the length of the day was 18 hours and the length of the year was 481 days.

The slow retreat of the moon meant that something remarkable happened about 150 million years ago. Before that time the moon appeared bigger than the sun. So on the occasions when the moon's orbit took it in front of the sun it completely obscured it. But because of the moon's slow retreat there came a time, first apparent when an eclipse occurred, when the moon was at the far point in its orbit and appeared exactly the same size as the sun. At that point there was a total eclipse which blotted out the visible disc of the sun, allowing its spectacular hot outer atmosphere, its corona, to be seen in all its radiant splendour. The dinosaurs were the first to see it. But, because the moon continues its outward trek, there will come a time, in about 150 million years, when it will appear too small to cover the disc and there will always be a circle of the sun visible that will swamp the elusive corona. The spectacular eclipses of the sun that we now witness will only be visible for about 2 per cent of our planet's life. We are lucky to see them.

Nendrum Monastery on Mahee Island in Strangford Lough, Northern Ireland, was one of the great maritime monasteries of Ireland between the seventh and the tenth centuries. Contemporary sources say it could have been home to over 400 monks as well as a large lay population. In a recent survey of the foreshore of Stangford Lough a series of gullies, stonewalls and rocks with grooves and holes ground into them was found in the intertidal zone. It seems that the monks, lacking any freshwater streams on the island, turned to tidal power to grind their bread. When the tide came they trapped the water behind a gate and released it through a channel that turned a waterwheel. From measurements made of the size of the water enclosure and its height it seems that the monks could have generated energy for about an hour and a half either side of the 642 tides of the year.

As they ate their bread or took sacrament, the Nendrum monks must have known about the moon's influence on the tide. I wonder, did they appreciate that they were being fed by a little power robbed from the moon that they had pushed ever so slightly further away from the Earth?

CHAPTER THIRTEEN

Lucian's Dream

The world held its breath as man took his first step upon the moon. Almost every TV and radio station carried the news minute by minute, waiting to hear what words would be spoken when the first footprint was made. Astronauts training for future moon missions at NASA's Johnson Space Center stopped what they were doing to follow events, as did cosmonauts at Star City near Moscow. World leaders watched, ordinary people watched, even those who thought the whole enterprise was folly watched. Heads of state had their congratulations already written, ready to be dispatched when the first man on the moon made his way down the ladder and off the footpad onto the lunar surface. Soon the world waited as he stood at the footpad, looked around, and prepared to step off.

Within moments of the first word spoken from the lunar surface, President Brezhnev, who had been watching from his suite in the Kremlin, received a call from Richard Nixon, President of the United States. The text of the call was released later. It went: 'First Secretary, this is a great day for mankind. I congratulate the Union of Soviet Socialist Republics on their magnificent achievement and salute Alexei Leonov, the first man on the moon.'

It could have happened. Nobody who has studied the Soviet space effort will deny that the Soviets could have beaten the Americans to the moon. In the final analysis they were beaten as much by themselves as they were by the better organized and richer Americans. The American triumph in the 'moon race' is well known and deservedly celebrated as one of the greatest achievements of all time. But what is less well known is that the Soviet Union also had an aggressive lunar programme that began before the Americans talked of sending a man to the moon and indeed continued long after America had turned its back on the moon. Undeniably, the Soviets had a head start over the Americans but they squandered it. On the one hand, the Soviet programme included an ambitious, and largely successful, series of robotic missions that included orbiters, landers, surface rovers, and even lunar sample-return spacecraft. On the other hand, there is their desperate attempt to put a cosmonaut on the moon. They tried it all – super-rockets (like the mighty Saturn 5 that took Americans to the moon), lunar landing craft, lunar rovers. They tried it all and suffered many deaths, launch pad explosions and failed spacecraft. But in the end, as if unable to admit they had failed, they denied they were ever in the race and, perhaps to their surprise, many in the West believed them.

Twenty years after the first American moon landing, in August 1989, the USSR officially acknowledged the existence of their manned lunar programme with an initial release of information in the Soviet newspaper *Izvestia*. Some western observers had known the truth all along, as had the inner circles of the United States civil and military space programme but now, in a semi-official way, the story could be told. Why was it not Alexei Leonov who became the first man on the moon? Some of what you are about to read was secret until the collapse of the USSR.

It took the most destructive war in history to make the dream of actually visiting the moon (first envisioned by the second-century Greek rhetorician Lucian of Samosata) a reality. The race for the moon between the Americans and the Soviets confirmed what Ariosto had written centuries before: that there were kingdoms, riches and fame on the moon as well as countless prayers, vows, tears and sighs, time and talent. It took the clash of two ideologies and a prolonged period of international tension to provide the spur for the first journeys to the moon and it took two remarkable men working on either side of the Iron Curtain. They never met but, from afar, they held each other in unbounded admiration. One of them said that they could have been friends.

On Saturday 5 October 1957 in a desolate region of the Kazakhstan steppes fifty-year-old Sergei Korolev was nervously waiting for a simple beep-beep-beep from the sky. He was the leading figure in the Soviet effort to explore space, a man whose designs and concepts are still influencing the space programmes of the twenty-first century, and a man who barely escaped the Stalinist purges with his life. He was as much a part of the story of the moon as Galileo. He was the driving force behind the first man-made object to touch its surface, and he discovered more of the moon than anyone before him.

Sergei Korolev was born in December 1906 in the village of Zhitomir not far from Kiev. As a young boy he was obsessed with aeroplanes and space travel and at the age of nineteen he had built and was flying his own glider. He preferred his flying machines and his dreams to other people. When he was twenty his parents moved to Moscow and he attended the Bauman Higher Technical Institute where his talents came to the attention of the great engineer Andrei Tupolev. He joined a private rocket group known as GRID (the Group for the Study of Rocket Propulsion Systems). Meeting at first in a wine cellar, they included the space visionary Friedrikh Tsander who shared his dreams of flying to the moon. A member of Stalin's staff heard about GRID and they received government funding. Korolev was a loner, a workaholic, whose only interest other than rockets was women. He was often melancholy, poorly dressed, resentful, angry, driven and brilliant.

But soon Stalin became suspicious of the intellectuals in the rocket group and had the head of the team shot. Korolev was arrested and in September 1938 he was sentenced to ten years in a labour camp. He spent two years appealing against the sentence and eventually the original verdict was thrown out. But, such was the corruption of the system, even though he was officially not guilty, he still had to serve the remaining eight years of his sentence. He was first sent to the mines at Kolyma in eastern Siberia, then to a prison ship at Magadan, and finally to Siberia to work as a slave in the goldmines. It was effectively a death sentence. To the end of his days he carried a scar on his head – a guard had struck him with a shovel when he was working as a river widener. After the labour camps' brutal discipline his health was never quite the same. He had a heart condition and had lost all his teeth.

There cannot be many people who owe their lives to Adolf Hitler. For Korolev, however, the threat posed by Nazi Germany to Soviet Russia was his salvation. As war came, the prison camps were scoured for anyone who could make a contribution to the war effort, and that of course included engineers and rocket scientists. Instrumental in rescuing Korolev was his old tutor Tupolev, who was himself a prisoner and had already been conscripted into a prison design bureau.

In September 1945 Korolev, now a colonel in the Red Army, was in Germany to study the V2, the impressive rocket that skirted the edge of space before raining destruction on London. As he watched test flights of the V2 and the surrender of its chief designer Wernher von Braun and most of his team to the welcoming arms of the USA, along with enough parts to make 100 V2 rockets, it was clear to Korolev that von Braun had gone further with rocket technology than anyone else and that the Soviets were going to need this technology. Korolev never met von Braun, the other man in our story of the race to put a man on the moon. But by the time he arrived in Germany von Braun was already in America. When Soviet troops reached the German rocket research base at Peenemünde they found only a heavily bombed site, a few badly damaged rockets and a handful of technicians. But Korolev knew that his dream of building rockets to go into space would eventually come true, if not for him then for the Americans.

It was at this time that mankind first touched the moon. In January 1946 engineers from the US Army Signal Corps used a 3 kilowatt transmitter to bounce a radio signal off the moon and pick up its echo. This feat was repeated a month later by a Hungarian by the name of Zak Bay. A few years later the US Army Corps used the moon to send a message between Iowa and Virginia. The message was the same as the first Morse Code message sent by Samuel Morse in 1844: 'What God hath wrought.'

In 1947 Korolev began talking about the possibility of putting a satellite into orbit but no one in the government was interested. The effort was to go into building Inter-Continental Ballistic Missiles (ICBMs). Korolev thought the rocket that was being developed as an ICBM, the R-7, could get an object into space. In 1954 he urged that work should begin on a satellite but no one was listening. Undaunted by official indifference, Korolev did a very risky thing in the USSR at that time; he sent a copy of his letter to Premier Khrushchev whose response was to back Korolev.

The USSR Council of Ministers issued a decree, number 149-88ss, on 30 January 1956, calling for the creation of an artificial satellite. The document approved the launch of a large satellite (designated the 'Object D') in 1957, in time for the forthcoming International Geophysical Year. But by mid-1956 the Object D project was beginning to fall behind schedule. On

14 September, the prominent mathematician Mstislav Keldysh made a personal plea to a meeting of the Academy of Sciences Presidium, 'We all want our satellite to fly earlier than the Americans.' By the end of November, Korolev was getting very anxious. He had been informed about a September 1956 launch of a missile from Cape Canaveral, Florida, which according to his incorrect information was a failed attempt to launch a satellite into orbit. While Korolev's information on US plans may have been wrong, his instincts were not. The United States could have launched a satellite by early 1957, but for turf wars, lack of interest and political obstacles – the same forces that stood in Korolev's way.

Korolev was also worried because the results of static testing indicated that his rockets were not powerful enough for the heavy Object D satellite. He soon realized that he was making things too difficult by attempting to put into orbit a 1½-ton scientific observatory. The R-7 could launch something smaller. So, on 5 January 1957, Korolev sent a letter to the government with a revised plan. He asked that permission be given to launch two small satellites, each with a mass of 40–50 kg, in the period April–June 1957, immediately preceding the beginning of the International Geophysical Year (IGY).

Throughout the early part of 1957 the design, construction and testing of the R-7 continued and it was transported to the Kazakhstan launch site in freight cars camouflaged to look like passenger trains. The first three launches of the R-7 in May–July 1957 were all failures. Korolev's plan, to launch a satellite before the beginning of the IGY, looked impossible. The days following the last failure were the lowest point for Korolev. He wrote: 'Things are very, very bad.'

But the fourth R-7 launch, on 21 August 1957, was successful. The missile and its payload flew 6,500 km, the warhead finally entering the atmosphere over the target point at Kamchatka in the far east. Korolev was so excited that he stayed awake until three in the morning speaking to his deputies about the great possibilities that had opened up, the artificial satellite, and beyond that the moon and the planets. Another test launch was successful and Korolev began to informally target the satellite launch for the one hundredth anniversary of Russian spaceflight visionary Tsiolkovsky's birth on 17 September. But it soon became clear that it would be impossible to meet that date, and it slipped to October.

An R-7 was transported to the launch pad in the early morning of 3 October, escorted on foot by Korolev and others. That night huge floodlights illuminated the launch pad as the engineers in the nearby blockhouse checked the systems. History was about to be made.

Command for the launch was entrusted to Boris Chekunov, a young artillery forces lieutenant. The seconds counted down to zero and Chekunov pressed the lift-off button. At exactly 22:28 Moscow time, on 4 October, the engines ignited and the booster lifted off the pad.

A relieved Korolev heard the beep, beep, beep from the orbiting satellite 101 minutes later as it completed its first orbit. They waited another 96 minutes to be sure and then made the call to tell Khrushchev. From the bunker someone called Major Dimitry Ustinov was put through to Nikita Khrushchev who, at just before 2 a.m. Moscow time, was fast asleep. Of the four phones in his bedroom it was the large white one that was ringing, the one reserved for the most senior members of the government. When told of the success Khrushchev said, 'Oh. Frankly, I never thought it would work' and went back to bed. Like many others, Khrushchev had not grasped the true importance of this historic event.

The Soviet media did not even give a specific name to the

satellite. It was generally referred to as 'Sputnik', the Russian word for 'satellite', often loosely translated as 'fellow traveller'.

A few hours after the launch the duty officer at the CIA phoned the White House to say that the Soviets had launched a satellite. President Eisenhower had left for his farm in Gettysburg to play golf. But Ike wasn't worried. Satellites are about science, he argued, not military might. A satellite did not have any effect on the United States' ability to defend itself against the Soviets. He was technically right but the public did not believe him. Ike had misjudged the effect that Sputnik would have on the American people. A TV reporter stopped a woman in Times Square and asked for her reaction. She paused and said quietly, 'We fear this.' The next person he approached said, 'Somebody has fallen down on the job, badly.' Dr Edward Teller, one of the most influential scientists in America, said the country had lost a battle more important and greater than Pearl Harbor. One astronomer said that he would not be surprised if the Russians reached the moon within a week. Wernher von Braun said that the Russians 'beat us only because we let them'.

With the successful launch of the first Sputnik and the furore that followed, Khrushchev became more interested and asked what other space spectaculars were possible. With Khrushchev's backing, Korolev's dreams of space exploration were to advance much more quickly than he could have ever imagined. Now he wanted to send a space probe to the moon.

After the success of Sputnik, resources were made available for the development of manned spacecraft as well as probes to the moon and planets. One thing was immediately clear: they needed a rocket more powerful than the one that had been used to launch the first satellite. By the summer of 1957 they had started developing an addition to the R-7, called Blok E. But, as with the R-7 that was to launch Sputnik, and just as Korolev had feared, the development of the rocket engines dragged on much longer than planned. Its first test took place on 10 July 1958.

The USA had responded to Sputnik very unimpressively. Their first attempt at putting a satellite into space (a satellite the size of a grapefruit) ended when the rocket exploded on the launch pad. The media called it 'Kaputnik'. Von Braun and his army team were then given the job and they successfully put the tiny Explorer 1 into orbit in January 1958.

By August of that year both the United States and the Soviet Union were preparing to launch their first probes to the moon. To get the United States there first, the Advanced Research Projects Agency (ARPA) started Operation Mona which went under the cover name of 'Pioneer'. The US Air Force planned to launch a Thor-Able rocket with a small probe from the Atlantic Missile Range (AMR) in Florida that would enter lunar orbit.

Meanwhile, engineers at the Soviet design bureau OKB-1, led by Sergei Korolev, were preparing their E-1 lunar probe. They planned to use their new rocket to hurl a probe of about 360 kg (ten times that of the small US Pioneer probe) towards a lunar impact. But the rocket was giving problems. Despite his misgivings, the rumours about the imminent Pioneer launch and pressure from his superiors forced Korolev to attempt a launch. But, in the event, the Pioneer launch took place first. On 17 August 1958, at 8:18 a.m. EDT, a Thor-Able rocket lifted off into a clear Florida sky. For the first time in the history of our species, mankind was seriously attempting to reach the moon.

All seemed to be going to plan but then, 77 seconds after launch, the rocket exploded. To everyone's frustration transmissions from the Pioneer probe were received until it plummeted into the Atlantic Ocean two minutes later. It was determined that the loss had been caused by the failure of a bearing in a turbopump.

Meanwhile in the Soviet Union preparations to launch the first

E-1 probe early the following day were falling behind. Frustrated by a series of malfunctions on the pad, Korolev finally called off the launch after hearing of the Pioneer failure. The unco-operative rocket was returned to the assembly building. The next launch would be in a month's time.

So it was that on 23 September 1958 the Soviets got their rocket back on the pad, ready to try for the moon again. But soon after it took off, severe vibrations gripped its fuel tanks. Then, 93 seconds after launch, its side boosters broke loose and the rocket and its E-1 moon probe headed back to Earth. The Soviets' first attempt to reach the moon had ended as ingloriously as that of the Americans. But, unlike the American attempt, their failure was kept quiet. Another rocket was hastily modified for the following month but Korolev again had the Americans to worry about; they were preparing another Thor-Able rocket with another Pioneer probe. But this time there was a crucial difference – ARPA was no longer in charge. An act of Congress officially established the National Aeronautics and Space Administration (NASA) to run the United States' civilian space programme, starting on 1 October 1958.

As before, the United States got off the pad first. On the morning of 11 October, Pioneer 1 was launched towards the moon just seconds after the opening of its launch window. This time the Thor first stage worked, allowing the high-speed Able stages their chance to operate. It seemed that the probe would reach the moon around midday on 13 October.

Word of the successful Pioneer launch arrived in the Soviet Union just as Korolev and his team were struggling to meet their launch window the following day. But, although Pioneer was the first into space, the faster trajectory of the E-1 would allow it to reach the moon a couple of hours earlier. After a night of hectic preparations, the E-1 lifted off and began its chase. But the so-called 'pogo' vibrations reappeared and after just 104 seconds, the rocket fell apart under the stress. It was obvious that a more thorough solution to the problem was needed and all launch attempts were put on hold. But would the American Pioneer probe reach the moon?

Fortunately for Korolev, it was soon discovered that Pioneer 1 was not headed for history after all. A simple programming error caused the rocket's second stage to shut down early, leaving the lunar probe travelling too slowly to reach the moon. Eventually, after a high elliptical arc, it fell back to Earth. Although Korolev, recognized the feelings that the Americans would be having he breathed a sigh of relief. But the Americans managed to salvage something from the mission. While reaching the moon was out of the question, Pioneer 1 used its instruments to investigate the Van Allen radiation belts that circle the Earth. It showed that they faded after 15,000 km and were not a barrier to manned lunar missions, as some had begun to fear.

If Korolev had a reprieve with the failure of Pioneer 1 it was only a brief one. The last of the original ARPA Pioneers was immediately prepared for launch in the hope of still beating the Soviets. And with his rocket problems Korolev had no way of making another attempt of his own. On 7 November a Thor-Able carried Pioneer 2 into space. Surely this time, the engineers hoped, they would get it to the moon. Sadly, while the first and second stages operated perfectly, the third stage failed and it fell back to Earth just 42 minutes after launch. But NASA still had one more card to play. They had a pair of smaller Pioneer probes that could be ready to launch in December. But Korolev may have smiled when he heard of this, because by mid-November he believed he had solved the pogo vibration problem and this time the laws of celestial trajectories would favour him. In December the Soviets could dispatch a moon probe two days before the Americans. Now *they* would have to nervously watch *him*.

His moon rocket lifted off on 4 December, carrying the third of the E-1 moon probes. This time the launch was flawless, the pogo problem had finally been solved and Korolev dared to hope. But after four minutes the main engine spluttered and failed and once again he faced a tense wait to see if NASA would reach the moon first. In the end they failed. The prize of touching the moon had yet to be claimed.

One last lunar probe was considered as part of the E series, the E-4. But its mission would be radically different. Its task was to deliver a nuclear warhead to the lunar surface – its detonation leaving no doubt that a Soviet probe had reached the moon. Korolev was not very keen on beginning an era of lunar exploration with a nuclear weapon but for a while it seems he had no choice in the matter. Incredibly, the United States had the same idea.

The US Air Force asked American scientists to plan a spectacular nuclear blast on the moon at a time when the Soviet Union was leading the space race. People would see a very bright flash, particularly if the blast occurred on the moon's shadowed side, and clouds of debris would probably also be visible. The classified project, which was worked on from late 1958 through to mid-1959, was known as 'A119, A Study of Lunar Research Flights (SECRET)' and was ordered by the Air Force Special Weapons Center. For lunar science it would have been a disaster, and for humanity as a whole it would have sent all the wrong signals about space exploration. Fortunately the United States plan evaporated after the final report in early to mid-1959.

But not the Soviet one.

The lunar nuclear explosion idea was the brainchild of a circle of Academicians. They reasoned that, if filled with conventional explosives, an exploding probe on the lunar surface would not be easily observable from Earth. But if a nuclear device was exploded on the moon's surface, the whole world would be able to witness the event and nobody would be able to question whether a Soviet spacecraft had really reached the moon. After such a demonstration, much of the world would surely cower beneath a symbolically nuclear-armed Soviet moon?

Korolev manufactured a mock-up of the spacecraft that would carry the bomb, its dimensions based on the bulky and inefficient nuclear weapons of the time. The container with the nuclear charge was to be equipped with detonation rods pointing in every direction, like an anti-ship mine, to ensure an explosion at the moment of contact with the moon. Fortunately, the project never advanced beyond the mock-up stage.

It was folly. As Shakespeare's King Lear said, we would have been making the moon guilty of our disasters. Nobody at that time, or indeed today, could provide a guarantee that the charge would be safely delivered to the moon. If the rocket failed, and most of them had failed up until then, the nuclear bomb would fall on the Soviet Union. If the rocket's third stage failed, it could land on another country, causing a highly undesirable international incident. What is more, the charge could end up in orbit, from which it would fall at a time and place that nobody could predict. To miss the moon would be to send the charge on a journey around the sun, returning periodically to the environment of the Earth, an unpleasant thought.

After this succession of failures Sergei Korolev wrote on 28 January 1958 to the Central Committee of the Communist Party of the Soviet Union. His letter set out two clear goals: a lunar impact and a flight around the moon to see its far side.

CHAPTER FOURTEEN

'My God! It Landed'

The year 1959 was the year mankind reached the moon. On 2 January the Soviet Union announced the launch of Luna 1, their first acknowledged moon probe. It was far larger than anything the United States could muster and although it was intended to strike the moon it actually passed within 6,000 km of it. The Soviets renamed it Mechta or Dream and it went into orbit around the sun. Now they had two more space firsts to add to their list: the first lunar flyby and the first artificial planet in the solar system. It did produce some useful science in finding out that the moon had no magnetic field.

In September mankind finally reached the moon for the first time. Luna 2 and its carrier rocket crashed on the edge of Mare Imbrium, near the crater Archimedes, carrying two small spheres made up of Soviet pendants engraved with the Soviet coat of arms. They were designed to be scattered across the lunar landscape but if you were to visit its impact site today you would see little apart from a small crater. Striking the moon at 10,000 km an hour would have melted and vaporized them all.

At the time, it must have been crushing for the Americans. Less than one month later, the Soviets launched the most advanced moon probe to date and in doing so solved one of the moon's eternal mysteries. On 4 October Luna 3 became the first to return images of the far side. It radioed back twenty-nine very indistinct pictures which showed that the far side was very different from the near side. There was, in general, an absence of large dark maria.

Soviet astronomers were the first for 350 years to gaze upon unseen lunar vistas, however indistinct. Like Galileo, Langrenus and Hevelius before them, they explored new regions of the moon and, as discoverers do, they started to name the features they saw. They did not consult the international body that names objects in space, the International Astronomical Union (IAU). At a subsequent meeting of the IAU, attended by many Soviet astronomers, the question of ratifying these unofficial names was raised. Many in the American delegation were not happy that Riccioli's long-established tradition of naming seas after states of mind was being flouted. But the Soviets were adamant; one large mare region was to be named the 'Sea of Moscow', they insisted. After a few moments someone came up with an ingenious solution. All would be well, and traditions honoured, if the IAU decided that 'Moscow' was a state of mind. After some light-hearted debate which, it is said, the Soviet delegation enjoyed, it was decreed that Moscow was indeed a state of mind and the name could remain on the moon.

The Americans had to bear their failures and the success of the Soviets while at the same time making ambitious plans for the future. It was clear to them that, for the next decade, the moon would be the focus for manned and unmanned exploration. While the Soviets had also suffered their share of failures, their successes were spectacular, and they had clearly won this first round of the race to the moon. In response to the Soviet effort and as part of President Kennedy's stated aim of landing a man on the moon before 1970, the United States developed three series of unmanned spacecraft to explore the moon: Ranger, Surveyor and Lunar Orbiter.

Ranger was designed to strike the lunar surface, taking closer and closer images as it headed for destruction. It was hoped that these pictures, showing features far smaller than could be seen with a telescope from Earth, would tell scientists what the surface was like. Would it support a spacecraft or would any vehicle sink into a sea of dust? At one time a rugged spherical capsule capable of withstanding such an impact was incorporated into Ranger. Engineers tested a range of materials, including aluminium honey-comb, cardboard – in fact anything crushable. To their surprise, the best material by far turned out to be balsa wood. So, by the summer of 1960, a 66 cm diameter sphere weighing 42 kg was built for Ranger. After separating from the Ranger it would fall just over 300 m to the moon's surface, roll to a stop and begin transmitting.

But the wooden lander never got the chance to prove itself. Rangers 1–6, including the only three to carry the ball, all failed. Several missed the moon because of malfunctions in the rocket launcher. Ranger 4 actually hit the moon just over the limb. But, en route, a speck of foil from the separation of the Agena Carrier rocket shorted it. All engineers could do was track the tiny bleep from the balsa wood ball. Premier Khrushchev was ecstatic. At a Communist Party meeting in Vladivostok he said that socialism was the only reliable launching pad for spaceships.

Back in the USA, while analysing the Ranger 4 problem, the Jet Propulsion Laboratory (JPL) modified a Ranger to visit Venus, calling it Mariner. Unfortunately its rocket malfunctioned and it ended up in the Atlantic. They tried again and, when Mariner 2 was halfway to Venus, Ranger 5 was launched towards the Ocean of Storms. It missed the moon.

The Ranger project was now in crisis. Three commissions were established to look into the failures, one from JPL, one from NASA and one from Congress. Perhaps it was only a spell of bad luck? So, just as Mariner 2 passed within 37,000 km of the Venusian cloud tops, twice as close as the Russian craft, the Ranger project was reorganized and given one last chance. The balsa wood ball was dropped, so to speak. And it was with high hopes that politicians and engineers watched the launch of

Ranger 6 on 30 January 1964. It worked fine, except for the camera. The humiliation was complete.

James Webb, the head of NASA, was about to cancel the project. But the head of JPL, William Pickering, argued and got one final flight. At that year's annual late-winter JPL party, the Miss Guided Missile Dance, Pickering had to perform the ceremony of crowning the winner. As he walked to the microphone there was spontaneous applause. 'We're going to make it work' was all he said.

That July, Ranger 7 was heading for Mare Nubium, an area crossed by the rays from two craters, Copernicus to the north and Tycho to the south. Its six cameras were each snapping five images a second. A lot was gleaned from the pictures which could show objects as small as 0.5 metres in size (a thousand times better than could be obtained from the Earth). There were no jagged features, just wide-open spaces with boulders supported on the surface; and craters, craters everywhere, in all sizes. This surface would take a lander. Within a few hours William Pickering was in the cabinet room in the White House showing the photos to President Lyndon Johnson. A month later the IAU recognized Ranger 7's success by renaming the impact site Mare Cognitium, the Known Sea.

The task of the next Ranger, number 8 in February 1965 was to study the central highlands looking for landing sites for manned missions. Having gathered the data, the final Ranger, number 9, was given to the scientists, and in March 1965 its crash into the fractured crater Alphonsus was shown live on TV networks. Although there were still some who believed that a lander would sink into lunar dust most believed that Ranger had established the basic nature of the lunar surface and it would most likely support the weight of a spacecraft, or an astronaut. Aeons of pitting by meteors had not turned the surface into a thick, weak dust layer after all.

Meanwhile the Soviets were having mixed success. Luna 5 was designed for a soft landing but the retro-rocket system failed, and the spacecraft hit the lunar surface in the Sea of Clouds. Luna 6, in June 1965, was supposed to travel to the moon but, because a midcourse correction failed, it missed. In October Luna 7 should have achieved a soft landing on the moon but, due to a premature retro-fire, it crashed in the Sea of Storms. Two months later Luna 8 was launched to soft-land on the moon but retro-fire was late, and again the spacecraft smashed into the lunar surface in the Sea of Storms.

Back in the USA, Surveyor made Ranger look simple. Surveyor would have to carry out a soft landing using a solid-fuel rocket to slow from its initial descent at more than 9,000 km per hour to 385 km per hour. What is more, the lander would have to aim the thrust of its braking rocket directly along its flight path to avoid tumbling. It was a daunting task. Then, at about 8,000 m above the moon's surface, Surveyor would use small, liquid-fuel rockets to slow to about 12 km per hour in vertical descent. To absorb an impact on hard ground its three landing legs were fitted with shock absorbers and the footpads were made of crushable aluminium honeycomb. Its scientific team hoped that an incident during Surveyor's tests would not be prophetic. In April 1964, a test version of the spacecraft had been suspended from a balloon and lifted 500 m above the New Mexico desert to test the landing system. Before the test could begin, a nearby electrical storm triggered the balloon's release mechanism and the test Surveyor fell to the desert and broke into pieces.

The resulting delays cost the Americans the second round in the race. On 4 February 1966, Luna 9 soft-landed on the Ocean of Storms. On the moon four petals opened and stabilized the craft. Spring-controlled antennae popped out and a television camera looking through a rotatable mirror took pictures and radioed them to Earth.

British radio astronomers at the Jodrell Bank radio observatory near Manchester, England, were waiting for the signals. Using the large radio dish (then the largest fully steerable dish in the world), they recorded Luna 9's signals and at first could not make any sense of them. Then someone said they sounded like a simple fax transmission used all the time by the press. The problem was that Jodrell Bank did not have a fax machine. So Sir Bernard Lovell, Jodrell's director, contacted the Manchester offices of the *Daily Express* newspaper and they sent a fax machine down. Although they got the proportions of the picture slightly wrong what emerged from that machine was remarkable. British scientists had picked up the first images from the surface of the moon before they had been released by the Soviets. The Soviets were furious and accused Jodrell Bank of stealing their pictures; the *Daily Express* got a scoop.

The pictures included views of nearby rocks and of the horizon just over a kilometre away from the spacecraft. The moonscape was like a rock-strewn desert.

As if this was not bad enough for the Americans, three months later Luna 10 became the first craft to orbit the moon. One by one, it seemed, the Soviets were ticking off the major lunar accomplishments: first probe to strike the moon; first images of the far side; first soft landing and pictures from the surface; and now the moon's first artificial satellite. There seemed to be only one record left, a manned landing. Luna 10 had an instrument called a gamma-ray spectrometer which made an initial survey of the composition of the moon and indicated that the rocks in the maria were basaltic. Kuiper's idea, that the moon was made of rocks that had been differentiated by intense heating, appeared to be confirmed. Harold Urey's idea, that the moon had been assembled from cold objects, was not.

Nevertheless the Americans fought back and on 1 June, less than three days after a flawless launch, Surveyor 1 reached the moon and scientists watched the automatic landing sequence. At 80 km above the moon, Surveyor 1's braking rocket fired a 40-second burn, then fell away. To everyone's relief, Surveyor wasn't tumbling. A mission commentator called out the diminishing altitude: 1,000 feet, 500, 50, 12 – then 'Touchdown'. At Mission Control, no one could believe it – well, almost no one. Geologist Gene Shoemaker, a Ranger veteran leading one of the Surveyor science teams, recalled saying, 'My God! It landed. Hell, I wouldn't have given you a 10 per cent chance that Surveyor 1 was going to land.'

Half an hour later, the first television images began to appear on the monitors at JPL, showing a round footpad perched on a dusty but firm moonscape. As Surveyor's pictures revealed a 30 m crater rimmed with boulders, it became clear that Surveyor had been lucky to come down where it had.

The luck held. Six more missions followed; all but two were successful.

Surveyor 1 had touched down near the crater Flamsteed on the western edge of the Ocean of Storms. On the morning of 2 June, when Surveyor 1 took its first 144 pictures, commercial television networks showed the 'live' lunar programme throughout the nation and the Early Bird communications satellite relayed the pictures throughout Europe. In addition, a number of experiments were conducted. A gas jet was turned on to study its blast-erosion effect on the lunar surface.

The pictures were better than Luna 10's and for the first time you could imagine yourself standing on the moon. Small craters and rocks and a line of boulders could be seen outlining the rim of a crater in the middle distance. When the sun set for the fourteen-day lunar night everyone thought that no more would be heard of Surveyor 1 but they were wrong; it survived five lunar nights. Surveyor 2 followed on 20 September but when one of the three-rocket engines failed it started to tumble and never made it.

Not since 1609, when the telescope was first turned towards it, had the moon seen a year like 1966. On 10 August came the first of the next set of missions. Lunar Orbiter 1 was launched and it entered orbit of the moon four days later, returning its first pictures four days after that. Five Lunar Orbiter missions were launched in 1966 and 1967 to map the surface before the Apollo landings. All five were successful, and 99 per cent of the moon was photographed with a resolution of 60 m or better. This was ten times what could be achieved by ground-based telescopes. The work started by Langrenus, Hevelius, Riccioli and Cassini and others was now finally over. The first three missions were equatorial orbits, dedicated to imaging twenty potential lunar landing sites. The fourth and fifth missions were devoted to broader scientific objectives and were flown in high-altitude polar orbits. Lunar Orbiter 4 photographed the entire nearside and 95 per cent of the farside, and Lunar Orbiter 5 completed the farside coverage.

On 23 August it took a picture that caused a sensation – the Earth hanging over the lunar limb. There was our planet, lonely and fragile, floating in the great cosmic dark. All known life was confined to a thin skin on that cloud-covered ball we could now all see. In the vastness of space it was an oasis. There are some who maintain that the strength of today's environmental movement stems from that picture. Strange that we had to go to the moon to find the Earth.

The Russians were still busy. Luna 11 entered lunar orbit on 28 August 1966, and Luna 12 achieved lunar orbit on 25 October 1966. These spacecrafts were equipped with a television system that obtained and transmitted photographs of the lunar surface but they were nowhere near as good as those from Lunar Orbiter. The balance between the superpowers was shifting.

Meanwhile, back in the USA Lunar Orbiter 2 was sent out on 18 November on an eight-day mission. After five days in orbit it was being prepared for its next mapping sequence when it turned to take a picture looking along the lunar surface. It had been looking at the ejecta ray systems around Copernicus; scientists were unsure if rayed areas were smoother or rougher than the surface they overlaid. The oblique image of the 100 km wide Copernicus was immediately hailed as the 'picture of the century'. In the foreground are the 300 m high mountains of the crater's central peak system. From what is understood about the dynamics of the impact that caused this crater about a billion years ago (young in terms of the moon's age), the rocks in those central peaks have been raised from far below the moon's surface. Analysing them would reveal much about the history and the origin of the moon. No wonder many astronauts looked at the picture, pointed at those peaks and said 'Land there.' Beyond the complex peak system are the ramparts of the crater, and beyond that the Carpathian Mountains.

Driven by the need to gather data for a manned landing on the moon, Surveyor 3 landed on 20 April, touching down near the crater Lansberg in Procellarum. It actually bounced several times before settling in a 200 m wide crater. It had a remote-controlled arm fitted with a scoop, and it found that the surface was soft with hard rock at a depth of 15 cm.

The next mission took place on 14 July 1967, when Surveyor 4 was launched from Cape Kennedy and aimed for a landing in the Central Bay. It was the second attempt to land a Surveyor in the centre of the moon and it failed. Whether the spacecraft crashed or landed intact will remain unknown until man sets foot in that region.

Surveyor 5, the first in the Surveyor series to carry a scientific instrument for analysis of the moon's surface, landed successfully on 10 September 1967 in the Sea of Tranquillity, not far from where men would walk less than two years later. During the two-week-long lunar day it operated perfectly and transmitted a total of 18,006 television pictures (more than the combined total from two previously successful Surveyors). The analysis indicated that the lunar surface near the spacecraft was composed of a basaltic rock similar to that found in Greenland.

Surveyor also achieved a minor first. Mission 6 soft-landed on 9 November in Sinus Medii, the Central Bay, and within a week had sent back nearly 10,000 images, as well as data on the composition of the lunar soil. Then its thrusters were fired once again, for just two and a half seconds, to lift it 4 m high and move it a few metres to one side; it was the first ever lift-off from another world. It landed upright and started taking pictures again 35 minutes later. Its stereo camera looked back at where it had rested and showed the imprint of the footpads at the original landing site – one small step for a machine . . .

With its mission goals now complete, Surveyor 7 was, like the last of the Rangers, given to the scientists. They chose to send it to one of the most spectacular objects on the moon, the crater with the magnificent ray system that so dominates the face of the full moon: Tycho in the Southern Highlands. On 10 January 1968 it touched down some 30 km from its rim. Scoops of the soil showed it to be like feldspar. This type of rock suggested that the entire surface had once been molten; the heavier elements seemed to have sunk out of a magma ocean, with the lighter elements floating to the surface to create a fine crystalline crust. It was a vital piece of evidence concerning the origin of the moon.

Of the seven Surveyors launched between 1966 and 1968, five landed successfully, giving the USA its own list of firsts. The first US soft-landing was Surveyor 1, from which came the first colour pictures from the surface of the moon. Surveyor 3 performed the first dig on an extraterrestrial body, Surveyor 5 carried out the first analysis of lunar soil and Surveyor 6 performed the first 'launch' from the moon. In total they transmitted almost 88,000 television pictures of the lunar surface and above all confirmed that the lunar surface could support a landing craft and that astronauts would be able to walk on the moon.

The Lunar Orbiter missions paved the way for the manned Apollo landings. They saved Apollo time and money; the cost of one Apollo manned mission to look for potential landing sites would have been far higher than the total cost of the whole Lunar Orbiter Programme. And there were those two famous pictures. Both were unplanned and unrelated to the Apollo manned lunar landing missions. They came two years before the first landing. Although they were not the first pictures of the Earth from space, they were the first to show Earth from the distance of its nearest neighbour.

The unmanned probes had shown the way. Man was to follow in their flightpath.

CHAPTER FIFTEEN

'It's Very Pretty Out Here'

There are many people who played a crucial role in landing a man on the moon. Neil Armstrong, the first person to walk on the moon, said he was at the top of a pyramid with hundreds of thousands of people supporting him. But Wernher von Braun has come to epitomize the story of how a great triumph of the free world emerged from the maw of a brutal dictator, how conflict and mistrust was turned into one of the greatest adventures of all time. If only it were that simple . . .

Wernher von Braun was born in Germany just before the First World War, son of Prussian aristocrats Baron Magnus and Baroness Emmy von Braun. The von Braun family had been famous since 1245 when they defended Prussia from Mongol invasion. From an early age he showed an interest in rockets. Germany's foremost rocket scientist was Hermann Oberth who had written a book, *Die Rakete zu den Planetenräumen* ('By Rocket into Planetary Space') in which he describes a rocket designed to go to the moon. A young von Braun read it and was captivated; he also read the science-fiction works of Jules Verne, especially 'From Earth to the moon'. He went to Berlin Technical University, and was already a member of an amateur rocketry club, the Raketenflugplatz Group. A year later Hitler came to power.

The parallels and the contrasts with Sergei Korolev are remarkable yet not exact. At NASA von Braun was a brilliant man among many brilliant men. In the USSR Korolev was the dominant personality; von Braun took his rocketry ideas to Colonel Becker, chief of ballistics and ammunition of the Reichswier. Perhaps to his surprise, Becker was impressed: 'We are greatly interested in rocketry, but there are a number of defects in the manner in which your organization is going about development. For our purposes there is too much showmanship. You would do better to concentrate on scientific data than to fire toy rockets.' Whereas von Braun wanted to use rockets for spaceflight, Becker wanted a long-range missile. Becker offered von Braun money to continue his work and von Braun, a civilian, found himself working in a secret army camp. Eventually he joined the army and worked under Captain Walter Dorenberger on liquid-fuel rocket engines. He later said: 'We needed money for our experiments, and since the army was willing to give us help, we didn't worry overmuch about the consequences in the distant future. We were interested in one thing, the exploration of space.' But, like Becker, Doren-berger wanted a missile rather than a spacecraft.

While 'working on his thesis', von Braun told his fellow amateur rocket enthusiasts that he had been conscripted into the army, and he started to lie to them about what he was really doing. The Army was soon the only organization developing rockets in Germany. Before long, Dorenberger needed a quieter and more isolated place for the rocket tests so they moved to a small fishing village on the Baltic sea called Peenemünde.

Peenemünde started echoing to the sound of rocket tests as the number of workers there grew. By 1944 they had a rocket they called the A-4, being mass-produced by slave labour. With the Germans losing the war, the military hierarchy changed its name to the V-2. On 8 September 1944 two V-2s were launched from a site near the Hague in Holland, aiming to hit a site about a mile from Waterloo Station, London. Instead they landed in Chiswick, killing two people. But von Braun told his staff: 'Let's not forget that this is the beginning of a new era, the era of rocket-powered flight. It seems that this is another demonstration of the sad fact that so often new developments get nowhere until they are first applied as weapons.' He later said, 'It behaved perfectly, but on the wrong planet.' But when they heard that the V-2 had hit London they drank champagne. 'Let's be honest about it. We were at war. Although we weren't Nazis, we still had a fatherland to fight for.'

It was soon obvious that Germany would lose the war. Just before the Americans captured the Nordhausen rocket factory several hundred scientists were escorted from Peenemünde under heavy German guard to Bavaria. When he got there von Braun ordered two men to find an abandoned mine in the Hartz Mountains and hide data about the rockets. A cave was found and several large boxes were buried. American intelligence heard about von Braun's whereabouts as they closed in on Bavaria. Dorenberger and von Braun knew their best chance of survival was to surrender to the Americans who would be interested in their work. Luckily the Americans were nearby.

Under the Yalta agreement, the Russians would occupy the region around Peenemünde. In order to prevent valuable rocket technology falling into Russian hands, the Americans packed away a hundred V-2s and shipped them to New Mexico only days before the Russians arrived. Von Braun and his team were moved to Fort Bliss, Texas. There they worked on rockets for the United States army, launching them at White Sands in New Mexico. A few years later they moved to the Redstone Arsenal near Huntsville, Alabama, where they built the monster rocket that took men to the moon.

In 1952 von Braun wrote an extremely influential article about spaceflight. In *Collier's magazine* he described the first lunar expedition. Due to land in 1977, he predicted, it would include fifty astronauts on a six-week visit to the Sinus Roris region. A year later von Braun, along with Fred Whipple and Willy Ley, wrote a book called *Conquest of the Moon*. They described a fifty-strong crew, showing that von Braun was influenced by the great naval expeditions of the past. When it really came to mount an expedition to the moon an army of people were involved but all but three stayed on the ground. Von Braun also wrote that television transmission between Earth and moon would be impractical. Sixteen years later Neil Armstrong's first footsteps were televised and seen by 500 million people.

Dr H. Percy Wilkins, the moon mapper we met earlier, read the article and was not impressed. He had his own ideas about a lunar expedition. He rejected the maria as landing sites, saying they 'are too open to be considered as really suitable sites. Why land on a congealed lava flow miles from any object of interest?' In the end that is just what America did.

If President Dwight D. Eisenhower had had his way, there might never have been a moon race at all; the Soviets would have had it all to themselves. He totally misjudged the mood of the nation after the shock of Sputnik 1. His standpoint was logical and technically correct, but he completely overlooked the political horror of the United States being seen to be inferior to the USSR in such a high-profile, futuristic endeavour. He consistently refused to approve space programmes justified on purely political grounds, including a $38 million manned mission around the moon proposed in December 1960. Eisenhower established a civilian space agency, the National Aeronautics and Space Administration (NASA), on 1 October 1958. Within seven days, NASA announced a man-in-space programme, Project Mercury. They were already talking about sending a man to the moon.

In 1960 John F. Kennedy, a Senator from Massachusetts, ran for president as the Democratic candidate, with Lyndon B. Johnson as his running mate. He said that the United States lagged far behind the Soviet Union in ICBM technology. In an election against Eisenhower's successor, Richard Nixon, Kennedy scraped through.

Kennedy was looking for something to make political capital

out of, and came to fix his attention on the moon. He was probably the most political person the moon had encountered since Langrenus had tried to save it for a Catholic Europe in the seventeenth century. At first Kennedy had little interest in the space programme. He was not a visionary with a great urge to explore the unknown; instead he was a consummate politician with the tricky task of maintaining American–Soviet relations and his own standing with the American people.

In his inaugural speech in January 1961 he appealed to Soviet premier Nikita Khrushchev, asking him to co-operate in exploring space. In his State of the Union address ten days later, he asked the Soviet Union 'to join us in preparation for probing the distant planets of Mars and Venus, probes which may some day unlock the deepest secrets of the universe.'

Then, just a few weeks later, on 12 April 1961, Soviet cosmonaut Yuri Gagarin became the first human in space, emphasizing how far the United States seemed to have fallen behind in the space race. Kennedy had to find a way to re-establish the nation's role as a world technological leader. Two days after the Gagarin flight he discussed the possibility of a lunar landing with James Webb, the head of NASA, but Webb's $20 billion estimate of the cost was too high. A few days later, during the Bay of Pigs invasion, Kennedy called Johnson, who chaired the National Aeronautics and Space Council. Kennedy asked: 'Do we have a chance of beating the Soviets by putting a laboratory in space, or by a trip around the moon, or by a rocket to go to the moon and back with a man? Is there any other space programme that promises dramatic results in which we could win?'

For two weeks Lyndon Johnson polled experts, just as he had done after Sputnik when he was majority leader of the House. NASA's deputy administrator Hugh Dryden said there was 'a chance for the US to be the first to land a man on the moon and return him to Earth if a determined national effort is made'.

Wernher von Braun, head of the big booster programme that would be needed for the lunar effort, added 'we have a sporting chance of sending a three-man crew around the moon ahead of the Soviets' and 'an excellent chance of beating the Soviets to the first landing of a crew on the moon.' With an all-out crash programme, he said the US could achieve a landing by 1967 or 1968. As always, von Braun was optimistic and grandiose.

With these discussions in mind, on 25 May 1961 Kennedy announced the goal of sending an American safely to the moon before the end of the decade:

> If we are to win the battle that is going on around the world between freedom and tyranny, if we are to win the battle for men's minds, the dramatic achievements in space which occurred in recent weeks should have made clear to us all, as did the Sputnik in 1957, the impact of this adventure on the minds of men everywhere who are attempting to make a determination of which road they should take.

He added: 'We go into space because whatever mankind must undertake, free men must fully share.' Then he said:

> I believe this Nation should commit itself to achieving the goal, before this decade is out, of landing a man on the moon and returning him safely to Earth. No single space project in this period will be more impressive to mankind, or more important for the long-range exploration of space; and none will be so difficult or expensive to accomplish.

Somewhere, listening to that speech, was the American who would be the first man on the moon. Project Apollo was born.

One of the critical early decisions NASA had to make was how to get to the moon. There were three basic approaches. The first was direct ascent. This involved using a very powerful rocket to go straight there. For a while this was considered by the Soviets but it had few advocates in the United States. The second was Earth–Orbit Rendezvous which involved the launching of various modules required for the moon trip into an orbit above the Earth, where they would rendezvous into a single system and be sent to the moon. The final choice was Lunar–Orbit Rendezvous. This involved putting the entire lunar spacecraft up in one launch. It would head to the moon, enter into orbit, and dispatch a small lander to the lunar surface. It was the simplest of the three methods, but since rendezvous was taking place in lunar, instead of Earth, orbit, there was no room for error or the crew could not get home. Von Braun wanted Earth–Orbit Rendezvous because it fitted in with his other plans for space exploration, providing a rationale for the space station he wanted to build. But no one else agreed and eventually he had to give in, admitting that further delay would jeopardize the president's timetable of reaching the moon before the decade was over.

Kennedy tried to back out of the deal more than once. The first time was when he had his first summit with Khrushchev in June 1961. Kennedy raised the question of going to the moon together but Khrushchev just did not believe that the Americans were serious about going to the moon. It was a big mistake on his part.

To gain experience, NASA devised two-man Project Gemini to build on the success of the one-man Project Mercury. One of its main tasks was to perfect techniques for rendezvous and docking but the two-man Gemini capsule would be inadequate for a lunar voyage. The Apollo spacecraft would be far more complex and, coupled with a lunar landing spacecraft, would need a far larger rocket to put it into space. That is where von Braun came in.

The Saturn 5, standing about 125 m tall, can claim to be the most complicated piece of machinery ever constructed. It had hundreds of thousands of parts, all with the same aim: to release sufficient energy to drive it and its payload upward, to take the astronauts to the moon. Its first stage generated 3.4 million kg of thrust from five massive engines. The second stage presented NASA engineers with enormous challenges and very nearly caused the lunar landing goal to be missed. It consisted of rocket engines burning liquid oxygen and liquid hydrogen. This stage could deliver about 450 million kg of thrust but it was always behind schedule. The third stage was an upgraded version of the smaller Saturn 1B rocket and had few problems.

But tragedy struck the programme on 27 January 1967. Three astronauts, 'Gus' Grissom, Edward White, and Roger Chaffee, were aboard a ground-based mock mission when, after several hours of work, a fire broke out in the spacecraft and the pure oxygen atmosphere. In a flash, flames engulfed the capsule and the astronauts died. The Apollo capsule had to be extensively redesigned and, while that undoubtedly contributed to the safety and eventual success of the Apollo mission, it also threatened Kennedy's timetable.

But if the Saturn rocket and the Apollo spacecraft were giving problems, the third part of the hardware for the moon landing, the Lunar Module (the part that descended to the moon and took off again), was the most serious worry. It was in reality two separate spacecraft: one for descent to the moon and one for ascent back to the Apollo Command Module. It was like no other manned spacecraft before as it only operated outside the Earth's atmosphere. It did not have to be aerodynamic or rugged enough to survive the rigours of re-entry. Thin foil made up its skin and it had no seats. Both engines had to work perfectly or the astronauts would not return home. The philosophy was that the rocket motor that would fire to get the astronauts off the moon had to be so simple that it could not fail.

For some, the most remarkable mission of Apollo was not the

actual landing on the moon. When Apollo 11 touched down in July 1969 two other missions had already been to within arm's reach of the moon's surface. For many it was Apollo 8 that was the most significant, the biggest single leap out into space. On 21 December 1968 man finally left the cradle of Earth. The Russian spaceflight pioneer Tsiolkovsky, who has a prominent far side crater named after him, once wrote that the Earth is the cradle of mankind, but that one cannot live in a cradle forever. Listening to the audiotapes of the Apollo 8 mission, one is struck by how matter of fact was the event. Ground Control and the astronauts talked of initiating 'TLI' (or Trans-Lunar Trajectory) and without comment or fanfare they just pressed the button and fired the engines. The third stage of the giant Saturn 5 rocket was re-ignited; and with the velocity it provided three men broke free of Earth's gravity for the first time and began a voyage to another world.

What would our moon mappers have said? How would Galileo or Hevelius have reacted to the news that mankind was orbiting the moon just a few kilometres above its craters, mountains and plains? Astronauts Borman, Lovell and Anders were the first to see beneath them a landscape like the aftermath of the final battle. Like pumice stone, they said. A great expanse of black and white. Well, they were astronauts not poets. Two more Apollo missions occurred before the climax of the programme, but they did little more than confirm that the time had come for a lunar landing.

Neil Armstrong and Buzz Aldrin were chosen to be the first almost by accident. In a roster of crew assignments drawn up before the date of the landing was decided they were given Apollo 11. By the time Apollo 8 had circled the moon it seemed likely that Apollo 11 would attempt the first landing. Armstrong believed the chances of a successful touchdown were only fifty-fifty and before launch, during a dinner with the head of NASA, the crew of Apollo 11 was given a unique promise. NASA's head Tom Paine said to them that if they failed to land then the next mission would be theirs as well, and so it would be until they were successful. I doubt that this promise would have been kept – the astronauts of subsequent missions may have had something to say about it.

Apollo 11 lifted off on 16 July 1969 and began the three-day trip to the moon. On the day of the planned landing, at mission control in Houston, Flight Controller Gene Kranz, who would oversee and orchestrate the landing, made a remarkable speech to his fellow controllers. The tape has been lost but he recalls what he said:

Hey gang, we're really going to go and land on the moon today. This is no bullshit, we're going to land on the moon. We're about to do something no one has ever done. Be aware that there is a lot of stuff that we don't know about the environment that we're ready to walk into, but be aware that I trust you implicitly. Be also aware that we're all human. So somewhere along the line, if we have a problem, be aware that I am here to take the heat for you. I know that we are working in an area of the unknown that has high risks. But we don't even think of tying this game, we think only to win. And I know you guys, if you've even got a few seconds to work your problem, we're going to win. So let's go have at it gang, and I'm going to be tagging up to you just like we did in the training runs. Forget all the people out there. What we're about to do now is just like we do it in training. And after we finish this sonofagun, we're going to go out and have a beer and say, 'Dammit, we really did something.'

True to Gene Kranz's word, at 4.18p.m. EST, after its abort alarms had been blazing, the spindly Lunar Module landed on the lunar surface while Michael Collins orbited overhead in the Apollo Command Module. Soon Armstrong set foot on the surface, telling millions who saw and heard him on Earth that it was 'one small step for man – one giant leap for mankind'. He later added an 'a', referring to 'one small step for a man', to clarify the first sentence delivered from the moon's surface. To be completely accurate, however, the first words spoken on the moon were 'contact light' and were said by Buzz Aldrin as probes jutting from the Lunar Module's legs touched the soil.

On the surface Armstrong commented:

> The surface is fine and powdery, I can pick it up loosely with my toe. It adheres in fine layers like powdered charcoal to the sole. I only go in a small fraction of an inch, maybe one eighth of an inch, but I can see the footprints of my boots and the treads in the fine, sandy particles.

A few moments later he reached down to a pocket just below the knee of his left leg and pulled out a telescopic rod with a scoop attached to one end. He began to scrape the surface, collecting what was called the 'contingency sample'. If for any reason Armstrong had to get back into the Lunar Module in a hurry he might not have time to collect any more moon rock. Eventually Armstrong and Aldrin collected about 40 kg of rock and soil samples. It was basalt-like, with breccia, a rock made of fragments of other rocks, glass, mineral grains. It also had a high titanium content, which nobody expected. Later analysis showed that the rocks were 3.7 billion years old but strangely the soil on top appeared to be even older, dating back 4.6 billion years, the age of the moon itself. Tiny white fragments in the breccia were part of the highlands. The soil was not related to the bedrock!

Armstrong gave his impressions: 'It has a stark beauty all of its own. It's like much of the high desert of the United States. It's different but it's very pretty out here.'

Soviet television did not broadcast live images of Armstrong on the moon and the Soviet daily *Pravda* carried only a brief mention of the historic walk on its front page. Inside, after an extensive article on twenty-five years of Polish socialism, it showed a fuzzy photo of Armstrong on the moon taken from a TV screen.

They left behind a seismometer and a laser reflector. The next day they launched back to the Apollo capsule orbiting overhead and began the return trip to Earth, splashing down in the Pacific on 24 July.

The first landing on the moon will be remembered long after most of the events of the twentieth century have been relegated to footnotes or completely forgotten. Yet why is it that my children have been taught in school about the voyages of Columbus and the travels of Marco Polo but not about Apollo? Sometimes I think the true significance of what happened has yet to sink in.

With the flight of Apollo 11 the United States and humanity touched greatness. At the time of the landing, Mission Control in Houston flashed the words of President Kennedy announcing the Apollo commitment on its big screen. Those phrases were followed with: 'TASK ACCOMPLISHED, July 1969'. Far away, at the Arlington National Cemetery, somebody quietly placed a note next to the eternal flame that flickers over President Kennedy's grave. It read simply, 'Mr President, the Eagle has landed.'

But after the triumphant return it was clear that for another president things were changing. At a celebration party President Nixon raised his glass and said, 'Here's to the Apollo programme. It's all over.'

CHAPTER SIXTEEN

How the Moon was Lost

Korolev was not the only designer of rockets and spacecraft in the Soviet Union; he had some co-operation and lots of competition from other groups. Vladimir Chelomei led one such group. He had developed military missiles but had no experience with rockets. However, Chelomei had cleverly hired Khrushchev's son, Sergei, giving him a great advantage in a political system where personal contacts were all-important. With Khrushchev's patronage, Chelomei soon had the biggest budget of all the Soviet bureaux and he was keen to take over Korolev's work. Furthermore, Chelomei found himself an extremely important ally when Valentin Glushko, the primary designer of Soviet rocket engines, allied his Gas Dynamics Laboratory with him, following a disagreement with Korolev.

Korolev and Glushko clashed bitterly over the new engines for the next generation of Soviet rockets but their conflict was also a battle for authority and perhaps something more personal. In the 1930s it was Glushko's evidence that had sent Korolev to the slave labour camp that almost cost him his life. Korolev had been a former deputy of Glushko's before becoming chief designer, and it is clear that Glushko resented him. This was a resentment that in no small measure contributed to the Soviet Union's failure to win the moon race.

In 1962 Khrushchev instructed Chelomei's group to prepare for a manned spacecraft intended for a flight around the moon. Landing on the moon was not a stated goal.

Korolev was by then working on his own large rocket, the N-series, to launch heavy unmanned and manned spacecraft to the moon and the planets beyond. He had started it in 1961 and he hoped it would be ready by 1965. But, according to his political masters, the aim of the N-series of rockets was not to go to the moon but to launch superbombs. What is more, Korolev's falling-out with Glushko meant he had to find another supplier of rocket engines. He had to use crude engines with little power, which meant that the final N1 version needed thirty such engines in its first stage to achieve sufficient power for a lunar mission. This was the reason why the project was doomed.

Korolev also needed a spacecraft. The one that Gagarin had used was too small to carry the supplies and equipment needed for lunar flight. So he conceived of the Soyuz – basically the same spacecraft that still flies today. He also had plans for a manned lunar landing craft that would have ferried cosmonauts between the lunar surface and a Soyuz craft in orbit around the moon. But, although this approach was eventually adopted by the Americans for good reasons, Korolev's lunar plans were rejected in favour of Chelomei's.

Korolev lobbied hard to get involved in the manned circumlunar mission but that too was refused. He knew time was running out; their head-start over the Americans was dwindling. It was more than three years after Kennedy's speech that the Central Committee finally passed a decree to put a single cosmonaut on the moon in 1967–68, before the US. In retrospect it was far too late, but for a while it seemed that the Russians might just stand a chance of winning the moon race. The same day that the decree was passed, the Chelomei bureau received approval to build a spacecraft, called the LK-1, to send two cosmonauts on a mission around the moon by October 1967, the fiftieth anniversary of the Bolshevik Revolution.

By late 1964, three Soviet design bureaux had proposals for a manned landing on the moon and each thought their idea was the best. Chelomei's lunar landing spaceship was based on his LK-1

The first photograph taken by a man on the moon. Neil Armstrong took this picture just after he had stepped from the Lunar Module's footpad into the lunar surface (*NASA*).

Back on earth with the moon rock. Buzz Aldrin, Michael Collins and Neil Armstrong, the crew of Apollo 11 (*NASA*).

Magnificent desolation. Man's last outpost on the moon. The landing site of Apollo 17 among the highland and valley of Taurus-Littrow. Mankind left the moon on 14 December 1972 (*NASA*).

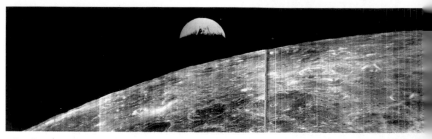

The first Earthrise ever seen over the moon as seen from Lunar Orbiter 1, August 1966 (*NASA*).

An Earthrise over the moon as seen from Apollo 8's Command Module, 22 December 1968 (*NASA*).

lunar eclipse in three exposures showing how the moon turns red when within the
Earth's shadow (*Stephen Barnes*).

The craters Aristarchus (the brightest crater on the moon), Herodotus and Schroter's
Valley as seen from Apollo 15. This region is the site of many strange glows, or
Transient Lunar Phenomena (*NASA*).

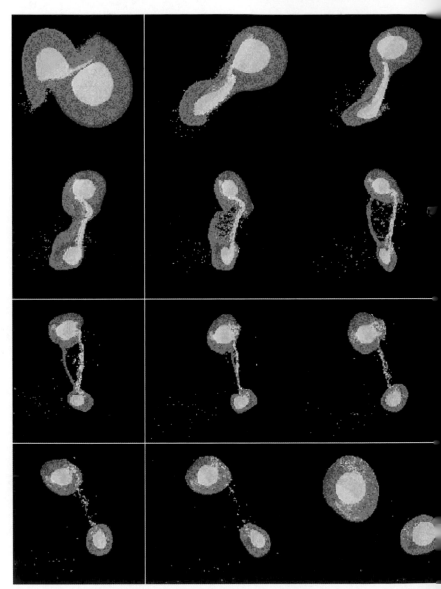

A series of computer simulations of the formation of the moon. At the top left the Earth Mark One and the impactor have just collided. Subsequent images show how the encounter might have progressed with streams of debris between the two world Eventually the Earth Mark Two and the moon become separate worlds (*Al Cameron*)

circumlunar spacecraft. It would place two cosmonauts on the moon with no need for any spacecraft rendezvous in Earth or lunar orbit. The big problem was that this spacecraft would need to be very heavy, since it would have to carry a lot of fuel and would require a very powerful booster to get it into space.

Korolev's group wanted to use the 'lunar orbit rendezvous' technique that the Americans were considering. To save weight, the heavy Soyuz mothercraft would be left in lunar orbit while a small one-man lander would descend to the lunar surface. Korolev's craft would require the mighty N-1 to launch it, something that one engineer said was 'on the edge of science fiction'.

But they still had a lead, as demonstrated on 18 March 1965, when Alexei Leonov became the first man to perform a space-walk. But take a good look at Leonov's spacesuit. It was over-engineered for the task. We now know that his suit was a prototype for an eventual 'moonsuit'. But the mission was fraught with danger and it was to be the last Soviet manned flight for almost two years. Meanwhile, the Soviet Union had finally made preliminary decisions as to how it would send men to the moon. The goal was now a first manned landing in 1968, and twenty-two new cosmonauts were recruited in October 1965.

In order to increase safety, it was decided to launch an unmanned precursor mission to the proposed site of the first manned landing that would leave a back-up capsule on the lunar surface in case the cosmonaut's original vehicle was damaged during landing. The first Soviet moon landing would thus consist of two launches – one unmanned precursor flight and one manned mission to the same site.

But the shifting tides of politics hampered long-term plans and those who live by the sword can also die by it. The Chelomei bureau fell from favour after Khrushchev was ousted from power; its contract for the circumlunar spacecraft was cancelled despite reports that many lunar landing capsules were being made. There was to be a new plan. Instead they would use Chelomei's new UR-500K booster (eventually called the Proton), supplemented by a Korolev upper stage being developed for the N1 rocket and a stripped-down version of the Soyuz spacecraft. Once again the Soviets just could not make up their minds about how to mount a lunar mission. Partly because of this, the moon was beginning to slip from their grasp.

Meanwhile the Luna soft-landing probes were also having serious technical problems. Luna 8 became the eighth straight failure in December 1965 and the entire series of unmanned lunar probes was nearly cancelled. It was a desperate time because Luna 8 was the first lunar probe to be constructed by the Babakin bureau. This had been established to manage unmanned lunar probes because Korolev was too busy with the manned lunar missions. Korolev kept the programme going but for him time was running out.

Did Korolev realize that, after years of delays, sloppy sub-contractors, underfunding, inter-bureau battles and one change of plan after another, things might be getting a little better at last? Just as the Soviet effort was picking up speed, confidence and a sense of direction, disaster struck.

Korolev had to have minor surgery to remove polyps from his rectum. It was a straightforward procedure and he had one of the best surgeons to perform it. But Korolev's general health was poor, probably as the result of years of stress following his time in the gulags. He started to haemorrhage on the operating table and it seemed there was nothing the surgeon could do. Frantic efforts to stop the bleeding revealed an unsuspected large cancerous tumour. Korolev never regained consciousness. Had he survived the operation, he would probably have had only a few months at most to live anyway. But it was tragic that he would never know who won the race to the moon.

He was succeeded by Vasili Mishin, who had worked with him since the end of the Second World War. But Mishin had neither Korolev's ability to lead nor his political clout. He was out of his depth in government circles and ineffective in doing battle with Chelomei and Glushko (who had not given up hope that their own moon ideas might be sanctioned). But the Soviets still managed to score two more impressive 'firsts' before the American moon programme finally moved ahead in 1967.

Two weeks after Korolev's death, Luna 9 finally became the first spacecraft to manage a soft landing on the moon and soon afterwards Luna 10 went into orbit. But Luna 10 was nowhere near as sophisticated as the American Lunar Orbiters. The Surveyor and Lunar Orbiter probes may have been second to the moon, but they were far more advanced and quickly completed ten successful missions to the moon in fifteen months. The Americans were catching up. Despite opposition in Congress and the cost of the Vietnam War, NASA spent almost $3 billion on the Apollo project in 1966 (far, far more than the Soviets could afford) and the giant Saturn 5 rocket was ready for tests in May 1966. In manned spaceflight, the Gemini spacecraft had been a success. Gemini 8 achieved the crucial first space docking in March 1966.

Without Korolev, the Soviet space effort was falling apart. He had barely kept it on track when he was alive but now he was gone they had to scramble just to keep pace. An important manned flight was delayed for two months, then cancelled within weeks of its planned lift-off in May 1966. The rest of the programme was cancelled to save time and to prepare for the first flight of the new Soyuz spacecraft. Chelomei was now openly challenging Mishin's authority as the leader of the lunar programme.

Their centrepiece had become the Soyuz spacecraft but, like

Apollo, it suffered serious development problems and was behind schedule. The first three unmanned test missions, launched between November 1966 and February 1967, all failed. But the new Soviet Premier Leonid Brezhnev demanded a first flight in April to test the new lunar spacesuits during a spacewalk as well as to perform the first-ever docking between two Soviet spacecraft. In the past the USSR had got away with flying three cosmonauts in a one-man capsule minus emergency equipment, having been forced to do so by Premier Khrushchev. This time political interference would cost a cosmonaut his life.

There exists a film of veteran cosmonaut Vladimir Komarov being driven to the launch pad on a bus, surrounded by his fellow cosmonauts. They are trying to be cheerful but his stern face shows without question just what he thought of his forthcoming mission. Soyuz 1 blasted off on 15 April. A record 203 faults had been detected in the spacecraft during the final tests. Plagued by serious problems in space, Komarov was commanded to return after just one day, and the launch of Soyuz 2 (carrying three more cosmonauts) was quickly cancelled. Komarov's spacecraft began tumbling wildly after one solar panel failed to deploy but miraculously survived the atmosphere re-entry. Then the parachutes failed to deploy and the capsule hit the ground at 600 km per hour. What remained of Komarov was buried in the Kremlin wall two days later. The accident set the Soyuz programme back two years. The moon seemed to be getting ever further away.

The Soviets planned to launch the lunar spacecraft unmanned into Earth orbit and send up its two-man crew on a Soyuz spacecraft instead. Both spacecraft would have docked in Earth orbit, and the crew would have spacewalked to the other craft. The Soyuz would return to Earth unmanned while the lunar craft blasted towards the moon. After two partly successful unmanned launches in March and April the Soviets decided to scrap this plan. The original goal of a manned circumlunar flight to commemorate the fiftieth anniversary of the Bolshevik Revolution had to be abandoned. In 1967, the year the Americans finally pulled ahead, the Soviets pressed on, knowing that the Americans would probably achieve the first lunar landing. But they had one more plan, as always. A manned circumlunar flight, before the Americans, would steal at least some of Apollo's thunder.

For those who could interpret them, the Soviets' intentions were revealed in March 1968 when a spacecraft called Zond-4, to conceal its true purpose, was placed in an elliptical orbit around the moon. Zond-4 had to be destroyed after a technical error. Another attempt in April did not even make it to Earth orbit and on 15 July a lunar spacecraft launch had to be cancelled when engineers over-pressurized the fourth stage oxidizer tank during testing. The explosion killed three workers. Such accidents became increasingly common in 1967–69, undoubtedly because overworked engineers were under great pressure to catch up with the Americans. But the cosmonauts training for moon flights still wanted to fly.

Meanwhile, in the United States, the redesigned Apollo spacecraft and its giant Saturn 5 carrier rocket were now ready for manned flight. On 19 August NASA shocked the Russians by announcing a revised Apollo schedule which included reassigning Apollo 8 as a manned flight to lunar orbit in December 1968, provided the forthcoming maiden flight, Apollo 7 in Earth orbit, was successful. Mishin must have thought it foolhardy to send a spacecraft on a moon flight on only its second mission. The Soviet goal had been two completely successful unmanned lunar craft tests, followed by a manned circumlunar flight in January 1969 at the earliest. Now they had little choice but to move it to December 1968 instead.

The moon race was finally decided in the autumn of 1968. First off the pad was the unmanned Zond-5 in September. It took the first living creatures to the moon, turtles and flies. It flew around the moon and caused a sensation when Jodrell Bank picked up a human voice from it! But it was only a tape-recorded experiment to test the communications system. The mission went well and a ship from the Soviet Navy picked up the capsule. The turtles and flies had survived. The relieved Russians released information which seemed to confirm NASA's worst fears. The Zond flights were for testing and development of an automatic version of a manned lunar spaceship.

On 11 October, three astronauts put the new Apollo 7 through its paces during an eleven-day mission in Earth orbit. The mission went well and Apollo 8 received the go-ahead for a trip around the moon. A day later the Soviets launched their first manned Soyuz flight since the Komarov tragedy when Soyuz 3 carried out docking manoeuvres with the unmanned Soyuz 2. Everything now depended on the Zond-6 flight in November. If it was a complete success there was still a small chance that the next Soviet flight to the moon in December would be manned.

Zond-6 was launched safely on 10 November and flew past the moon three days later. On its way back to Earth all seemed to be well. The Soviets knew that any manned follow-up would be a severe risk but, with cosmonauts willing to take that risk and with such a prize at stake, there were many who were ready to forge ahead come what may. But Zond-6's landing went totally wrong. The spacecraft depressurized, killing all the turtles and flies that had been placed on board, and crashed onto Soviet soil.

Officials at NASA were nervous, and some feared they might be upstaged as they prepared the Apollo 8 lunar orbit spacecraft in December. Celestial mechanics dictated that the Soviets would be able to launch a lunar spacecraft two weeks before the US. And many Soviet cosmonauts wanted to try, whatever the risks. They sent a letter to the Politburo asking for permission to launch a manned mission to the moon and some of them travelled to the

Baikonur Cosmodrome to be ready to fly at short notice. But the Kremlin never replied and two weeks later Apollo 8 and its crew of three (Frank Borman, Jim Lovell and Bill Anders) became the first men to fly around the moon.

Beaten at the only lunar goal they could possibly have achieved, the Soviet manned lunar project ceased to be a high priority. A few more test missions took place but only Zond-7 (launched the month after the Apollo 11 moon landing) was a success, passing within 1,500 km of the moon before landing safely back on earth. Encouraged by this, three months later the Soviets tested a man-rated mooncraft on an unmanned test flight but the launch ended in yet another failure. One step forward, followed by one step back. It had been the same story all along. Zond-8 ended the lunar flyby programme by making an unplanned ballistic re-entry into the Indian Ocean after an attitude sensor failed.

Soviet attention now turned to the N1 superbooster but it was all too little, too late. In February 1967 the Soviet government finally committed significant funds to it but, given its technical complexity and design compromises, it could not possibly have been ready in time. Since March 1968, cosmonauts had been training for a moon landing. At their Star City training base near Moscow they had a moonwalk simulator installed in the gymnasium and the cosmonauts practised lunar landings with a modified version of the Mi-8 helicopter. But they still had no reliable lunar spacecraft to fly.

In January 1969 the decision was taken to test the N1 by launching an unmanned lunar craft, to perform high-resolution reconnaissance of potential landing sites from lunar orbit. The first landing was slated for eighteen months' time and was to be commanded by the Voskhod 2 veteran, Alexei Leonov, with Oleg Makarov serving as the pilot in lunar orbit.

The Soviets had one last hope: that the Apollo programme

would be delayed long enough to permit a Soviet cosmonaut to get to the moon first. But, with the Apollo 8 circumlunar mission, it was clear that the United States would almost certainly achieve a landing in 1969. The Soviets were forced to prepare for the worst.

One way for the USSR to save face would be if they could return a small amount of lunar soil to Earth automatically. That way they could say that they were being driven by science and would not risk the lives of cosmonauts to bring back a few rocks when an unmanned spacecraft could do the job just as well. So, when it was obvious they would lose the race, the Soviet government asked the Babakin research bureau to revive one of their earlier proposals. Such a mission had been proposed in 1966 or 1967 but had been discounted, another lost opportunity. It was another sign that the Soviet moon effort lacked long-term vision and cohesion.

Although they had lost the race to the moon the Soviets did not want to abandon manned spaceflight, it was too much a source of national pride and prestige. So they changed the rules. Chelomei's idea of a military space station was approved and for a while he even thought some of the hardware he had designed for the doomed moon landing might be adapted and augmented with a new nuclear-powered rocket to go on a manned Mars flyby. Once again, such thinking revealed fault lines in Soviet space thinking. The Mars idea was clearly a no-hoper, given any realistic assessment of the technology.

But something seemed to be working. In January 1969 two manned Soyuz flights finally achieved the goals of the failed Soyuz 1/2 mission almost two years earlier. Soyuz 4 was launched on 14 January 1969, with Vladimir Shalatov on board; this was followed on 15 January by Soyuz 5, carrying three more cosmonauts. They tested the new moonsuits by performing a spacewalk to Soyuz 4. The Soviets claimed the link-up was the 'world's first space station' and they lied, saying that they had no plans to go to the moon.

It might have worked, but luck had long since abandoned them. In February 1969 the Soviets were ready to test their various lunar-landing spacecraft for the first time. The first N1 booster roared to life and began to lumber upward. But, just over a minute after launch, a leaking fuel pipe started a fire at the rear of the first stage and the flight was doomed. It was later suspected that vibrations from the first stage's thirty engines had damaged the rocket. The Soviets were not running out of time any more; they were beaten. The moon belonged to the Americans.

Apollo 9 astronauts successfully tested the Lunar Module, the craft that would touch down on the moon's surface, in Earth orbit one month after the N1 disaster. And two months later the crew of Apollo 10 ventured to within 15 km of the lunar surface in a dress rehearsal of the Apollo 11 landing mission. Nothing the Soviets could do could match that.

Most Soviet analysts and engineers knew they were beaten but they did not give up. Perhaps a miracle would happen and Apollo would fail so badly that the entire US moon effort would be put on hold, just as the Soyuz programme had been delayed by two years after Komarov's death. But it must have seemed to them that nothing would go right. The failure they experienced reflected their desperation and the fact that the Soviet moon effort was fundamentally out of control. One of their most desperate plans was to have a sample of lunar soil brought back to Earth before the first Apollo moon landing. That would go some way, they thought, towards taking the shine off the American triumph. But two missions to return lunar samples failed to reach Earth orbit in April and June.

After some changes, a second N1 launch was attempted on 3 July but it lasted just nine seconds before it exploded. Their last hope to upstage the Americans was a mission called Luna 15.

Luna 15 was the sub-plot to the Apollo 11 landing. Launched three days after Apollo 11, it reached lunar orbit safely. Jodrell Bank analysed its signals and said they were like nothing ever seen before. After fifty-two orbits it fired its rockets and began its descent to the surface. As it headed for a landing in Mare Crisium it seems that its landing systems failed and it smashed into the moon. The same day, on 20 July, Neil Armstrong became the first man to walk on the moon. It is believed that Luna 15 was an attempt to automatically bring back some lunar rocks. But even if it had worked it would not have got back to Earth until a day after the Apollo 11 crew. It would have been a footnote to history. The Russians did manage this task the following year with Luna 16.

It was going to take at least two years to repair the N1 launch pads following the explosion. Although some wanted to cancel all efforts regarding the moon, Mishin would not give up while he still had the support of the Politburo. Using the N1 idea, work began on a new manned landing concept on the premise that if they were not first to the moon they could still be the most impressive – perhaps they could stay on the moon longer than the two or three days Apollo could manage?

But the successes they had were unmanned. In September 1970 they managed to bring back a few grams of soil from the Sea of Fertility and Luna 17 landed the first successful rover on the moon. The vehicle, called Lunokhod 1, lasted nine months on the lunar surface and travelled almost 11 km.

The USSR claimed that the unmanned Luna sample retrievers were ten times cheaper than Apollo and far less risky than a manned mission. These were valid arguments but, rather hypo-critically, behind the scenes they were ready to try a manned mission again. Although their lunar spacecraft was tested secretly under the Cosmos label western observers suspected a link with the manned space programme. Soon the lunar lander was declared ready for manned flight. In December 1970, Cosmos 382 successfully tested the rocket that would be used by the mothercraft during lunar orbit insertion and the descent to the surface. Before long, they were ready to fly the N1 again. As three cosmonauts flew overhead in the new Salyut space station they launched another N1 on 27 June 1971.

But the curse struck again. Soon after lift-off the rocket twisted, causing the support structure between the second and third stages to fracture. The third stage and lunar spacecraft complex toppled over, crashing near the launch pad, while the rest of the N1 crashed 20 km downrange. To many engineers, even those who were passionately committed to the programme, this must have seemed like the end. But no. Mishin presented a new plan to the Council of Chief Designers, who approved it. It envisioned two N1 rockets with new high-energy upper stages placing a large lunar lander spacecraft into lunar orbit. The second N1 would deliver a three-man lunar craft into lunar orbit where both payloads would dock and descend together to the lunar surface. Two cosmonauts would spend up to a month on the surface, using a Soyuz capsule for the return to Earth. It sounded over-ambitious and impractical, but they went for it.

Extensively modified since its last failure, the fourth N1 rocket blasted off from pad number two at Baikonur early in the morning on 23 November 1972. All went well for 90 seconds until an oxygen fuel line broke. A fire broke out, engines started to explode one by one, the escape rocket pulled the payload, an unmanned lunar orbiter, away from the rocket, which was then blown up. Surely, this had to be the end of the manned moon effort? In January 1973 Luna 21 landed, carrying the Lunokhod 2 rover, and in May the following year Luna 22 was launched to carry out a survey mission from lunar orbit. Two further unmanned lunar missions failed.

But Mishin pushed for one last chance. Two new N1s were

constructed, with the first set for an August 1974 launch. Their purpose was now to fly the entire moon mission in an unmanned mode, including a lunar landing. If it worked there were plans to put a Soviet cosmonaut on the moon. More N1s were on the drawing board as part of a rejuvenated series of missions but Mishin's always scarce supply of luck had run out. In May 1974 he was dismissed and replaced by Valentin Glushko, Korolev's old enemy. Within days, Glushko suspended the lunar programme, instead presenting his own plans for a lunar colony. For the next few years he worked on an entirely new heavy-lift rocket called Vulkan that would have used oxygen and hydrogen fuel just as Korolev had wanted in 1962. He planned a large manned lunar rover that would have carried cosmonauts across the lunar surface. But his plans were opposed by Mstislav Keldysh of the Academy of Sciences who correctly said they were expensive and premature and that neither the government nor the military were interested. Both regarded the new American Space Shuttle as a bigger threat.

Glushko was ordered to plan a similar Soviet space shuttle and all moon work ceased. His Vulkan booster became the Energia booster and would be used to launch the Soviet shuttle. Both of those programmes were to become disasters in their own right. The remaining six N1s were destroyed. Luna 24, the final Soviet lunar probe, departed for the moon in October 1976.

Fragments of the superbooster were scavenged and used as makeshift hangars and storage sheds at the Baikonur Cosmodrome where many can still be seen today. The launch pads and rocket assembly buildings were converted to support Glushko's ill-fated Energia superbooster programme which only made two flights. But many of the N1's rocket engines survived and in 1996 they were sold to two American companies to be used on the first stage of new reusable spacecraft. Perhaps, many years after they were designed, they may help something be delivered into space.

Four surviving lunar landers ended up in museums or space engineering institutes, where today they are a historical curiosity. One friend of mine, who saw one in the basement of the Moscow Aviation Institute, said he was glad it wasn't used as he considered it a deathtrap. Mishin was also sent to lecture at the Moscow Aviation Institute and, following Glushko's death in 1989 and *glasnost*, he started to tell his story.

One major reason why the Soviet space programme failed was lack of money. It is estimated that the Soviets spent only $4.5 billion on their manned moon programme, compared to Apollo's $24 billion. The other reasons were the lack of co-operation and duplication between design bureaux, poor management and the failure to grasp the significance of President Kennedy's challenge. There was also a lack of proper ground-testing of rockets and other equipment. The technical reason why the N1 failed was the imbalance across its thirty first-stage rocket engines. They were never tested together outside a launch; to save money and time a test stand was never built. And even if it had worked, it would almost certainly have been too late.

But look at what they *did* achieve: the first probe to reach the moon; the first images of its unseen far side; the first soft-landing and pictures from the surface; the first probe to orbit it; the first living creatures to fly around it; the first and so far only automated sample return; and the first automatic rovers.

But they could have put a man on the moon. Alexie Leonov could have been better known than Neil Armstrong if they had formulated a good plan and stuck to it. History could have been different.

The story has a sour end. Years later Mishin was still bitter about what had happened. In the new open era he admitted that they had made mistakes and he resented being airbrushed out of photos in the 1970s when the Soviets were denying that they ever intended to put a man on the moon. It was not a fair race he says, adding that the Americans were richer and the USSR had been weakened by the fight against German fascism as well as by the cost of the arms race. Surprisingly, he also says that as soon as they knew the Americans were in the moon race they realized they could not win. This is rewriting history.

Today Alexei Leonov has on his office wall a small USSR flag as well as a matching USA one. They were taken to the moon on the Apollo 11 mission. He could have been the first man on the moon, but now he sees things differently. He does not agree that the USSR did not have enough money. He says Mishin misspent it and the failure to land on the moon was Mishin's mistake. 'We had everything we needed to fly around the moon,' says Leonov. 'We had the rockets, the space ship, the crew was ready, but we didn't have Korolev. But even with Korolev we would not have beaten the Americans to be first on the moon.' In response Mishin calls Leonov a mouse who understands nothing. It is a sad and undignified end to the Soviet attempt to land a cosmonaut on the moon.

Although Apollo 11 had returned from the moon to a tremendous welcome and many future landings were planned, President Nixon said it was all over and in a way he was right. Having achieved a manned landing, many couldn't see what else there was to do. You wouldn't ask Lindbergh to fly the Atlantic again, it was said. But NASA had enough hardware for nine more landings, leading up to a grand finale. This was to be Apollo 20, a landing in the dramatic Copernicus crater, on that central peak in that spectacular Lunar Orbiter photograph.

It didn't help that it looked easier than it was. Months later Apollo 12 descended into the Ocean of Storms and when Dick Conrad stood on the surface he looked into the mid-distance. There, 200 m away, on the slope of an ancient crater was Surveyor 3 which had landed two and a half years earlier.

He walked over to Surveyor 3 and removed a few pieces of it for analysis to see how they had stood up to over two years on the lunar surface. Upon its return, a small colony of bacteria, only 50–100 of them, were found nestling on the inside of Surveyor's camera in some polyurethane foam. In the lab they grew and multiplied when placed on a nutrient solution. They were sent to the Communicable Disease Center in Atlanta where they were identified as *Streptococcus mitis*, a common harmless bacteria from the nose, mouth and throat in humans. Were these tiny creatures the first lunar colonists and how had they survived nearly three years on the moon?

Today scientists appreciate that life can survive in very hostile conditions and their study of such organisms, termed extremophiles, who live in the mouths of volcanoes, in the polar ice and many kilometres under the ground, has told them much about life itself. Perhaps these bacteria were the most extreme extremophiles yet found? Alas, many scientists today do not think so. From their standpoint, looking back to the previous generation of less than perfect clean room technology, they generally believe that the bacteria are contamination that never left Earth.

The basalts of Apollo 12 were lower in titanium than those of Tranquillity base and were 500 million years younger. This suggested that Mare did not erupt from a single massive eruption but were formed over a considerable length of time. Fragments of highland rock in the Apollo 12 breccias (rocks made up of several rocks) were different from those of Apollo 11. Evidently the highlands varied in composition from place to place. There was a strange enrichment in certain elements – potassium and phosphorus. The material was given the name KREEP, an acronym made from the chemical symbols for potassium (K), rare earth elements (REE) and phosphor (P). And it was an important clue to the formation of the moon's crust.

But when Apollo 12 returned Apollo 20 had been cancelled and 18 and 19 looked uncertain.

Apollo 13 limped back to Earth, having suffered an explosion that destroyed all hopes of a landing. Until that drama, public interest in the mission was low. But keeping the crew alive for 87 hours afterwards in their thin flight-suits with the interior temperature dropping to that of a refrigerator; with their fatigue and lack of sleep; and seeing them through the fiery re-entry – that was a tour de force that gripped the world. But when they returned the White House let it be known that henceforth space exploration would no longer hold such a high position in the national list of priorities.

Apollo was wound down. Two more moon landings were cancelled. For those back on Earth the desolate moon held no fascination any more. The Stars and Stripes had been planted on its barren plains, the Soviets beaten and now there were other things on people's minds. Nixon was reducing America's global responsibilities as it faced new limits on its resources and will. The 'pay any price, bear any burden' attitude of Kennedy and Johnson had gone. Inflation was raging unchecked. The head of NASA, Tom Paine, resigned. The USSR failed to grasp the moon, the USA abandoned it.

Apollo 14 was redirected to the Fra Mauro site which was on a blanket of debris thrown across the moon by the titanic impact of the Imbrium basin. It carried small explosive charges they used to seismically probe the subsurface. The astronauts walked 3 km to collect the ejecta from Cone crater, but they walked past it without realizing. They became lost and disoriented; it was difficult to judge the distance of features in the airless environment with its lack of distance perspective. Subsequent crews needed a rover with a computer to keep track of where they were. Apollo 14 found some of the most complex rocks ever returned from the moon, all breccias including some containing breccias from previous events. All were enriched in the strange KREEP chemicals. The breccias showed that lunar volcanism began early in the moon's history. Tiny pieces of basalt that were 4.2 billion years old, nearly as old as the crust itself, were found in the breccias.

Harrison Schmitt, a geologist trained as an astronaut, considered the idea of landing on the moon's far side. He described himself as a member of a 'lunar mafia' at NASA's Manned Spacecraft Center in Houston. They met in each other's apartments over beer and popcorn to talk about ways to modify the Apollo moon missions so that they could produce more science. According to Schmitt, it was this group that persuaded NASA to alter the Apollo 10 launch date by a day so that it flew over regions of the moon that were not photographed by the Apollo 8 mission. One of the new areas that had been photographed included the Apollo 11 landing site on the Sea of Tranquillity. But their most ambitious idea was to send geologist Schmitt to Tsiolkovsky crater on the lunar far side. Schmitt was scheduled to land on the moon with Apollo 18.

But when Apollos 15 and 19 were cancelled and the remaining Apollo missions renumbered, Schmitt was moved to Apollo 17. Schmitt again proposed Tsiolkovsky as a landing spot, saying it was an 'end of the beginning'. Some planning for the expedition took place. There would be three traverses near dark-floored Tsiolkovsky's central peak and continuous communication would be possible with a communications satellite positioned in a so-called halo orbit at the Lagrange-2 point, 64,500 km behind the moon. But NASA planners considered that being out of direct line-of-sight radio contact with the Earth was too risky.

With mission 15 the Apollo programme really got into its stride. It landed near a vast chasm in the lunar surface called Hadley Rille. Hadley Rille and the towering Apennine Mountains, one of the steepest and highest mountain ranges on the moon, make up the rim of the Imbrium impact basin. Hadley is a huge chasm, 900 m wide and 2,000 m deep, that winds across the Mare surface bordering the mountains. Apollo 15 brought back breccias and basalts, and a strange emerald green glass was discovered scattered around the site (a deposit from a volcanic eruption 3 billion years before). A large ridge called Silver Spur showed a layered structure (ancient, deeply buried layers of rock), testimony to the lava filling of the Imbrium basin.

During a moonwalk David Scott saw a small white rock which he immediately recognized as anorthosite, part of the moon's primordial crust, the so-called, 'genesis rock', 4.5 billion years old.

Apollo 16 touched down in April of 1972 in the central highlands near the ancient crater Descartes. Here they found many kinds of breccias instead of the ancient volcanic rocks that had been expected. The highlands, it seemed, were a geological patchwork quilt.

Apollo 17 landed in a steep walled canyon on the rim of the ancient Serenitatis basin where lavas had flooded a mountain valley. The astronauts travelled 30 km and explored for over 25 hours, collecting more than 120 kg of rocks. To this day, three of the core drillings that Apollo 17 returned to the Earth remain unopened. They sampled giant boulders that had rolled down mountainsides, possibly after the formation of Tycho over 2,200 km away. They found an orange soil that was a type of glass, formed in an old volcanic eruption 3.6 billion years ago. There were lavas in the valley, basalts from many different flows, rich in titanium. They also looked at the melt-sheet formed during the impact of the Serenitatis basin. And the seismic experiments they left behind told us that the moon has an aluminium-rich crust about 60 km thick, below which is an iron and magnesium-rich mantle.

And then it was over. The cold grey moon was alone again. One flight controller back on Earth remarked that it must have felt the same when they finished the Pyramids.

Then the great adventure ended. And, looking back, we are left with the feeling that we did not know what we had until it was gone. Many, even today, haven't truly comprehended the historic nature of our first journeys to another world. It was an undertaking as heroic and as perilous as any in history. No other explorer, no Jason, Marco Polo or Columbus, no Vasco da Gama, no Cook, Amundsen or Hillary, can match the voyages to the moon.

But, apart from history, what else did Apollo leave us? It inspired a generation to become involved in a grand engineering feat which cross-fertilized many other areas of American industry. Microelectronics, computers, avionics, advanced materials all benefited from Apollo. Indeed, extraordinary manufacturing proc esses had to be developed to produce the mighty Saturn 5 rocket without which the moonflights would have been impossible. Apollo, more than any other space project, showed us where we live in the universe and gave us a global ecological awareness that lives on today. Of course Apollo also gave us the moon.

Thanks to Apollo, we know more about the moon than we do about any other object in space, with the exception of our own planet. We have the testimonies of those who went there, and what tales they are. We have over 2,000 samples from nine sites: 382 kg from six Apollo landings as well as 0.3 kg from three Soviet automated sample return probes. The samples tell us that the moon is rich in minerals and that there is plenty to do when we return.

CHAPTER SEVENTEEN

Our Accidental Moon

There was a time when the Earth was alone in space but it was not our Earth. Without the moon our world would not have developed the way it did. The Indians of North America have a saying, 'No moon, no man', and in a way they are right. The Earth, the moon and mankind are bound together in deep ways.

It took the secrets held in moon rocks to reveal the moon's surprising and spectacular birth. When the precious cache of rocks was brought back from the moon their analysis showed that all the theories about the moon's origin were wrong.

During the first hundred million years of the life of our solar system the sun had an unruly empire. The formation of the planets was at times a gentle process and at others an act of raw violence. At one stage there were huge rocky proto-planets, hundreds of kilometres in diameter, moving in jumbled orbits that intersected one another. Titanic collisions were inevitable.

I will call one of these worlds the Earth Mark One for reasons that will become apparent. It was smaller than the Earth is today and it was a very different world. Earth Mark One was suffering from a constant bombardment of rocky debris that melted its surface as it swept up leftovers from the formation of the planets. As we shall see, the Earth Mark One is not our world and probably could never have been. We live on Earth Mark Two. To tell the story of the moon's origin and how Earth Mark Two came into being, we have to understand how stars and planets form and how our world and its moon emerged from the mayhem at the dawn of the solar system.

Compared to moons orbiting other planets in our solar system, our moon is unusual in many respects. It is large relative to the Earth and the pair have sometimes been called a double planet. Only distant, icy Pluto and its moon Charon are larger in comparison. Although there are many moons elsewhere in our solar system that are larger than our own moon they circle worlds that are thousands of times bigger. What is more, our moon is made of relatively lightweight materials, and has an abnormally low density compared to other rocky worlds in our solar system. The Earth–moon system also has an unusually large amount of rotation (technically called angular momentum) in both the Earth's spin and the moon's orbit. Before scientists were able to analyse rocks from the moon, these were the basic facts that any theory of the moon's birth had to explain.

Before the moon landings there were three different theories for the origin of the moon. The fission theory, proposed in 1878 by George Darwin, son of Charles Darwin, suggested that the moon was spun out of the Earth's mantle when the Earth was young and rotating more rapidly than it does today. As the Earth spun, it became distorted, teardrop-shaped, and tore off a piece of itself. Some advocates of this theory even suggested that three pieces had been formed. The larger was the Earth, with a smaller offshoot, and a tiny blob formed in between. The second largest blob would be Mars and the moon, the bit in between. There was, they argued, even a planet-wide scar that could be the region where the fissure took place – the Pacific Ocean. But such 'fissure' models for the moon's origin cannot explain the angular momentum of the Earth–moon system. If Darwin's idea was true then both the Earth and the moon would be spinning about four times faster than they do. Even with the kindest interpretation it was a difficult theory to take very seriously, as the Earth would have needed to spin extremely rapidly to throw off a moon-sized lump. But it made predictions that could be tested, as all theories must.

It predicted that moon rocks should be broadly similar to Earth rocks.

There was also the capture theory. This supposed that the moon had formed somewhere else in the solar system and later been captured into an orbit about the Earth. But for the Earth to capture a wandering world would not be easy. The general rule is that if two worlds approach each other then, unless they collide, they will deflect each other's trajectory but will not be captured. For one to go into orbit around the other, just the right amount of energy must be lost by the approaching world at just the right time. That would probably require a third world to be present. This theory predicted that the make-up of lunar rocks would be different from the Earth's because the moon was a world that had formed elsewhere in the solar system.

Finally, there was the co-accretion or 'double planet' theory. This proposed that the Earth and moon had grown alongside each other as the other planets had formed. According to this idea, Earth rocks and moon rocks should be roughly similar. Of all the theories we have encountered so far, this is the most appealing but it cannot explain why the moon is made of lighter stuff than the Earth.

Scientists hoped that analysis of lunar rocks brought back by the Apollo astronauts would reveal which of the three theories was correct. But when they got their hands on the Apollo moon samples they found, to their surprise, that none of the three theories could be confirmed or ruled out. It was a humbling experience. The Apollo programme was a great technological and political triumph but, even with moon rocks to study and a wealth of new data, astronomers could not solve one of the most important questions the moon landings had set out to answer: how was the moon born? As they examined the lunar samples, they realized that they did not understand the moon as well as they thought they did. No theory was favoured or ruled out and nobody was suggesting the way we now believe the moon was formed.

Arriving in their sealed boxes at the specially constructed lunar sample receiving laboratory in Houston, the moon rocks were initially treated as a severe biohazard. Nobody seriously believed that they harboured any form of life but, for the first Apollo samples at least, they had to be treated as such. Then, as now, they were kept in a closed inert nitrogen environment and handled remotely or through thick rubber gloves. Several scientists have told me of their desire to handle a rock from the moon. Some have studied moon rocks for years, if not decades, yet are denied close contact with them. Some long to touch their roughness and perhaps rub a thumb satisfyingly over them, feeling the fine powder come away from their surface. Geologists are used to close contact with their specimens. They like to bring them close to their eye and, using a magnifying glass, look for granularities or crystal structure or familiar minerals. This time that was impossible. But there were some who did touch the moon rocks.

On the lunar surface, as the moonwalkers peeled off their spacesuits in the cramped lunar module everything became covered in a fine layer of moon dust exposed to oxygen for the first time. Astronauts tell of how it smelt of gunpowder that seemed to have reacted in some way with the oils on their skin and how it penetrated every crack and crevice in their hands. One told me that for weeks after he came back from the moon, the washbasin in his garage was grimy with the moondust that lingered on his hands. Some astronauts gave parts of their moondust-soiled spacesuits and equipment to relatives.

The rocks were indeed fascinating but, regarding the problem of how the moon had formed, they raised more questions than answers. However, they did reveal the fact that the moon had been heavily bombarded during the first half-billion years of the solar system's life 4.5 billion years ago. They also suggested that the moon was heated at that time, perhaps even becoming completely molten. But the most important and most puzzling conclusion was that the moon rocks lacked so-called volatile elements, those that vaporize and escape easily when heated. Further analysis suggested that this depletion of volatiles happened within a relatively few million years after the formation of the solar system. Something unusual had happened to these rocks, something that had not happened to rocks from our own planet.

The ratio of radioactive elements in moon rocks gave the moon a birthdate; the interval between the birth of the solar system and the birth of the moon was about 50 million years. In addition, there was an abundance of siderophile, or 'iron liking', elements in lunar rocks. Some of the lunar highland rocks brought back by Apollo appeared to be very old, older than 4.4 billion years. Geologists speculated that they might be from the crust that formed on the first magma ocean as light plagioclase floated on top of dense basaltic magmas. But what was even more confusing was that the moon rocks were in many respects very similar in composition to the Earth's mantle; indeed the ratio of oxygen isotopes (elements) in the moon rocks was identical to the Earth's.

So how did the moon form? To find out we have to go back to the birth of the sun.

Stars are born in great clouds of gas and dust. The gas is enriched with elements made in previous generations of stars and recycled back into space by stellar explosions. The dust grains are also from earlier stars, having been formed in the atmosphere of a star or in jets from a star that streamed material back into interstellar space. When we look across space at these vast clouds we see dark regions in them where the gas and dust segments are contracting and forming an opaque cocoon where the star birth process takes place, like human birth, in private. Looking at these stellar birthsites, we see, scattered against them, a dusting of hot newborn stars. Stars are born in families. The brothers and sisters of our sun, which formed alongside it some 4.5 billion years ago, have long been scattered into space and could by now be on the far side of the galaxy.

The age of our solar system is easier to determine than the age of the Earth. One way to measure it is by looking at the oldest known meteorites. They contain the residue of radioactive elements that were active when the solar system was young but which have long since vanished. Short-lived radioactive atoms of aluminium in primitive meteorites indicate that the solar system did not exist for more than about a million years before the inclusions in these ancient rocks formed. The chemical clocks that started ticking near the time of the sun's birth tell us that our solar system is 4.57 billion years old, roughly a third of the age of the universe. Curiously, some studies of radioactive isotopes of hafnium suggest that this element was formed in a nearby region of space before the gas cloud that became our sun started to collapse. It may be that a star from a previous generation exploded not far from our sun's placental cloud. This not only triggered its collapse with its shock wave but seeded our birth-cloud with a smattering of radioactive elements that had been synthesized in the high-temperature ejecta from the explosion.

Stars and planets are formed gently at first. The gas and dust cloud slowly gets smaller and denser, and in the diffuse, cold and extremely low-pressure solar nebula all matter must have existed as gas or as tiny grains of dust and ice. Imagine an enormous cloud of snowflakes and ice-coated dust.

The density and pressure gradually increases at the centre of the solar nebula, as gravity tugs ever more tightly. As the concentrations increase, atoms collide frequently with each other, generating heat. If this process had continued in isolation the whole gas cloud would have fallen into one object and there would have been just a sun with no planets. But because the solar nebula must have been rotating, its angular momentum sculpted the nebula into a flattened disc, warm in the centre, cold at the edges. When they formed, all the planets would have been in the same flat plane, at least in the beginning.

Temperatures near the proto-sun have now climbed to over 2000°C, whilst the outermost regions of the nebula stay frosty at about minus 200°C. The high temperatures near the proto-sun were not due to radiation from the emerging star because the inner dust cloud was highly opaque, meaning that little starlight could reach the nebula to warm it. Instead, the heat came from the decay of highly radioactive elements in the dust. In the inner regions the icy substances must have vaporized, leaving streams of tiny grains. In the outer regions, snowflakes and ice-coated dust survived in the cooler temperatures. They would eventually form the methane, ammonia and water-rich giant planets of the outer solar system.

Computer simulations reveal three stages in the formation of the planets. During the first stage, dust grains from the cloud that formed the sun stuck to each other until objects were formed that were large enough to begin to attract material with their gravity. Eventually this process produced objects the size of asteroids up to a few hundred kilometres in diameter. During the second stage, a period of runaway growth took place, with objects colliding and coalescing, possibly leading to many tens of objects much larger than the moon. Most of the mass of the inner solar system was contained within these planetary embryos. It all happened relatively rapidly in cosmic terms because gravity never relents.

It may have taken only about a million years for the first two stages to be completed. But it was the third stage that was the worst. During this final stage, huge objects smashed into each other, creating larger worlds.

At this stage, the dim sun cast its then feeble light over a very different scene from the one it illuminates today. The few dozen worlds that had accreted from the planetesimals (building blocks of planets) were themselves colliding. Those few tens of millions of years of stage three were full of violence from which the Earth, the moon, and ultimately you and I came. If there is any lesson that emerges from this early chaos, it is that the moon and the beings that stare up at it from our world are here by chance. We have this particular Earth, with this particular moon, because our first home was destroyed in the violence of its birth. Let me now tell you about the brief lives of two worlds, both of which died billions of years ago but whose influence is all around us today.

I have previously called one of these worlds the Earth Mark One and it was very different from the other rocky worlds that circle the sun today. Today we see only the long-term survivors and few of them emerged intact. The four so-called terrestrial planets that nestle close to the sun form an unlikely family. Moon-like Mercury is mostly iron, covered with a bit of rock, and has no atmosphere. Venus, in terms of its size and composition, is a twin of Earth, but it is smothered by an inferno of an atmosphere and is drier than any desert. Earth's surface is mostly liquid water, continents drift across it and life in its various forms has colonized every corner. Mars, a tenth the mass of Earth, is a world from the past with an ancient, immobile face, now dry and lifeless but with hints of an earlier, more hospitable era when life possibly started (and may still cling on in pockets of moisture beneath the surface).

This motley crew are a study in the effects of chaos. When the solar system was young dozens of Mars-sized proto-planets were

roaming menacingly around the inner solar system. Minute variations, trivial changes in their trajectories, decided if they collided
or just missed each other. These variations, as unpredictable and
as chaotic as the forces that control a ball in a roulette wheel, are
responsible for the state of the inner planets we see today.

Until recently, planetary scientists couldn't calculate the individual fate of these scores of miniplanet-sized worlds. In computer programs errors accumulated until they swamped the final
answer, rendering the simulations meaningless; virtual planets
were constantly being flung out of the solar system or falling into
the sun. Now that we have far more powerful, accurate computers, several groups of researchers are able to run the required
100-million-year simulations and study what might have happened. In one simulation, twenty-two planetary embryos, each
about the size of Mars, merged to become a few terrestrial
planets, typically with a pair of planets, each at least half the mass
of Earth, orbiting between the distance of Earth from the sun or
inside Venus's orbit. A third, less massive planet tended to form
near the orbit of Mars. Some of these imagined planetary systems
have many planets; some have none. That there would be planets
circling our sun was highly likely; that they would be the
particular planets in the particular positions they occupy today is
just a matter of chance.

Imagine that two large planetary embryos remain after Mercury, Venus and Mars have taken shape. In one simulation, the
two embryos collided with great violence to form a primitive
Earth and splashed off material to form a smaller world. In
another they settled into stable orbits as two small planets and
there was no Earth in this solar system. In other runs of the
simulation, one of the planetary embryos collided with the virtual
Venus and turned it into a double planet. What these simulations
are telling us is that the greatest accident in Earth's history was no
accident at all.

★ ★ ★

Our accidental moon was born like this.

In a solar system that was less than 100 million years old the leftovers of planetary formation were still bombarding Earth Mark One. It had grown through the accretion of tens of thousands of smaller bodies and, by some estimates, had reached a size about half as large as our Earth is now. Each bombardment brought with it, firstly, material to make the Earth Mark One grow and, secondly, energy for the kinetic energy of planetesimals travelling typically at 16 km a second. Despite the punishing impacts, the Earth Mark One was on its way to becoming a planet we would recognize. It had an iron centre formed from melted rocks that had separated into their constituents and from which the heavy iron had sunk to form the metallic core. The outer layers of Earth Mark One were made of silicate rocks formed when the molten surface cooled and there may have even been oceans of steaming water in the periods between the catastrophic impacts that vaporized them and turned the surface back into bubbling magma. No planet could escape the violence. All the proto-planets smashed into one another again and again, forming boiling oceans of molten rock enveloped in white-hot silicate atmospheres.

The other world in our story has no name, or at least not one that I am going to reveal just yet. It was smaller than Earth Mark One, probably a few times larger than the present-day planet Mars but it had had a similar upbringing to the Earth Mark One. It too had an iron heart, though it was somewhat smaller than the Earth's and it was similarly overlaid with a rocky crust from time to time. This smaller world is commonly referred to by astronomers as the 'impactor'.

On their computers, researchers regularly scatter rocky bodies of various sizes in various orbits in the early solar system and watch as they sometimes pass close to each other, and sometimes collide. Eventually the myriad of small worlds is replaced by a few larger ones and then the collisions between them become truly catastrophic.

It is even possible that the first stages of life may have been taking place in the short-lived oceans of Earth Mark One and possibly in the oceans of the impactor as well. Looking at samples of the world's earliest rocks, scientists cannot help but be impressed at the swiftness at which primitive life started on our planet. As soon as the surface rocks cooled, it seems that life began. It is possible that life arose several times when the Earth was young, only to be snuffed out as a giant impact melted – and sterilized – the Earth's surface yet again. Both the Earth Mark One and the impactor were to be denied their futures one fateful day over 4 billion years ago.

From a distance of 40 million km it would have been one of the brightest things in a sky full of menacing moving points of light. The impactor is only 1,000 hours away, heading for the Earth Mark One, and there is almost nothing that can stop it. Travelling through space its own diameter every ten minutes or so, it will traverse the last million kilometres to its death and rebirth in less than two days. The energy a planet carries by virtue of its motion, its kinetic energy, is enormous. The collision between the impactor and the Earth Mark One unleashed an energy 100 million times greater than the impact that wiped out the dinosaurs (a million billion megatons worth of TNT explosive). And when the impactor collides with Earth Mark One that energy has to go somewhere.

Imagine being a witness to the last few hours before these doomed worlds collide. Until the last hour or so it would be difficult to make out the motion of the impactor but each time you looked back it would loom a little larger. In the last 20 minutes or so its motion would become frighteningly obvious. In just a few seconds it would cut through the atmosphere, forcing it out of its way in supersonic winds. For a second or so the atmosphere would be full of sonic booms until the two worlds came together in an embrace of death. Tidal forces would cause them to become slightly pear-shaped as they approached, and there would be an instant when the two worlds were just touching, filling each other's skies. Then hundreds of cubic kilometres of rock would be vaporized in a split second and blasted into space as the two worlds ground themselves together. In minutes a major part of the Earth would be missing, the rest would be turning ruddy and soon an ever-brightening red. Streamers of superheated rock vapour would stream into space as shock waves embraced what was left of the two shuddering worlds.

Computer-generated images do not adequately convey the magnitude of what happens when two planets collide and are torn asunder. Such simulations cannot show the sheer grandeur of the planet-wide destruction. In the instant that Earth Mark One and the impactor were destroyed, our Earth and the moon were born, and nothing would ever be the same again.

Within minutes a plume of superhot rock vapour stretched 16,000 km into space; half the Earth is missing and the rest is a distorted riven mass. In one scenario the impactor survives, barely. Its energy sapped, it staggers into a low orbit. For a while the two wrecked worlds are connected by a thin bridge of glowing material that starts to fall onto one or the other or fragment into a string of beads. The distorted impactor withdraws to a maximum distance of a few Earth Mark One diameters and then falls back a second time. This time it is fully destroyed. All things considered, it would have been a bad weekend to be on Earth.

In some simulations the second impact is at a shallower angle than the first and creates a dumb-bell shaped planet surrounded by a cloud of vaporized rock. Now the impactor's iron core has insufficient energy to escape. Distorted and boiling, it is drawn swiftly by gravity to the centre of the Earth where the iron hearts of these two worlds merge. Any water on either world has been vaporized and lost to space, the Earth's oceans are gone. Within hours of the impact a ring of debris forms around the Earth which is still far from spherical. Its shifting molten surface is now surrounded by an opaque, white-hot silicate atmosphere. The mean temperature is in excess of 4000°C out to about eight Earth radii. Of all the material thrown into space after the collision most of it was eventually drawn back to Earth, but not all. The fraction that remained in space became our moon which was born, initially, in just 15 minutes.

Whether a moon forms depends on the size of the impactor and how off-centre the impact is. Dead-centred impacts do not throw much material into space with enough velocity to allow it to stay in orbit. Some of the simulations resolve a nagging problem with the giant impact hypothesis. The problem is that of producing a collision large enough to get a moon-sized body into orbit with the correct amount of angular momentum. Most plausible impacts produce a much larger lunar orbit. But one solution, in this game of making planets, is that the Earth was only about half to two-thirds of its present size when the impact occurred. If it occurred early enough in planetary history, plenty of extra debris would have remained to fall on the Earth afterwards, allowing it to start growing again. Some astronomers disagree with this suggestion, believing that the Earth was not brought to its present size that way. They point out that comparisons of the chemical compositions of the Earth and moon suggest that the Earth was fully formed, or nearly so, when it spawned the moon.

Whatever the answer, the aftermath of the impact would have been a cloud of rock vapour surrounding the new Earth with possibly a string of rocky bodies in orbit. The impact would also have left a ring of very hot debris circling the young Earth.

Calculations indicate that the moon could have formed from that debris in ten years or less. The moon would have formed very hot, possibly entirely molten, and such a scorching state is consistent with the idea that it was initially surrounded by an ocean of magma. The magma ocean idea has been a central tenet of lunar science for decades, and data from the 1994 Clementine lunar mission to the moon finally proved it.

In many simulations two moons are formed, circling the Earth at a distance of only about 20,000 km (or about twenty times closer than the moon orbits the Earth today). Two moons gracing the skies of the angry Earth would have been quite a sight but it wouldn't have lasted long. In every simulation either the inner moon crashes back to Earth or the two moons collide within about a thousand years.

After the large proto-moon had been formed it probably continued to accrete material, including some objects up to about half its size. These big impacts would have maintained the magma ocean, and scrambled any crust that tried to form between impacts. It could also add rock with a composition different from the rest of the moon, accounting for some unexplained features of the lunar interior.

Being much closer together, the tidal forces between the Earth and the new moon would have been much stronger than they are today. Both worlds would have bulged towards the other, a bulge that traversed each world as it rotated. These forces would have dissipated orbital energy, causing the moon's orbit to expand. Within a few hundred million years it would have receded to half its present distance. It is still receding. Laser beams bounced off reflectors left on the lunar surface by the Apollo astronauts confirm that it is moving outward at about 4 cm each year, slower than the rate at which continents drift around the surface of Earth.

As well as being consistent with what we know the early solar system was like, it could also explain why the moon has a chemical make-up very similar to that of the Earth but different in some respects. The rock vapour ejected into space would consist predominantly of material from the outer regions of the two objects and should therefore exclude iron-rich core material. Elements that are easily boiled off would be lost due to the high temperature. This could explain why moon rocks are devoid of elements that can be driven off by heating and why the Earth has a large iron core but the moon does not.

It is an appealing theory but in the recent past not many astronomers have been willing to believe that our moon was formed in such a dramatic way.

It was astronomers William Hartmann and Donald Davis who, in a paper published in 1975 in *Icarus*, the journal of solar system studies, first put forward the impact hypothesis. They knew about previous work done in the Soviet Union in the 1960s by Viktor Safronov who was interested in how planets had formed out of countless smaller bodies called planetesimals. Picking up on Safronov's ideas, Hartmann and Davis ran computer simulations of the rate of growth of these primitive objects. Their conclusion was that, as the Earth was forming, several threatening bodies up to about half its size would have been lurking in menacing orbits. Another paper on the same topic had been written by Alfred Cameron and William Ward of the Harvard-Smithsonian Center for Astrophysics, Cambridge, Massachusetts. Although they took a different approach both groups suggested that the moon formed when a huge impactor smashed into the Earth. To account for the angular momentum, Cameron estimated that the object would need to be about 10 per cent the mass of Earth (about the size of Mars). It was an interesting theory but few took it seriously.

At about the same time other scientists were suggesting that the dinosaurs had been wiped out by the catastrophic impact of a giant meteor. The evidence was a worldwide rock layer formed at the time of the dinosaur extinction about 67 million years ago. This layer was enriched in an element that is rare on Earth and more common in meteorites. Astronomers did not like that idea either.

Hartmann and Davis presented their calculations to other scientists at a conference on planetary satellites in 1974. Hartmann's logic was compelling. He approached the problem from the perspective he had gained from his work on the objects that had struck the moon throughout its history. He reasoned that if there were huge impact craters on the moon, made by objects about 160 km across, then there must have been others – perhaps ten or more times larger. If one hit the Earth, perhaps sufficient material would be lifted into orbit to form the moon.

For those with eyes to see, there is evidence of gigantic collisions all around us. Mercury, for instance, is a small rocky world with a large core of iron. An impact with a large planetesimal may have removed much of Mercury's iron-deficient rocky exterior, leaving the relatively huge iron core. And Venus has an unusual rotation period of 243 days which could also have been caused by an impact. Further out in the solar system we see moons with huge scars. For example, Miranda, orbiting Uranus, looks like a small world that was torn into many pieces and then put back together the wrong way. And the large axial tilt of Uranus looks as if it may have been the after-effect of a collision with another giant body.

Over the next few years the giant impactor theory languished somewhat. Then in 1984 an international meeting was organized at Kona, Hawaii, about the origin of the moon. Before Kona the three competing theories about the moon's origins each had their advocates but by its end almost all the scientists were convinced that the giant impact hypothesis was the best explanation, and it has remained so ever since.

However, there was one sceptic. American astrophysicist Jay Melosh heard about the impact theory of the moon's origin at the 1984 conference and thought the idea was ridiculous. As he made his way home he decided to devote that weekend to writing a paper that would refute the theory. But when he sat down a few days later he realized things were not quite that simple.

Firstly, the impact would produce a great deal of vaporization. The material ejected from the Earth would not be solid. That was significant. Melosh was aware of the suggestion that the peculiar composition of the moon could be explained if the mantle of the Earth had vaporized and condensed in a vacuum.

He ran through series after series of calculations in his notebooks, trying to determine just how much material would be vaporized during a giant impact. Soon he decided that he needed to perform a computer simulation of the impact and he knew just the computer to use. It was one of the fastest computers in the world. It was at the Sandia National Laboratories in New Mexico and it was mainly used to simulate the detonation of nuclear weapons.

Not long afterwards a friend ushered him into the main computer control room where the nuclear codes were developed. These codes (computer programs that simulate nuclear detonations) are regarded as items of the highest importance to national security. Three teams of scientists at three national laboratories have developed independent versions of them so that their veracity can be verified. The inner sanctum of the Sandia computer is usually off limits but, due to Melosh's contacts and his previous work, he was allowed in. The computer itself is not connected to any other, to eliminate the prospect of hacking.

Melosh knew that the equations the Sandia computer used to study the effects of nuclear detonations only involved metals. The data needed to run simulations involving rock should use

so-called equations of state for rock but they were not available so
Melosh had to improvise. He therefore considered a metal planet
with an iron core and an aluminium outer shell. (This was a good
first model as, in terms of shock physics, aluminium is a pretty
good match to Earth materials.)

Not being allowed to touch the computer himself, he was
asked what figures should be keyed in. He gave the mass and size
of the Earth as the target. A few ears pricked up when they heard
this. He was then asked what would be the mass of the projectile?
He gave the mass and size of Mars. By this time heads had turned,
as others working in the control room realized that this was no
ordinary simulation. What about the closing speed was the final
question and Melosh gave the typical speed of a body moving in
outer space. Now everyone had crowded around the computer
terminal, anxious to see the outcome. What they saw on the
screen (a crude, cartoon-like display compared with today's computer graphics) showed an impact that did indeed splay material
out into space, enough material to possibly form the moon.
Melosh was converted.

Since then computers have become more powerful and calculations more refined and attention has turned away from *if* it
happened to *how* it could have happened. Other factors have
fallen into place as well: for example, the mysterious tilt of the
moon's orbit is probably a consequence of the moon's formation
from the giant collision. Today's lunar orbit can be backtracked in
time to show that, when it formed near the Earth, its orbit was
inclined by approximately 10 degrees relative to the Earth's
equator. Most other planetary satellites in the solar system have
orbital inclinations smaller than 1 or 2 degrees. The cause of the
moon's large orbital tilt has long been a mystery. For years, the
so-called 'inclination problem' had been one of the last remaining
obstacles to complete acceptance of the impact hypothesis of

moon formation. Computer models of the moon's formation from such a disc of debris predicted that the lunar orbit should have been nearly aligned with the Earth's equator, with only about a 1 degree tilt at most. However, it has recently been realized that the moon acquired its large tilt soon after it formed because of a gravitational interaction with debris left over from the impact event. Modelling results show that the moon could indeed have acquired its 10 degree tilt as a consequence of the moon-forming impact.

To yield a lunar-sized moon, the giant impact must place two lunar masses of material into an Earth-orbiting disc. Vaporized rock in space does not behave like ordinary particles. Because it can expand under its own internal pressure, the vapour can stay in orbit when colder rock particles would fall back to Earth. In the most sophisticated computer models, debris in the inner regions of such a disc are prevented from coalescing by Earth's gravity, which tends to pull objects apart.

The proto-moon rapidly coalesces at the outer edge of the debris disc, at a distance of about 20,000 km from the Earth (or about twenty times closer than our moon is today). For a while the close environs of the newborn Earth Mark Two must have been highly dramatic, with the newly formed moon co-existing with an inner disc of gas and debris. As the proto-moon coalesced, its gravity would generate ripples in the inner disc. The waves generated at one region, where the orbital period of the moon is approximately three times that of the disc particles, produce a so-called resonance effect that interacts with the moon to amplify the tilt of its orbit. This can exaggerate the lunar inclination to values as high as 15 degrees before the disc dissipates. Some detailed studies indicate that the required tilt of about 10 degrees could be achieved if the disc contained at least 25–50 per cent of a lunar mass and persisted at least several decades. So, rather than being a conflicting piece of evidence, the lunar inclination may now represent an additional corroboration of the impact event.

There may even have been spiral arms in the debris disc surrounding the Earth. Some simulations show that when such a spiral arm is extended beyond the so-called Roche limit (inside which tidal stresses prevent any moon from forming), the tip of the spiral arm collapses to form a small moonlet. The rapid accretion of these small moonlets might form a lunar seed that would grow by sweeping up particles. When the moon became large enough to gravitationally dominate the disc, it would push the rest of the inner disc onto the Earth. As it grew, the moon would have gone through a succession of orbital resonances. And 1,000 years after its birth the first resonance would have squeezed the orbit into a narrow ellipse. The intense tidal forces in this orbit would have raised tremendous tides, generating enough heat to melt the surface again.

Once an angry moon, or possibly two, loomed fifteen times bigger in our skies than it does today. The tidal interaction between the two wreaked havoc on both worlds. In the oceans of Earth every wave was a tsunami, every piece of land was molten. This was a far cry from today's serene silver light; it was a blotched blood-red fiery moon. Yet it was a gift that had a profound effect on our world.

What if it had never happened?

There are some scientists who believe that without the moon we would not be here and the Earth would be a very different place. Perhaps it would have been an ocean world with very little land and what land there was would have been barren. Or perhaps it would have become a baking-hot or freezing-cold world on which life may have started but been forever under siege in a hostile and changing environment. Perhaps other sentient beings would have developed here if by some chance the Earth had remained Mark One. What would they have been like? What could they have achieved? What would their legends and myths have been without a moon?

Ten thousand years ago the Sahara Desert was fertile and covered in grasslands. But then the climate started to change, and the region turned drier and started to become the inhospitable place it is today. Some of its inhabitants moved east, settled on the flood plains of the River Nile and founded the great civilization that was Egypt. Several millennia later a Greek traveller called Herodotus wrote that the 'Nile obeys the moon', yet he and the Egyptians had no inkling that the moon might have played a part in the founding of the Egyptian dynasties.

Some scientists believe that the climatic change that created the Sahara was due to a slight shift in the inclination of the Earth's rotational axis with respect to its orbit around the sun (less than 1 degree from its current axial tilt of 23.5 degrees). It is the presence of our large moon that acts to stabilize the variation of the Earth's rotational axis. Were it not for the moon, the influence of the giant planets in our solar system would cause Earth's obliquity to vary wildly. Thus, having a large moon may be one of the key characteristics necessary for a habitable Earth-like planet.

Simulations show that if the moon was removed there would be times when the Earth's axis would swing 50 or 60 degrees, causing the sun to pass directly over the poles. Clearly, the balance of our world would be upset as everywhere on the planet would experience dramatic extremes of climate. Without the moon, the Earth would also be rotating faster. How would any form of life have been able to evolve and adapt to these conditions?

The impact with Earth Mark One might have driven a lot of water on the planet into space so if the impactor sailed by we might now be living on a water world where the sea level was many thousands of metres higher than it is. Few patches of land would poke above the waves. So, without a moon, any advanced intelligence would have to have evolved in the sea and it is interesting to speculate how they might have developed technology in an aquatic environment.

The presence of the moon might well have altered the course of life on Earth. Every 100 million years or so, our planet suffers a mass extinction of life. Look back at the fossil record and they are plain to see: sudden events when one layer of rock shows an abundance of life that is mostly gone in the next. Such events alter the course of evolution. For example the giant meteor that struck the Earth 67 million years ago and wiped out the dinosaurs cleared the way for tiny mammals to evolve out of their small niches to become the dominant life forms on the planet.

What would have happened if that particular meteor had missed the Earth? Palaeontologists say there were signs that the dinosaurs were on the way out anyway, having been dominant for over 100 million years (I wonder if humans, having emerged in only the past few million years, will be so successful). But it is clear that things would have been different if the impact had not occurred. Nobody can prove this but many suspect that at some time in the past the moon deflected or intercepted a large meteor or asteroid that would otherwise have collided with the Earth. If such an impact had occurred 200 million years ago it would have wiped out the dinosaurs just as they were getting started. And if the dinosaurs had been destroyed, would the mammals have been able to step in?

In recent years we have found many worlds (over sixty at the last count), circling many of the nearby stars. Present technology limits us to detecting gas giant worlds like Jupiter and Saturn but soon, using space-based techniques, we may be able to detect Earth-sized worlds. If we find one, the first thing we will want to know about it will be its colour for, from its spectrum, we can gain clues as to its physical state and whether it could support life. Is the presence of a large moon a prerequisite for life to develop on such worlds?

The impact simulations that show how our moon may have been formed also provide astronomers who are searching other stars for planets like our own with an extra tool. The birth throes of moons like our own might be visible in other solar systems. Calculations suggest that a moon-forming impact should be detectable from a distance of 400 light years, so perhaps we should start surveying newly forming stars in the same way that we survey old galaxies for exploding stars. Who knows, perhaps some day we may detect the afterglow of such a cataclysm.

The moon was formed in a dramatic way but the violence did not end with its birth. It was still being bombarded by the leftovers of planetary formation for the best part of half a billion years before the planetesimals that punished its surface became more and more infrequent. The scars they left remain on the moon today. It was those impacts, so long ago, that are responsible for all the tales and legends about how the moon got its spots.

Some of the most interesting evidence for the bombardment of the moon comes from moon rocks that were not brought back to Earth by the Apollo astronauts or the Russian automated samplers. It comes from an analysis of four of the twenty or so known lunar meteorites. We have lunar meteorites to study because the moon's escape velocity is 2.38 km per second, only a few times the muzzle velocity of a rifle. Any rock thrown up by an impact on the lunar surface to lunar escape velocity or greater will leave the moon's influence. Some of this material will be captured by the Earth's gravitational field and land swiftly on Earth. Most ejected material, however, goes into orbit around the sun. Some of that material may eventually strike Earth but it can take a long time. The record-holder, lunar meteorite Yamato-82192/82193/86032, remained in space for about 9 million years before landing in Antarctica.

The Apollo and Luna samples are drawn from particular places on the lunar surface which do not necessarily represent the moon as a whole. An analysis of a handful of lunar meteorites carried out at the University of Arizona, and reported in *Science* in 2000, looked at the ratios of isotopes in them. The conclusion was that the samples were almost completely melted about 3.9 billion years ago during the big bombardment.

The energy from these impacts formed a magma ocean over 480 km deep. Inside this bubbling, convecting molten mass, tiny crystals containing aluminium, silicon, oxygen and calcium were being formed. Geologists call these particular crystals plagioclase and, being lighter than the surrounding magma, they began to ascend, forming a scum on the surface that began to cool, creating the moon's first crust. The resulting rock, which is virtually all plagioclase, is called anorthosite and forms the extremely ancient lunar highlands. In addition, the highlands are also made of another dominant rock group that contains magnesium as well as the iron-rich mineral olivine.

Beneath the surface of the magma ocean, more components were crystallizing out of the mix (in particular, iron in the form of the mineral olivine promptly sank to the core). So-called 'rockbergs' may have formed over regions of the molten rock that were moving downwards towards the interior of the moon, as partially solidified and lighter rocks struggled against the downflow to remain on the surface. Between the impacts a solid crust attempted to form and in some places managed to persist. Indeed, within minutes of molten rock being exposed to a vacuum, a crust started to appear. It took years for the top few metres to solidify after the impact rate declined and perhaps 50 million years for it all to grow cold and immobile after the bombardment tailed off. The final crystallization of the magma ocean is thought to have produced so-called KREEP rocks. In a few hundred million years these rocks would change the face of the moon forever. As the skin that was to become the bright-coloured lunar highlands solidified, more material was being added to the crust from below. And as it did, some streams of magma managed to punch their way through the crust, erupting onto the surface and producing volcanoes in the highlands.

An iron-nickel core formed, similar to but far smaller than the Earth's (recall that the iron heart of the impactor had already been captured by the Earth, leaving the material that made the moon depleted in iron). Initially the core was molten and convective motions within it would have produced a weak magnetic field. Evidence for this can be found in some of the rocks returned by Apollo. The moon's magnetism appears to have been strongest approximately 3.8–3.6 billion years ago, but eventually the core solidified and the 'dynamo' which powered its magnetism faded.

During this time numerous large impacts sculpted many of the major basins. In the 500 million years between 4.5 and 4 billion years ago asteroids, typically 100 km in size, struck and formed the Australe, Nubium, Tranquillitatis and Fecunditatis basins. They were then festering scars on the surface that had not yet been filled with dark maria lava flows. There were certainly numerous impacts whose effects have been erased by later cataclysms. Some lunar geologists believe they can see the ghostly outlines of very ancient structures barely discernible against a billion years of subsequent impacts. Even if they cannot truly see them they are definitely there, for the giant basins we see, the dominant features of the lunar landscape, are the last of many, surviving only because none came afterwards to obliterate them.

One structure on the moon is remarkable because its formation may have come close to breaking it up. It seems that the moon was almost subjected to the same fate as the Earth Mark One as a giant impactor struck it. The moon survived but left on its surface as a reminder was the biggest hole in the solar system. You cannot see it from Earth because it is in the moon's southern hemisphere, mostly on its far side. The South Pole–Aitken Basin is 2,700 km in diameter and over 11 km deep. One way it can be seen is as a region that is darker and richer in iron than the rest of the lunar highlands. Such was the intensity of the impact that the floor of the basin may well be composed of rock gouged up from the mantle of the moon. The existence of this giant basin was suspected as early as 1962. But as the Galileo spacecraft flew by the Earth and moon in 1992, gaining speed for its long trip to Jupiter, its camera showed it in all its shattered desolation. A few years later the United States Defense Department's Clementine mission confirmed that the only impact basin that comes anywhere close to it in size is the Chryse Basin on Mars.

Geophysicists are puzzled by this big hole. Such an impact should have dug up vast amounts of mantle material from below the crust, yet there seems to be only a relatively modest amount. To explain it, some have suggested that it was formed by a low-velocity asteroid that hit at a low angle and therefore did not dig very deeply into the moon. This particular impactor, like its counterpart that struck the Earth, would have thrown into orbit a disc of debris that, when raining back down on the moon, could have made other lunar basins.

Scientists look at the moon and, by seeing what basin, crater or other structure overlays what other feature, they can work out a rough order of events on the lunar surface. But ascertaining absolute dates requires the analysis of samples from the moon. Some of the Apollo 14 samples, dated at about 4.5 billion years old, are from the peak of the period of intense bombardment. Samples returned from Apollo 17 are highland breccias which help date the Serenitatis Basin-forming impact at 3.98 billion years ago. Less than 100 million years later, the basins Nectaris and Humorum were created. Most of the craters we see were formed during this time. Samples from Luna 20 date the Crisium Basin at 3.9 billion years ago and those from Apollo 14 and 16 date the formation of the mighty Imbrium basin marginally later. The enormous Orientale followed swiftly. Although there is evidence of a late burst of impacts about 3.9 billion years ago, which overwhelmed the impacts that preceded it, the supply of large objects roaming the solar system generally started to dwindle. So ended the era of the massive basins. But shortly after Orientale was formed and the external bombardment declined, something began to happen inside the moon.

From deep within the moon, rocks that had fallen inward during the magma ocean phase were becoming active again as they were heated by the decay of radioactive elements. These were the KREEP rocks. What may have happened is that in the magma ocean minerals did not always crystallize in order of density. Some of the densest minerals may have crystallized late to form a thin dense layer just underneath the crust, near the end of the magma ocean solidification. This material, known as an ilmenite cumulate, would have been denser than the surrounding rock and would have slowly sunk through the rock beneath it, dragging the still-lingering molten KREEP down hundreds of kilometres. In effect the moon turned itself inside out! This rock, heated by radioactive decay, then melted and forced its way upwards under pressure and in some places reached the surface and began to ooze out and fill the basins. Apollo 11 samples date the first phase of the filling of the Sea of Tranquillity with material from about 100 km deep at about 3.8 billion years ago. This process went on intermittently for hundreds of millions of years.

But the lava could not reach all parts of the moon's surface, only the low-lying basins. For some reason, not yet understood, the battering of the previous billion years had not been exactly even across the moon. Slightly more impacts on one side than the other had resulted in a crust that was on average 110 km thick but which was 32 km thicker in the far-side one hemisphere. It was obvious that there was something strange going on when Luna 3 sent back the first fuzzy pictures of the far side in October 1959 showing no widespread dark maria. The slightly thicker crust on the far side of the moon seems to have prevented the lava from reaching the surface. But why do the dark maria all face the Earth?

It's probably best to approach the question from the other direction. For years scientists wondered why maria had formed on the side of the moon that faced the Earth and not on the side that faced away. Now we know how the lava was prevented from reaching the surface by the far side's thicker crust, we can ask the related question: how did the crust on the side facing the Earth become thinner? It is the wrong question.

We cannot be sure of the dates exactly, but many scientists believe that the moon has not always kept the same face towards the Earth in the past. Sketchy calculations suggest that it only became tidally locked when it was perhaps a billion years old and that, crucially, the side of the moon that ended up facing the Earth was the side with the thin crust. So, the thin crust is not there *because* it faces the Earth. The asymmetry in the thickness of the lunar crust came first and independently of the direction of the Earth. Only later did it end up pointing this way, as the moon's rotation was captured. Whatever the cause, the great outpouring of lava onto the surface did not happen completely until some 3.5 billion years ago. So the man on the moon is at least 3 billion years old!

The solidified lava flows that form the maria average a couple of hundred metres in thickness, thinner nearer the rims. The mass of each layer of basalt pushed down on the crust so usually the next layer of lava pooled in the middle, producing concentric rings in each impact basin. This implies that the youngest basalts are on the top and in the middle. Indeed the greatest thickness is at the centres at about 1.6–4.8 km. The lava also sometimes leads to compression in the centres of the maria and stretching at the edges. Hence the wrinkle ridges and rift valleys that can some-times be seen.

Since the filling of the maria, not that much has happened to the moon. Lunar geologists now divide the moon's history into phases determined by the major impacts. Young rayed craters are said to be of the Copernican system, while older craters that predate the formation of the maria are of the Erastosthenian system. Older craters, flooded and unflooded, belong to the Imbrium system. There is the earlier Nectarian system and even a pre-Nectarian. There is some evidence for local volcanism in Mare Imbrium about 2.5 billion years ago and the occasional impact: Copernicus just over a billion years ago, Tycho just over 100 million years ago. But essentially the moon has been cooling and becoming more and more inactive.

So what are we left with? A world covered in rock that formed as a crust riding on a magma ocean; a world bombarded with giant meteors that formed giant impact basins; a world scarred with craters of all sizes; a world that briefly awoke and oozed lava from its insides to fill low-lying basins on one side with dark, smooth lava; a world still occasionally struck and scarred by meteors; a world where igneous rocks make up over 90 per cent of the crust, and mare basalts cover about 17 per cent of the lunar surface but constitute only about 1 per cent of the moon's crust. Above all, geologically, it is a world that is dying.

Yet this dying world may hold vital clues to another mystery. Measurements made of a speck of lunar dust may tell us how life first blossomed on our own planet. A recent analysis of the history of impact cratering on the moon suggests that the rate of meteor impacts had dropped steadily after the period of heavy bombardment but then increased rapidly about 400 million years ago. The clear inference is that the Earth would have experienced a similar frequency of impacts over the same period.

The team that carried out this work looked at a gram of lunar soil brought back by the Apollo 16 astronauts in 1971. In it they found 155 glassy spherules, formed when droplets of molten basalt are splashed out of a crater by the force and heat of an impact. The spherules came from approximately 146 different craters. The age of the spherules determined by isotope measurements, yields a record of lunar bombardment. Even though we do not know which crater was the source of which spherule, the distribution of the ages of the spherules from a single lunar site should reflect the age distribution of craters on the moon. The moon, although geologically a dying world, may also have influenced geological activity on the Earth.

Agatha Christie once wrote that any coincidence is worth investigation, then afterwards you can always discount it if it remains just a coincidence. The sudden cratering increase coincides with the so-called 'Cambrian explosion', a period which also saw a dramatic increase in the number and diversity of species on Earth. Although most people assume that impacts always cause death and destruction, it is possible that the additional stress of the impacts forced life to become more diverse and flexible. Just as we stress trees, through pruning, to make them give more fruit, so the stress caused by catastrophic impacts may have forced evolution into new directions.

Meanwhile French scientists have put forward another thought-provoking theory to explain what caused catastrophic volcanic activity on our planet hundreds of millions of years ago. This volcanic activity, they argue, changed the course of life on our planet and led to the rise of the dinosaurs.

In a report published in *Science*, researchers from Paris and Strasbourg suggest that three times in the history of life on Earth, the moon, together with the sun, caused oscillations inside the Earth, perhaps with volcanic results. This could account for some of Earth's more dramatic geological events, such as the splitting of continents and oceans. One of these, around 300 million years ago, perhaps wiped out the majority of animal species and paved the way for the rise of the dinosaurs. Oscillations at certain points in history created tension in the heart of the Earth, according to the French team's model. This was converted into heat, causing molten rock to spill out of the ground, changing the face of our planet. It sounds very dramatic but it might just be true.

CHAPTER EIGHTEEN

Fort Luna

O n 29 May 1961, just four days after President Kennedy told the American people he wanted a lunar landing by the end of the decade, the US Air Force finished compiling a secret report on military plans to colonize the moon.

The lunar fort would consist of pressurized empty fuel tanks 3 m in diameter by 6 m long, buried in the lunar soil by a tractor. Seven such tanks would be used for barracks, air locks, a hospital, a command post and a mess room. An extra three tanks could be used as a laboratory. On the perimeter of the base would be the arsenal, housing explosives, munitions and chemicals. A region at the end of a well-defined path leading away from the main habitation centre would be the waste dump, where refuse would be bagged and left in piles. On the other side of the fort four small nuclear reactors would be placed in pits to provide electricity. Next to the habitation modules would be emergency weapon bays housing Davy Crockett missiles and handheld Claymore mines in case the Soviets attacked. Some of the missiles were specifically designed to puncture pressure suits. Another option was to construct a fenced-off region where nuclear weapons would be stored.

This, and the idea of exploding a nuclear bomb on the moon, was among many military proposals for the occupation of the moon. Many in the United States military believed that routine manned spaceflight would soon be possible and they wanted the military to control it. In particular, some wanted to establish a bridgehead on the moon. The moon, it was believed, would be the ultimate high ground in the battle for strategic supremacy.

Now that the Cold War is over, it is hard for us to imagine just how the fear of nuclear war dominated American society in the 1950s. During the Second World War America itself had been safe but that would not be the case in any future conflicts. From the late 1940s it was being said that the nation that controlled the moon would not only control the Earth but a large part of the solar system. It was also said that the moon was the 'fortress of the next conqueror of the Earth'. The magazine that von Braun had used to set out his grand vision of lunar and planetary exploration, *Collier's*, once ran an article headed, 'Rocket Blitz from the Moon', showing missiles similar to the V-2 emerging from lunar silos.

One of those who most fervently believed this was USAF's General Homer A. Boushey. In a lecture to Washington's Aero Club, he outlined two military uses of the moon: as a missile base and as a place from which to spy on the Russians. He said that missiles fired from the moon could be guided from start to impact. He believed that the moonbase would be almost invulnerable. Any attack on the United States would be easily seen from the moon, and 'sure and massive retaliation' would follow. If the Soviets attempted to destroy the moonbase they would have to fire missiles towards the moon two and a half days before they attacked the United States. He went on to describe how energy, rocket fuel and oxygen could all be extracted from lunar rocks and concluded, 'We cannot afford to come out second in a territorial race of this magnitude. This outpost, under our control, would be the best possible guarantee that all of space will indeed be preserved for the peaceful purposes of man.'

General Dwight Black, the Air Force's director of guided missiles and special weapons, told Congress, 'I would hate to think that the Russians got to the moon first. The first nation that does will probably have a tremendous military advantage over any potential enemy.' The United States Army also had its eye on the moon; they listed their requirements as a manned lunar outpost and a lunar tank.

Another study was carried out for the Ballistic Missile Division. It said, 'the lunar base possesses strategic value by providing a site where future military deterrent forces could be located' and that 'a military lunar system has potential to increase our deterrent capability by insuring positive retaliation.' It added that such a base could become operational in June 1969.

The Army Ordnance Missile Command called its study 'Project Horizon'. It was produced by a group headed by Wernher von Braun and it was typically big in scale. The report said a lunar outpost was 'required to develop and protect potential United States interests on the moon, to develop moon-based surveillance of the Earth.' It said that an outpost was of such importance that it 'should be a special project having an authority and priority similar to the Manhattan Project'. It warned that the Soviet Union had openly announced that some of its citizens would celebrate the fiftieth anniversary of the October 1917 revolution on the moon. If the Soviets were to be the first to establish a moonbase, it 'would be disastrous to our nation's prestige and in turn to our democratic philosophy'.

It added chillingly:

Throughout the recorded history of human endeavor, the military outpost has been the hub around which evolved the social, economic, and political structure of civilization. During early US History, the establishment and maintenance of routes of communication to the far west was made possible by Army outposts.

The Wild West had come to the moon.

But President Eisenhower, with his growing fear of the military-industrial complex as he described it, was having none of this.

And he was right to dismiss the military significance of Sputnik even if few of the American people saw it that way. None of the apocalyptic predictions of the military significance of space have so far come true. As far as lobbing nuclear bombs onto the Soviet Union was concerned, a satellite was not the best way to do it. A satellite was vulnerable, and not all that accurate upon re-entry into the Earth's atmosphere. Ballistic missiles were far more convenient and reliable. There was no real military advantage in having a base on the moon. It was too visible and too far away. Missiles from it would take over two days to reach Earth, during which time they were theoretically in danger of being intercepted. In addition the cost of a moonbase was astronomical. It was, according to one report, a 'clumsy and ineffective way of doing a job'. To his credit, Ike set the tone for future manned space endeavours when he awarded the responsibility for manned, earth-orbiting spaceflight to the newly created civilian NASA.

Throughout the Apollo era, NASA planned for a moonbase which was seen as the next logical step after the landings but, as we have seen, Nixon nixed all that when he forced NASA to choose between future projects. Soon after Apollo 11 had landed, a Nixon-appointed task force looked at America's future direction in space. They asked von Braun who talked of a base on the moon and a manned mission to Mars. They all but laughed at him and von Braun resigned from NASA and went to Fairchild Industries to sell helicopters.

NASA had no option but to go for a scaled-down reusable space shuttle in the early 1970s. Not much was said, at least officially, about a return to the moon until the *Ride Report*, in 1986. This was written by a task force assembled by NASA, led by Sally Ride, the first American woman in space. It outlined four 'Leadership Initiatives' as a basis for discussion. It took as its premise the existence of a space station. The report states that the moon is 'not absolutely necessary' as a 'stepping stone' to Mars, nor is Mars necessarily the ultimate goal if the United States opts for a lunar base. One of its four initiatives was an outpost on the moon: 'a program that would build on the legacy of the Apollo Program to continue exploration, to establish a permanent scientific outpost, and to begin prospecting the moon's resources.' Tellingly it commented, of a proposed mission to Mars, that it should 'not be another Apollo – a one-shot foray or political stunt'. From its 1986 viewpoint, it envisaged returning to the moon in the 2000–2005 timeframe. The early outpost would allow a two-week lunar night stay in 2001. By 2005 the outpost would be supporting five people for several weeks.

The return to the moon idea stayed out of sight after the *Ride Report* until it was raised again in the preparations for the twentieth anniversary of the Apollo 11 moon landing. To President George Bush, it must have seemed an ideal opportunity to make a Kennedyesque speech and set the course of America's future space efforts. On the day of the anniversary he stood outside the National Air and Space Museum in front of the three Apollo 11 astronauts. But his speech had no long-term influence because he failed to identify any particular direction he wanted the American space programme to take. He was in favour of the space station that his predecessor, President Reagan, had started; he also wanted to put a man on Mars by 2019, and about the moon he said it was 'back to the moon, back to the future and this time back to stay'. Congress later voted away any significant funds for a back to the moon study.

After a few more years a new NASA administrator, Dan Goldin, initiated another study of when and how we should return to the moon. It was called the Human Lunar Return Study and it began in September 1995. But on the day that its conclusions were presented to NASA by, among others, Apollo 16 moonwalker

John Young, another NASA team made the sensational announcement that it had found evidence of fossilized micro-organisms in a meteorite from Mars. NASA shelved the Human Lunar Return initiative and has ever since been fixated on the red planet. The moon has been overlooked.

But if it had gone ahead the first phase of the Human Lunar Return (HLR) would already be underway. The first HLR mission was targeted for Aristarchus crater, selected because it is one of the most geologically interesting regions on the lunar surface and one of the most frequent areas for the mysterious glows that hover on rare occasions over the moon. The area includes the Aristarchus Plateau, a tectonically uplifted region nearly 100 m above the surrounding terrain. There is also Cobra Head, an intriguing volcanic structure. Add to that the spectacular 100 km long lava channel that is Schröter's Valley and other craters that are partially submerged by ancient lava flows, as well as sundry rilles, scarps, and volcanic domes and vents as well as blanket deposits of iron-rich glassy material spewed from ancient volcanic fire fountains and you have one of the most scientifically appealing regions on the moon.

By now we could have been watching astronauts walk over this ancient terrain. The space shuttle would have delivered to the International Space Station components for the reusable lunar transfer spacecraft that incorporated a crew cabin and a propulsion module. A short while later a Russian Proton rocket would put a lunar habitat module into a lunar trajectory from where it would eventually land in Aristarchus. This habitat module would be an inflatable structure that automatically opens up and waits for the crew to arrive. The crew, along with their lunar landing craft, would have been ferried up to the International Space Station and would have entered the lunar transfer spacecraft preparing it for flight into lunar orbit. From there the mission would become especially interesting.

In lunar orbit the crew would don spacesuits because their lunar landing craft would be open-topped. This concept was often considered in the period when Apollo was being designed and the Soviets thought it had many advantages. After all, why build a complex life support system for a small landing craft when you have spacesuits? But what a ride it would be, strapped onto the open lander as the lunar mountains and plains raced beneath you, getting so close that you would feel you could almost reach out and touch them.

The crew would spend about eighteen days at Aristarchus base during their first mission. And the cost, an estimated $2.5 billion, would be only about 3 per cent of the Apollo programme. As I write this, the International Space Station is in orbit with its first crew of three spending three months onboard. The ISS is an interesting project but it would be fair to say it hasn't exactly captured the imaginations let alone the hearts of the public, especially the young. How much more exciting and inspiring would be the Human Lunar Return.

Whenever we go back, wherever we land, the moonbase will definitely need a source of power. If they could be safely transported to the moon small nuclear power plants would be ideal. They would be rugged and compact and could be buried some distance away from the main sectors of the base with a power cable connecting it to an electrical grid. The power would be continuous and available throughout the two-week lunar night. But any launch involving nuclear components is bound to be controversial. For many, a more acceptable energy source would be sunlight converted into electricity by solar panels. Less than the area of a football field (2,000 square metres of panels) could produce about 100 kilowatts of electricity. The cells could be mounted on flexible backing, transported rolled up, and unfurled across the lunar surface. But they would obviously only work during the lunar day. To survive the long lunar night, recharge-able fuel cells – which combine oxygen and hydrogen to make electricity and water – would be needed.

Apollo showed us that the moon has all the minerals and resources we need to build a moonbase. It's all there in the rocks and we just have to find ways to get it out: oxygen to breathe, rocket fuel and construction materials could all be extracted. As well as being 42 per cent of the material, oxygen is the most abundant of many useful substances, including silicon (21 per cent), iron (13 per cent), calcium (8 per cent), aluminium (7 per cent) and magnesium (6 per cent).

Aluminium could be obtained from the feldspar mineral plagioclase which is abundant in the lunar highlands. Its processing is a conventional technology on Earth but it prob-ably won't work exactly the same way on the moon. The standard method involves constant supplies and resupplies of electrodes and electrolytes, including sulphuric acid. There is a simpler method but that releases corrosive chlorine gas. It would be useful as a building material and perhaps even as a rocket fuel but, because of its complexity, aluminium production would perhaps be postponed until the moonbase was more established.

One of the main things the lunar astronauts could do is look for the mineral ilmenite (a mixture of iron, titanium and oxygen), which would probably be the raw material for oxygen production. This mineral makes up 10–20 per cent of some lunar mare basalt rocks. Scoop it up, crush it and heat it. Making glass would be possible but it requires acids to leach out undesirable metals and temperatures above 1700 degrees.

The oxygen and hydrogen from the water at the poles could be liquefied – not a tremendously difficult task in the lunar cold – and used just as it is for rocket fuel. Some of the rockets the Apollo astronauts used to get to the moon, as well as the space shuttle's main engines, used liquid hydrogen and oxygen as fuels. We have the rocket engines, we have the fuel.

But there are hazards on the moon. When astronauts venture beyond low-Earth orbit they are at risk from radiation from solar flares. One particular flare in August 1972 released an astounding amount of radiation that luckily occurred when no lunar mission was underway. Had it occurred during an Apollo expedition the astronauts would have been incapacitated immediately and dead within hours or days. Flares large enough to demand some form of protective shielding occur often, several times per year when the sun is at its maximum level of activity. So the first thing the lunar inhabitants would have to do would be to bury their living and working quarters. They could scoop lunar soil around it or, more likely, scoop the soil into long tube-like sacks that can be coiled around the outside of the base. Burying the base under 2.6–7.9 m of lunar dirt reduces exposure to levels experienced on Earth's surface 3000 m above sea level. An earth-built shelter, with aluminium walls many centimetres thick, could be used as a stopgap but bringing it from Earth would be tricky. When astronauts went for traverses across the surface they would have to be careful about sudden bursts of radiation – sometimes they would get less than three hours warning. Perhaps they would have to carry an emergency inflatable shelter that could be buried under a metre of lunar dirt at short notice.

Another hazard would be dust. The highly abrasive lunar dust gets everywhere and can destroy moving parts in machines, such as bearings, joints and linkages. Dust can also cover vehicle headlights and camera lenses. The experience of the Apollo astronauts was that a moonbase would need a 'dust lock' as well as an airlock.

And of course they would need food to eat. For the first missions they would live off rations but experiments have been conducted into growing food on the moon. Wheat is an excellent candidate for a lunar crop because its vertical leaf orientation permits highly efficient conversion of solar energy into carbohy-drate and protein in a limited space. In addition, it is a plant that responds well to continuous light. Some scientists have calculated that a lunar farm with an area of 1,000 square metres could feed 100 people. The atmosphere in the agricultural module would contain excess carbon dioxide to assist the plants' growth and transparent or translucent windows would admit sunlight. High-pressure sodium-vapour lamps would provide lighting during the two-week lunar night.

Another crop that could be grown on the moon is rice. Japanese researchers have developed a rice that matures in 100 days so that lunar colonies could have three crops a year. Normally the rice variety *mutsu-homare* takes 160 days to mature but if you fine-tune its growing conditions its starch production and growth speed can be increased. The researchers say the taste is not quite as good but on the moon I do not suppose there would be many complaints.

Scientists have had a little success in growing plants in lunar soil. It would be better, however, if the lunar soil was augmented with human waste materials. In the long term, the colony would have to have as near a self-sufficient life support system as possible and that would be a whole lot easier with access to the ice at the poles.

Apart from solving the problems of living on the moon, there is also the fascinating prospect of the moonbase helping us to live on Earth. One of the greatest problems we face on Earth is finding sufficient energy for our ever-growing numbers and utiliz-ing it in a way that does not damage the environment. The solution could be on the moon, in the form of a substance that could contain more than ten times the energy stored in the fossil fuels of Earth.

Nuclear fusion – the process of squeezing two atoms together to make one heavier atom – liberates a prodigious amount of energy. This is the process that generates energy deep in the heart of stars that slowly makes its way out and reaches us as starlight. The stars shine because of distant, concealed fusion fire. For fifty years we have attempted to generate sustained, controlled fusion, which promises cheap electrical power from clean nuclear fusion reactors. But, while researchers have achieved much, we cannot say we are close to that goal. It will take a few more decades yet to build a commercial fusion reactor, if we ever do.

In contrast, conventional nuclear reactors based on fission or the break-up of atoms require fuel in the form of uranium or plutonium which is expensive and hazardous, and has dangerous and problematic waste products. Nuclear fusion requires less troublesome ingredients. Helium-3 (He-3), an isotope of helium, could be an important fusion reactor fuel. But unfortunately it is rare on Earth; there are only several hundred kilograms of it obtained from the radioactive decay of tritium in atomic weapons. Combined in a fusion reactor with the isotope deuterium, He-3 could produce abundant fusion energy with few radioactive by-products. Our meagre supply would be useful for developing a prototype helium-3 reactor but not much more. But our sun has enormous amounts of He-3 that it sprays into space in the solar wind and over the past 4.5 billion years the moon has captured some of it. Lunar soil is an excellent collector of He-3 from the solar wind because it is extremely fine-grained. It could have trapped a million tons of it.

It is thought that older regions of the moon's surface should be better sources because they have been exposed to the solar wind for longer, and contain greater amounts of fine-grained aggregates that are good at absorbing helium-3. Even though helium-3 is more abundant on the moon than the Earth it is still very rare, amounting to only 4 or 5 parts per billion in the lunar soil. To extract 1 tonne, it is estimated that 200 million tonnes of lunar soil would have to be processed (equivalent to mining the top 2 metres of a region 10 kilometres square).

To get at it, you would need to strip-mine the lunar surface with robotic excavators, collecting lunar soil to a depth of 2 metres. Robotic conveyors would transport the soil to a nearby processing plant. There it would be heated to 1100 degrees, at which time the helium would evaporate. The remaining soil would then be heated to 1650 degrees, when the oxygen would be given off and collected. The helium-3 could then be extracted from the common helium using a cryogenic distillation process.

If and when we have solved the considerable technical problems and built a commercial fusion reactor it might be worth it. It would only require 25 tonnes of helium-3 to provide all the power that the United States needs in a year. And you could fit all this into the payload bay of a single space shuttle.

Ultimately we may get our helium-3 from Jupiter which contains vast amounts of it. But while we can dream about that for the far distant future, we can also ponder the intriguing idea that humble lunar soil may help us meet our growing energy needs and solve our pollution problems in the shorter term.

Because of the moon's slight tilt on its axis, there are regions deep in craters near its poles that never see the light of the sun. In several studies over the years it has been suggested that ice could accumulate there providing an invaluable resource for future exploitation. If the ice is there, many have argued, it would completely alter the prospects for settling the moon.

It is.

CHAPTER NINETEEN

The Eighth Continent

A t around 09.50 GMT on Saturday 31 July 1999 hundreds of telescopes from all over the world were pointed towards the moon's South Pole looking at the regions that are in perpetual shadow. The astronomers were waiting for the crash of a spacecraft that had been circling the moon for eighteen months; a spacecraft that had made an astounding discovery about the moon. It was on a suicide trajectory and was within minutes of passing over the surface for the last time and crashing onto the polar regions. Its last task was to fall into the eternal dark of a permanently shadowed crater. Scientists hoped that the estimated 6,100 km per hour impact would disturb the lunar soil and throw into space water vapour from the shards of ice they believed lay scattered like diamonds in the lunar topsoil. They were also witness to a burial.

The big players were all watching and waiting, the Hubble Space Telescope and the Submillimeter Wave Astronomy Satellite in orbit as well as ground-based instruments including the McDonald Observatory in Texas and the Keck Telescope in Hawaii. All agreed that it was a long shot. The spacecraft, called Lunar Prospector, would have to strike a region where there was ice, if there was ice. Few expected to be so lucky as to see anything but it was worth a try. As the spacecraft came closer and closer to the moon's surface, headed for one of the darkest spots in the solar system, they knew that – regardless of the outcome of this final bold experiment – Lunar Prospector had yielded a goldmine of scientific data. It had provided global maps of the moon's gravitational and magnetic fields, and the distribution of its key elements, giving us a much better understanding of the origin, evolution and composition of our rocky neighbour. It might also have discovered the moon's most precious resource, ice.

Lunar Prospector had been launched in January 1998. After a few days it entered orbit over the lunar poles and its five science instruments began their survey. The mission had been chosen by NASA in February 1995 as part of its Discovery Program, established to send frequent, low-cost space probes to the planets. Some were to study the sun, Venus and a comet, as well as Mars. After many years of neglect two space probes in succession had orbited the moon, showing us that there was much to be discovered on this seemingly dead world.

The other probe was called Clementine and it circled the moon for a while in 1994. It was a military mission intended to evaluate space technologies. But astronomers jumped on too, saying that they could use it without interfering with its technology aims. It did not carry instruments designed to look for lunar ice but during its mission its controllers improvised an experiment based on the fact that radio waves are reflected from planetary surfaces differently depending on the composition of those surfaces.

Radio waves are scattered in all directions from surfaces made up of ground-up rock, like those found on most of the moon, Mercury, Venus and Mars, but they are reflected more strongly from icy surfaces which act like a mirror. The Clementine team used its radio transmitter to beam radio waves into the dark regions of the South Pole of the moon. The data returned suggested there could be deposits of ice in the permanently dark regions, perhaps as much as 1 billion cubic metres, the volume of a small lake. However, the results were not conclusive.

A year later, astronomers at the Arecibo Radio Telescope, the world's largest radio dish, reported that their radar observations of the south polar regions showed no evidence of ice, reversing the conclusion of a year earlier. But both Clementine and Arecibo would only have definitely detected ice if it had been in the form of slabs on the surface. Perhaps it was in the form of ice splinters mixed in with the lunar soil? What was needed was to take another look.

So it was with great anticipation that astronomers awaited the launch of Lunar Prospector. It had taken only twenty-two months to build and was just 1.38 m in diameter and 1.23 m long. It had sensors on deployable arms, and six thrusters controlled its direction in space. For simplicity and to save money it had no onboard computer. The hopes of finding ice on the moon rested with the neutron spectrometer built at Los Alamos Laboratory. If there was water on the moon and it was within about 1 m of the surface, that sensor stood a good chance of finding it. To find the ice, it would need the help of particles that fly through space from other parts of the galaxy and beyond. These high-energy cosmic particles slam into the moon's surface, throwing up sub-atomic particles called neutrons. If hydrogen, a component of ice, is present then some of the neutrons would be slowed down. The neutron spectrometer was designed to capture a sample of those neutrons and measure their energies, looking for the low-speed neutrons that scientists said were the signature of water. The researchers thought they would know within a month or two. One said, 'If we see water, I suspect the land rush is on.'

Although all the attention was on Prospector's search for ice, the spacecraft also carried a range of other sensors including a gamma-ray spectrometer that would provide a global map of the major rock-forming elements on the lunar surface. The last time scientists had carried out a similar survey of our neighbour was during the Apollo missions a quarter of a century earlier. And because Apollo followed a near-equatorial orbit it sampled only 20 per cent of the moon. Prospector was going to look at all of it.

After just three weeks in orbit rumours began circulating in the media that Prospector had detected slow neutrons as it passed over the lunar poles. I knew a few people working on the mission and, on condition of anonymity, they briefed me about what Prospector had discovered. They were not willing to say definitely but after each passing the evidence was stacking up. So on Thursday 5 February I ran a story on BBC radio that Prospector had probably found ice. It featured high on the midnight radio news but my TV colleagues were unimpressed and decided not to mention it at all. The Lunar Prospector team had imposed a tight clamp on news releases and their official status reports made no mention of the water ice. NASA finally made the official announcement on Thursday 5 March; Prospector had indeed found ice. The story led the TV News. The following day newspapers all over the world said it was the biggest breakthrough in space exploration since Neil Armstrong had stepped onto the lunar surface.

The tiny spacecraft had found between 10 and 300 million tonnes of water, not only as expected in the dark depths of the Scott–Aitken Basin but also in the dark craters of the North Pole. To many people's surprise there was 50 per cent more water in the craters of the North Pole than those of the South: some 5,000–20,000 square kilometres at the South Pole and 10,000–50,000 at the North. Lunar Prospector's chief scientist Alan Binder said, 'We have the first unquestionable results indicating that there are significant quantities of water at both lunar poles.' The view was that the water was in the form of ice crystals at a concentration of about 1 per cent by volume of the lunar soil. They estimated that there was about 300 million metric tonnes, enough to form a 12 m-deep lake of 10 square kilometres. The implications are tremendous. For the first time we can go to a planetary body and we can fuel up. That fuel can be used to go to Mars and anywhere in the solar system,' said Dr Binder. He added that if you picked up a cubic yard of lunar soil from the ice field then you might find 1, 2, maybe 5 gallons of water.

The Times of London said, 'Galileo's vision of a watery moon is proved right.' The *Washington Post* said that, although there were no plans to colonize the moon, the presence of the ice would make all the difference. The British *Daily Mail* had a full front page headed 'Man may live on moon within 30 years.' The associated article predicted that 'The moon could become a vast launching pad for missions to Mars and the rest of the solar system.'

The following day those writers who do not normally write about science recognized a good story when they saw one and pitched in. *The Times* said, 'The only point in going there is to come back and say we have been.' On Saturday 7 March the *Guardian* carried a leader calling for the moon treaty to be brought up to date and for the exploitation of lunar resources to be approached in a 'green' way.

This article was referring to the treaty proposed by the United Nations in 1967 governing the activities of states in the exploration of outer space including 'the moon and Other Celestial Bodies'. It set out the rules for lunar exploration, said that its use should be for peaceful purposes and prohibited any form of military activity. A later agreement in 1979 extended the proposal saying that the moon should be 'the province of all mankind and [exploration] shall be carried out for the benefit and in the interests of all countries.' It also ruled out property rights on the moon and said that the lunar environment should be protected.

When the media comment died down, the case for the ice rested on two lines of evidence. The Clementine radar measurements showed the unusual radar signature of ice only in the permanently shadowed regions near the poles and slow neutrons were only detected over those same regions. The case is not conclusive but it is very good. To prove it, we will have to go there.

Until the ice was discovered, lunar bases had remained in the realms of science fiction, partly because of the enormous cost of sending up water supplies from the Earth. Lunar rocks lacked all trace of water, and although they contain a great deal of oxygen the hydrogen to make water is very scarce indeed. The discovery of ice could mark the first step towards science fiction turning into science fact. NASA said there was enough water to support 2,000 lunar colonists for more than a century. A few months later the researchers increased their estimates of the amount of ice. The new analysis also showed that the water was confined to localized areas near the poles, rather than spread out more evenly as was assumed. The ice appeared to be buried about half a metre beneath the lunar surface with slightly more at the North than the South Pole.

Prospector found between 11 million and 330 million tonnes of water which sounds like a lot of wet stuff, but it isn't really. Around 45 billion tonnes would fill 12,500 Olympic-size pools. Imagine the water spread over some 65,000 square kilometres which is roughly the area of Lake Huron in North America; 45 billion tonnes of water poured evenly over that area would hardly wet the ground – a depth of 6 mm. But despite its limited extent, lunar water could be very, very useful.

For those watching the Lunar Prospector, the final few minutes of its life ticked by. The estimated time of the impact passed. What had happened 400,000 km away? The controlled crash did not throw up any signs of water. There could be many explanations: the spacecraft might have missed the target area, or it might have hit a rock or dry soil, or there might be no ice at all. After looking at Prospector's final transmissions NASA said it landed on target, deep within a lunar crater near the moon's South Pole. Even given the most favourable circumstances, the dust plume would have stretched only 22 km above the moon's surface and would have been 100,000 times fainter than the brightness of the lunar limb. It was later estimated that the water plume would never have been detectable from Earth. Only one satellite in Earth orbit had any chance of seeing it.

But, as well as looking for ice, Lunar Prospector did something else as it plunged onto the moon's surface. It also buried someone. A secondary mission for the spacecraft was to deposit 1 ounce of the cremated remains of Eugene Shoemaker, making him the first person to be buried on another world. The renowned astro-geologist, had been killed in a car crash two years earlier.

Shoemaker was a legend among geologists. Almost single-handedly he invented the science of the study of cosmic impacts, and he played a key role in training the Apollo moonwalkers to explore the moon in a scientific manner. Shoemaker's work meant that the scientific gains from Apollo were remarkable. He had wanted to be an astronaut himself and perhaps today he could have been. But in the early 1960s health qualifications were more stringent than they are now and he was turned down because of a minor medical problem. Shortly before professor Shoemaker died he said, 'Not going to the moon and banging on it with my own hammer has been the biggest disappointment in life.' In death he got his wish.

'I don't think Gene ever dreamed his ashes would go to the moon,' his widow Carolyn Shoemaker said shortly before watching Lunar Prospector blast off in January 1998. 'He would be thrilled. We will always know when we look at the moon, that Gene is there.'

The water on the moon probably collected over 4 billion years ago when comets smashed into the lunar surface and molecules of water collected in the super-cold areas of the shaded crater. There it has been ever since, trapped in the cold and the dark. There are few places in our solar system like those found in the depths of certain polar craters. Calculations indicate that they may not have seen a ray of sunlight for billions of years. The ice has lain there undisturbed since the moon was young and life was not yet a dream.

Its presence transforms the case for a base on the moon. Hydrogen was always hard to find in moonbases that were situated near the equator but here at the poles it can be obtained easily. Just scoop up the soil and heat it. But to get it, you first have to venture into the eternal night and perhaps the eternal day as well. At the moon's South Pole, high on a mountain or lip of a crater, may be a region that is able to catch the sunlight all lunar-day long. No one has seen it but astronomers have given it a name, 'The Peak of Eternal Light', a place where the sun never sets.

NASA's Goldstone Deep Space Network Radio Telescope in California usually communicates with distant space probes scattered throughout the distant parts of the solar system: the Galileo probe orbiting Jupiter, Cassini on its way to Saturn, Voyager and Pioneer far beyond the most distant planets. But it can also turn its giant radio eye on the moon, and in conjunction with smaller radio telescopes nearby it can bounce radar echoes off the lunar surface and map its topography. In this way it has looked for the regions near the pole that may be in permanent shadow or permanent light.

The moon's axis of rotation, unlike the Earth's, is not markedly tilted compared to its orbit around the sun. This means that the moon does not have strongly different seasons and that the sun never rises very far up in the polar skies. You can stand at the lunar poles for a whole year and the sun would only move up or down about 1.5 degrees. Imagine a place of long shadows, which every month point in all compass directions. Some of the shadows are present all year round. The sun skirts the horizon, as does the Earth. Sometimes they are seen together, sometimes one or other dips behind a distant mountain peak.

The topographic map shows that the north polar area displays relatively little relief, whereas the south polar region has much more rugged terrain. In the north the permanently shadowed regions may be concentrated at the bottom of large craters or forming a crescent in the wall and floor areas that are furthest from the pole. Hermite, at 86 degrees north, may be one such crater. Several small lunar craters on the floor of Peary (88.6 degrees north) and three larger craters aligned roughly along the 315 degree longitude line are also protected from sunlight. These five regions constitute the largest potential deposits at the North Pole.

At the South Pole, virtually all the floors of three craters with diameters in the 39–51 km range appear to be in shadow: crater Faustini and some unnamed craters are also dark, as is Shackleton. Cabeus may also contain regions of permanent shadow, although its outlines cannot be specified because they are dependent on the unknown height of the northern part of its floor.

The radar data, combined with height measurements made by Clementine, show that there is probably no 'Peak of Eternal Light' as some had hoped. The maps reveal that no part of the South Pole is in constant sunlight but there seem to be some areas that are almost in the permanent glare of the sun. (This is not a definite conclusion because we have not observed this region over an entire year.) The rim of Shackleton crater is particularly interesting because it is illuminated more than 80 per cent of the time. Nearby there are two other places, only 10 km apart, which collectively receive illumination more than 98 per cent of the time. They are 'peaks of almost eternal light'. So there is a part of the moon that has, within walking distance, regions that are in almost permanent sunlight and regions that are in permanent darkness; and in that darkness can be found the resource most essential for a colony, water. This then, not the equator or anywhere else, is the place to put a base on the moon.

Electricity-producing solar arrays could be placed in the brigh ´
areas and connected by a microwave or cable link to the
habitation region, producing constant energy. Nowhere else is
this possible on the moon.

Another interesting fact is that the South Pole thermal environment is less harsh than that found at the lunar equator. There are
few dramatic temperature shifts. Surface temperature remains
close to −30 degrees C. (Outside the polar regions, surface
temperature spans about 400 degrees over the course of the
28-terrestrial-day lunar day.) The 14 days of hot sunlight and 14
days of frigid darkness do not occur at the poles. Instead, the sun
is on the horizon for most of the lunar day. This would also make
designing a lunar base easier here.

Many hoped that the discovery of ice would give a boost to
planned lunar missions. But, over three years later, it seems that
governments and space agencies are lukewarm about the idea of
going back to confirm the discovery and do some more exploration.

At one time the European Space Agency (ESA) had plans for a
soft-lander and an orbiter but both have been shelved because
they were too expensive and lacked political support. But the ice
discovery did add some impetus to another concept that was
being championed by a former astronaut. This ambitious proposal, called Euromoon 2000, was the brainchild of Wubbo
Ockels in 1996. Ockels, who flew on Space Shuttle Challenger in
1985, had spent seven years preparing it.

However, the space science interests of ESA are dominated by
astronomers who are fixated on clouds of superhot gas, either
those swirling around our planet or in distant galaxies. They did
not support the moon mission. So Wubbo Ockels took his case to
European Industry. He carted a three-dimensional model of the
Lunar South Pole into the offices of space executives and used a

flashlight to demonstrate why parts of it were in eternal darkness and to show the regions where a spacecraft could land. His strategy worked. Eventually he had fully three-quarters of the $200 million cost paid for by the private sector. Aerospace and high technology companies as well as other sponsors wanted to be associated with a high-profile return to the moon. It was unprecedented for a mission to be so well supported by non-government funds. When Lunar Prospector was being mooted private companies in the United States were asked to sponsor it but when they were uninterested, the concept was taken to NASA who were. Euromoon 2000 was several times more expensive than Prospector. The director general of ESA, Antonio Rodata, wrote to the head of NASA, Dan Goldin, suggesting co-operation on the mission.

The Euromoon mission was to have a small orbiter called Lunarsat to scout the South Pole for landing sites. The following year a lander would be launched to the rim of Shackleton crater to begin setting up what Ockels called a 'robotic village' for scientific studies and technology demonstrations. It would land on the western rim of Shackleton at a point where it intersects the rims of two other craters, 1,200 m above the basin floor. Ockels wanted to start by sending a small video camera to celebrate the millennium.

The mission was particularly challenging because it required a landing accuracy of 100 square metres in terrain that has an 11,000 metre level of vertical relief. Just achieving the pinpoint touchdown capability would help those probes that would follow. As well as Shackleton crater it could also head for the 6 km high Malapert Mountain, 120 km from the pole, from which the Earth can virtually always be seen, thus allowing continuous communications for any future outpost. The regions of almost perpetual light are in direct view of Malapert.

The project had captured the imagination of many and seemed

to be gaining momentum in March 1998 as representatives of ESA's fourteen member nations met to consider the future of Euromoon 2000 just weeks after the announcement that Lunar Prospector had found ice. Before the meeting Euromoon 2000 was said to have the support of the director general Antonio Rodata and Britain's science minister. Rodata said, 'The appeal for me is not purely the scientific side. The other appeal is that we are trying to approach this problem in an unconventional way. The image of an initiative like Euromoon could appeal to sponsors.' But after two days of discussions, with most of the money for Euromoon secured from private sources, ESA's council turned the funding request for £32 million down.

After the meeting Ockels said:

We are basically sitting here crying. I don't know what happened. When the director general of ESA asked who supported Euromoon there was silence. Nobody said anything. Everybody got scared. I was sitting there thinking. I can motivate industry. I can motivate the public. But the politicians just don't get the point.

Later ESA did sanction a mission to the moon. Called SMART-1, it is a low-cost high-tech spacecraft that combines science and the testing of new technologies. It will be launched as an auxiliary payload on an Ariane 5 booster at the end of 2002 and will use an ion-thruster to take it to the moon on a low energy expenditure trajectory. It will take almost 18 months to reach lunar orbit, where it will carry out a geochemical scan of the surface and take a lot of pictures.

Others have talked about a lunar return. In the United States several private companies have plans to go to the moon. Some want to put a small rover on the surface and have it driven from a console in a theme park; some talk of placing a rover on the lip of a dark polar crater and, floodlights on, moving slowly down into it. Japan has had small science missions on the drawing board for years but they do not seem to be getting closer to launch. China, which may put its own astronaut into space in a year or two, has also expressed interest in going to the moon. Some of these initiatives may be realized but most will not.

There is a word seldom heard these days at NASA head-quarters, a word that some believe, if allowed into common usage, might distract attention from the main tasks facing the organization – to continue the construction of the International Space Station in Earth orbit and to search for life on Mars. That word is moon.

It's a word that dare not be said because without doubt humans could return to the moon with relative ease. Advancing technology in the years since the first manned landing means that the next lunar explorers will not run the risks of Apollo. They will be able to take more with them and stay longer and there is plenty for them to do when they get there: science, engineering, exploration. There are wonders and surprises waiting for us right on our cosmic doorstep, accessible for a fraction of the cost of building a space station or a manned flight to Mars. So why is the idea of returning to the moon such a neglected issue among the world's space agencies? If they have lost their way it is because we have let them.

We know more about the moon than we do about any other object in space. We have the records of observers for hundreds of years; we have the data from dozens of space probes; we have the testimonies of those who have been there; and we have over 2,000 lunar samples from nine sites (382 kg from six Apollo landings as well as 0.3 kg from three Soviet Luna automated sample return probes). The surface has also been examined at ten additional sites by other probes. We have measurements made in orbit by the Apollo spacecraft, we have a partial photographic survey carried out by the Lunar Orbiter probes in the 1960s, a complete multi-spectral survey performed by the Clementine mission and the geochemical and ice survey by Lunar Prospector . . . and we have our dreams.

The International Space Station is a dramatic, multi-national large-scale construction in low Earth orbit. It could do wonderful science. But it's not space exploration because it's not going anywhere. Those seeking funding for the space station have often called it a stepping stone to space. If that is so then consider this. When did you last really look at a stepping stone? It is in the nature of stepping stones that they are in themselves uninteresting and overshadowed by what they lead to. If space advocates in the United States expect that public interest will be sustained by the space station so that a mission to the moon or Mars will be easier to lobby for, then they are mistaken.

Returning to the moon, I contend, is the only real way to get the public all fired up about space again. To the public the space station is worthy but dull, and a trip to Mars is just too expensive and, appealing as it is to scientists and astronauts, it would never be voted for in these times. It just has to be a trip to the moon.

Some would say that we have been there and done that. They would be wrong. There may be footprints on the lunar surface but we have only camped there overnight, we've hardly done anything on the moon. Nevertheless it's not just for a grand space adventure that we should go back to the moon. There are many other reasons.

The science possible on the moon is astounding. Just think of how it differs from the Earth: low gravity, no magnetic field, no atmosphere (a good-sized room holds as much gas as the entire lunar atmosphere), no water, high vacuum, low or high temperature depending upon whether you're in shadow, seismic stability, no radio interference on its far side, and total, total sterility.

A telescope has already been put on the moon. The Apollo 16 astronauts set up a 7.5 cm Ultra Violet scope in 1972. It looked at several UV sources including the Earth's upper atmosphere and nearby galaxies. As a follow-up, NASA scientists designed LUTE (the Lunar Ultra Violet Telescope Experiment). It would have been placed on the moon by an unmanned lander but Congress never funded it. With its 1 m mirror, LUTE would not have had the ability to move. It would have stared at a swath of sky 1.5 degrees wide every 28 days as the moon rotated.

Orbiting observatories may be cheaper than lunar ones and have many advantages but the moon has some important things to offer certain astronomers. It would be a good place to put an array of precisely positioned telescopes, a so-called interferometer. Optical telescopes on the lunar surface separated by just 1 km but linked could have a resolving power hundreds of times better than the Hubble Space Telescope. They could see the width of a coin at 2 million km.

One group of scientists have proposed the Lunar Synthesis Array. This is an interesting concept involving two concentric rings of 1.5 m telescopes. The outer ring would consist of thirty-three telescopes in a circle 10 km across. The inner ring would be 0.5 km across and would contain only nine instruments. It would have a resolving power 10,000 better than the Hubble Space Telescope and could detect Earth-like planets orbiting other stars.

Also, the moon's far side could be the quietest place in the solar system for radio astronomy. The far side could open up very low frequency radio astronomy – frequencies below 15 megahertz (wavelengths longer than 20 m). These frequencies never get through the Earth's atmosphere, and this is one of the few remaining unexplored windows in the electromagnetic spectrum. Relay satellites in lunar orbit could get the data back to Earth in less than two seconds. In lunar one-sixth gravity telescopes could be larger, with lighter mirrors. And if positioned at the poles they could carry out longer exposures of certain objects than are possible on instruments elsewhere.

There could also be an underground isolation facility. Situated in a man-made cavern 10 m below the surface, it would be shielded from all radiation except neutrinos and the radioactive decay products from naturally occurring potassium, uranium and thorium. These could be reduced by coating the inner lining of the chamber with low radiation materials. This combination of low gravity, high vacuum, low radiation environment would be unique. Indeed the stability of the moon would make it ideal for constructing the long arms of a gravity detector to try and pick up the faint gravity waves that ripple through the cosmos, so far undetected.

There are some disadvantages with the moon, however. The Earth's magnetic field protects us from cosmic rays and the solar wind, but the moon has no such protection. Micrometeoroids would be a problem as well. There is the long lunar night and the dust clings to every surface. An astronaut walking near an observatory could cause a disturbance.

It is clear that we will not go to the moon for astronomy alone. Some argue, but not me, that the reasons for building a moonbase will be like those justifying the International Space Station. Looked at individually, each stage involved in building the ISS is not in itself worthwhile. But at what point does a collection of individually inadequate reasons add up to a compelling reason?

To build the first moonbase we need take nothing with us except our ingenuity. There, in the lunar rocks, is everything required to support life and many industries as well. It is all in the rocks – aluminium, iron, hydrogen, helium and especially oxygen.

Travelling through space is all about the economics of energy. By far the hardest, most energy-intensive phase of any space journey is the initial step from the Earth's surface to low Earth orbit – just 200 km. At the moment every drop of rocket fuel required to send a spacecraft onward and outward has to be lifted up Earth's deep gravitational well, and of course you need rocket fuel to lift the rocket fuel.

Because the moon's gravity is much lower than the Earth's it requires far less energy to ship rocket fuel from the moon to low Earth orbit than it does to get it from the Earth. In fact it requires far less energy to send rocket fuel from the moon to Mars than it does to get it from the Earth's surface into orbit! Someone once said that, energy-wise, getting into Earth orbit not only gets you halfway to the moon but halfway to anywhere in the solar system. The rocket fuel (oxygen and hydrogen) found at the moon's poles could form the basis of a solar system wide transport network.

What would you say if I told you there was a new Africa to explore? The moon's land area is about the same as that of Africa. It is just as rich in minerals as Africa, and I believe it will make fortunes for as many as Africa has.

The last man on the moon was Gene Cernan. When he had completed his last moonwalk he grabbed the TV camera and pointed it at his lunar craft's front landing gear. Here was a plaque with words that sounded so final. He removed the cover and read the message: 'Here man completed his first explorations of the moon, December 1972.' But Cernan went on to say, 'This is our commemoration that will be here until someone like us, until some of you who are out there, who are the promise of the future, come back to read it again.' With one last look around, he climbed onto the ladder and made his way into the lunar spacecraft to begin his journey home. The Earth was high in the south-western lunar sky.

The moon is indeed Earth's eighth continent and we need no reason to go there other than our precious human drive to explore. The Cold War took us there once. Next time we should return for our spirit.

CHAPTER TWENTY

The Moon Stone

S he has been toiling up this slope for 20 minutes now; her colleague, one of the recently arrived astronauts from the non-spacefaring nations, wanted to look at the grand view as it is called. Behind her face mask her breathing sounds loud and laboured, for even in one-sixth of Earth's gravity the climb is an exertion. There is no danger of getting lost – light pipes have been placed on either side of the path for this is a route travelled frequently. Soon they reach the rounded summit and turn around.

Everything around her is inky black – not a black like night-time back on Earth but a black that's like looking into the infinite. The crater floors and valleys are in shadow as they always are in this part of the moon. They are standing on the rim of Shackleton crater whose southern side is bathed by the rays of the sun. She can see the tops of nearby peaks jutting out of the shadows like nunataks poking above the Antarctic ice cap or ancient mountains protruding from the lunar maria.

She points out the crescent Earth above one of them. It is always in roughly the same direction and, although a thin crescent, it is four times brighter than the full moon appears in the Earth's skies. She says that the phase of the Earth seen from the moon, and the phase of the moon seen from the Earth are complementary. In the skies of Earth the moon will be gibbous tonight. The sun is brilliant and low on the horizon. She has to adjust her visor.

Attached to nearby peaks are rows of solar cells propped up to catch the sunlight. Cables relay electricity back to base, though there is talk of an experimental microwave energy link being tested sometime in the future. That would enable them to spread out to further areas that receive almost constant light. On the flanks of nearby Mount Malapert is an antenna farm, their communications link with Earth.

Down the slope, also in semi-permanent sunlight, her colleagues are moving around the small, soil-covered dome that is their home. Stretching beyond the moonbase is a single track attended by a trail of lights supported on poles, like street lamps back on Earth. They go downhill, into the darkness.

For it is what lies in the darkness that has drawn them here. At the end of the lights she can see movement as astronauts scurry around the diggers and drills testing the regolith for traces of ice. To one side she can see the now lifeless hulks of miniature rovers that were sent here from Earth before the colony was established. The ice they mine is the most precious thing on the moon, after themselves of course. It makes this desolate and forbidding place one of the most important off the Earth. In the permanently shadowed area she can dimly see the ice store. When the ice is extracted some of it is stored as liquid oxygen and hydrogen, some as liquid water, but most lies in ingots, surrounded by a faintly glowing location stick.

One of her tasks on this rounded peak is to service the webcam. Its panoramic view is one of the highlights of the moonbase's website. Millions of schoolchildren, among others, log in every day to see how things are going and to chat with the crew or watch a broadcast.

Beyond the main living quarters, she can see the farm. Most of the food comes up on the lunar shuttle once every six weeks but they have some promising experiments and novel foods genetically tailored especially for them. In the distance she can see the automated lumbering Ice Searcher using its ground-penetrating radar to survey for ice.

Many more people know what it is like to stand on this peak

than have ever been here. The new generation of virtual reality helmets allow environmental data to be downloaded from the web. Many years ago some of the earlier space missions were funded this way, by the sales of such 'entertainment' data. 'Disney is larger than NASA' was the slogan. Nowadays the VR kits allow you to walk on the moon or the Sandy plains of Mars and there is even a passable reconstruction of Neil Armstrong coming down the ladder of his lunar module to make the first footprint. You can watch from over his shoulder or from Buzz Aldrin's viewpoint.

She wonders if, in years to come, spaceships bound for Mars and Jupiter will call here to pump onboard the fuel they need for their journey.

I am on my belly, slithering through mud, then squeezing through a triangular-shaped crack in the rock barely large enough for me to crawl through. Several times I think I am stuck but manage to wriggle through. In front of me is Professor George Eogan of the National University of Ireland. He has been this way countless times. Eventually the narrow passage opens up into a central chamber many times taller than I. It is the centre of a vast ancient burial mound and I am about to come face to face with one of its most intriguing mysteries. It is a map of the moon ten times older than anything known before.

It has been identified by Dr Philip Stooke of the University of Western Ontario in Canada. He spends most of his time preparing maps of asteroids based on spacecraft observations, but he has also prepared detailed maps of the moon. He could not believe that no one had drawn the moon before Leonardo da Vinci's sketch sometime around 1505. So he started searching records of ancient rock carvings and came across something amazing when he was studying the archives of a burial chamber at Knowth in the Irish midlands. 'I was amazed when I saw it. Place the markings over a picture of the full moon and you will see that they line up. It is without doubt a map of the moon, the most ancient one ever found,' says Dr Stooke. 'It's all there in the carving. You can see the overall pattern of the lunar features from features such as Mare Humorum through to Mare Crisium.'

I was here to see it for myself. Professor Eogan gestured to me from the other side of the central chamber, into one of four recesses that protrude from it. Crouching in front of a rock perhaps 1 m high, I could see that there were markings on its surface. The markings had been made by 'pitting' the rock with a lump of quartz (of which there was plenty to be found in the vicinity). The pattern of the pits was hard to see so I swung the torch around and moved back a little. Then the shapes carved into the rocks were obvious. I cannot be certain but it looked like a carving of the dark spots that can be seen on the moon with the unaided eye.

'The people who carved this moon map were the first scientists,' said Dr Stooke. 'They knew a great deal about the motion of the moon. They were not primitive at all.'

Knowth, constructed 5,000 years ago, is the largest and most remarkable ancient monument in Ireland. Though Newgrange is more famous and Dowth is older, Knowth has turned out to be a treasure trove of information, engravings and ancient artefacts. Built on a ridge 1 km north-east of Newgrange it is the biggest chamber cairn in Ireland. The mound has two passages, one facing east and one facing west. After being blocked for thousands of years they were excavated and re-opened by its chief excavator, George Eogan. They turned out to be the longest cairn passages in Europe. Knowth also has the largest collection of megalithic art in Europe, strange circular and spiral patterns that I was told are believed by some to be lunar symbols.

In another of the recesses off the central chamber is a large stone basin. Professor Eogan told me it could have been used to place the cremated remains of the king. Carved into the dished part of the basin is a rayed solar design. Its sides are decorated with a series of seven grooves which run around the basin, giving way to an emblem at the front which could be either the sun or the moon. Seven grooves on each side: that is a total of twenty-eight, the number of days in a lunation. But it is the wall behind the basin that leaves me amazed. A multitude of stars and lunar crescents face me; undoubtedly the moon, and so beautiful.

It may be that it was originally intended that sunlight, and moonlight, would shine down the passage into the central chamber. If this were true then there would have been times when moonlight would have shone on the back stone of the eastern passage and onto a map of itself.

Other ancient lunar maps may lie unrecognized among neolithic monuments. It has been noted that the plan of Stonehenge is like the shapes of the spots on the moon, a circle containing a horseshoe. Could it be considered a very simple map of the moon or is that too fanciful? Its famous solar alignment happens every year, but at certain times the full moon rises over the Heel Stone, and would again illuminate a map of itself. And this is in addition to its other lunar alignments.

The historian Diodorus Siculus (writing about the time of Christ but quoting Hecataeus, some five centuries earlier) wrote of our lands in the 'Island of the Hyperboreans':

> . . . there is also on the island both a magnificent sacred precinct of Apollo and a notable temple which is adorned with many votive offerings and is spherical in shape . . . They say also that the moon, as viewed from this island, appears to be but a little distance from the Earth and to have upon it prominences, like those of the Earth, which are visible to the eye. The account is also given that the god visits the island every nineteen years . . .

Back on the outside of the Knowth chambered mound, I reflect for a few moments on what I have seen. Was it really a map of the moon and is this place one of the most important lunar sites in the world? Lost in thought, the solitude of this place and its boundless views carry me back a multitude of centuries. The moon has never seemed stranger than when rising through the gathering mist above such an ancient structure.

At last, I have learned that you can gather all the facts about the moon but the facts alone will never give you the full picture or tell you the complete story. You cannot strip it of its myth and mystery and say it is just a ball of rock. It is far more precious than that. It has a unique place in people's hearts – just look at what they have done to discover it. In a way Leonardo was wrong. It *is* a mirror, not of the Earth but of our hopes and fears.

In every civilization, every age, mankind has looked up at the moon. Four thousand years ago, huge stones were moved to mark its motions. Four hundred years ago, crude telescopes were turned towards it. And just a short time ago, we walked upon the surface of the silver shrine of Hecate.

It is no 'lesser light made to rule the night'. How strange and wonderful it is, casting its silver mantle on the sidereal world.

Index